graphis annual 74|75

Edited by Walter Herdeg

This is the 23rd annual edition of a work that has been consistently called 'a visual feast'. This year's collection, from all over the world, continues its survey of graphics in advertisements, annual reports, booklets, book jackets and magazine covers, trade marks, letterheads, packaging, record covers, film and television, and now editorial design—selecting and beautifully reproducing what is happening in all design fields. Here is an endless source of ideas and a perfect 'swipe file' for art directors, illustrators and designers, keeping them up-to-date as well as offering new ideas and solutions to graphic arts problems.

The Two Companion Annuals, Edited by Walter Herdeg:

GRAPHIS POSTERS

The International Annual of Poster Art

The second edition of this new ANNUAL again presents an exciting cross-section of poster art throughout the world. 'The contemporary poster in its diverse usage for art, the stage, trade and industry and political propaganda, fills the need for many purposes,' reported *Creative Signs & Displays*. 'Technical advances have added to the richness and multiformity of the modern poster, which has risen to the position of an evolving art form.' This volume offers visual evidence, arranged in four major categories: *Advertising* posters, *Cultural* posters, *Social* posters, *Decorative* posters.

Published each year in early Spring.

PHOTOGRAPHIS

The International Annual of Advertising, Editorial and Television Photography

If one picture is worth a thousand words, then this book is easily a dictionary of photography—the reference annual of the best work from around the world. As such, it is invaluable to art directors, artists and photographers, who refer to it again and again as a permanent 'swipe file' for their own work. Published each year in late Spring.

Other Graphis Books, Edited by Walter Herdeg:

A new series in 'Square Books' format (9-¼" × 9-³/8"):

GRAPHIS/RECORD COVERS

GRAPHIS/DIAGRAMS

The Graphic Visualization of Abstract Data

In 9-½" × 12" format:

FILM AND TV GRAPHICS
Text by John Halas

GRAPHIS/ANNUAL REPORTS
Text by Richard A. Lewis

GRAPHIS/PACKAGING 2

Write for a complete catalogue:

VISUAL COMMUNICATION BOOKS

Hastings House, Publishers, Inc., 10 East 40th Street, New York, N.Y. 10016

graphis annual

74|75 graphis annual

The International Annual of Advertising and Editorial Graphics

Das internationale Jahrbuch der Werbegraphik und der redaktionellen Graphik

Le répertoire international de l'art graphique publicitaire et rédactionnel

Edited by: / Herausgegeben von: / Réalisé par:

Walter Herdeg

Walter Herdeg, The Graphis Press, Zurich

Distributed in the United States by

Hastings House, Publishers, Inc.

10 EAST 40TH STREET, NEW YORK, N.Y. 10016

PUBLICATION N° 137   (ISBN 8038-2667-2)

Contents

Inhalt

Sommaire

Abbreviations

Australia . . . . AUL
Austria . . . . AUS
Belgium . . . . BEL
Brazil . . . . BRA
Canada . . . . CAN
Czechoslovakia . . . . CSR
Denmark . . . . DEN
East Germany . . . . GDR
Finland . . . . FIN
France . . . . FRA
Great Britain . . . . GBR
Hong Kong . . . . HKG
Hungary . . . . HUN
India . . . . IND
Israel . . . . ISR
Italy . . . . ITA
Japan . . . . JPN
Kenya . . . . KEN
Netherlands . . . . NLD
Norway . . . . NOR
Poland . . . . POL
Senegal . . . . SEN
South Africa . . . . SAF
Spain . . . . SPA
Sweden . . . . SWE
Switzerland . . . . SWI
Turkey . . . . TUR
USA . . . . USA
West Germany . . . . GER
Yugoslavia . . . . YUG

Abkürzungen

Australien . . . . AUL
Belgien . . . . BEL
Brasilien . . . . BRA
Dänemark . . . . DEN
Finnland . . . . FIN
Frankreich . . . . FRA
Grossbritannien . . . . GBR
Hong Kong . . . . HKG
Indien . . . . IND
Israel . . . . ISR
Italien . . . . ITA
Japan . . . . JPN
Jugoslawien . . . . YUG
Kanada . . . . CAN
Kenia . . . . KEN
Niederlande . . . . NLD
Norwegen . . . . NOR
Ostdeutschland . . . . GDR
Österreich . . . . AUS
Polen . . . . POL
Schweden . . . . SWE
Schweiz . . . . SWI
Senegal . . . . SEN
Spanien . . . . SPA
Südafrika . . . . SAF
Tschechoslowakei . . . . CSR
Türkei . . . . TUR
Ungarn . . . . HUN
USA . . . . USA
Westdeutschland . . . . GER

Abréviations

Afrique du Sud . . . . SAF
Allemagne occidentale . . . . . . GER
Allemagne orientale . . . . GDR
Australie . . . . AUL
Autriche . . . . AUS
Belgique . . . . BEL
Brésil . . . . BRA
Canada . . . . CAN
Danemark . . . . DEN
Espagne . . . . SPA
Etats-Unis . . . . USA
Finlande . . . . FIN
France . . . . FRA
Grande-Bretagne . . . . GBR
Hongkong . . . . HKG
Hongrie . . . . HUN
Inde . . . . IND
Israël . . . . ISR
Italie . . . . ITA
Japon . . . . JPN
Kenya . . . . KEN
Norvège . . . . NOR
Pays-Bas . . . . NLD
Pologne . . . . POL
Sénégal . . . . SEN
Suède . . . . SWE
Suisse . . . . SWI
Tchécoslovaquie . . . . CSR
Turquie . . . . TUR
Yougoslavie . . . . YUG

Cover design/Umschlagentwurf/Couverture: André François

When JEROME SNYDER writes about the graphic design scene, as he does in the following introduction, he can be relied on for some thoughtful observation that does not stay on the surface of developments but puts today's endeavours into perspective both against the background of art history and in the context of our own many-faceted world of rapid social and scientific change. Jerome Snyder is himself part of this graphic scene; he first came into the limelight as a prize-winner in competitions for murals and posters, he later distinguished himself as art director of SPORTS ILLUSTRATED and THE SCIENTIFIC AMERICAN; but he has also—for instance—written a book about New York restaurants with Milton Glaser as co-author, and is now almost as well known for his writings about graphic design as for his own contributions to it. His thorough first-hand knowledge of the subject is greatly enriched by his wide range of interests and a truly cosmopolitan outlook.

Wenn JEROME SNYDER, wie in der folgenden Einleitung, über die Graphik-Szene schreibt, kann man sich wohldurchdachter Bemerkungen sicher sein, die nicht an der Oberfläche der Entwicklungen haltmachen, sondern die Leistungen von heute vor dem Hintergrund der Kunstgeschichte und im Rahmen unserer vielfältigen Welt raschen sozialen und wissenschaftlichen Wandels ins richtige Verhältnis setzen. Jerome Snyder ist selbst Teil der Graphik-Szene. Als Gewinner von Wettbewerben für Wandgemälde und Plakate trat er erstmals ins Rampenlicht, später zeichnete er sich als Art Director von SPORTS ILLUSTRATED und THE SCIENTIFIC AMERICAN aus. Er hat aber auch, zusammen mit Milton Glaser, ein Buch über New Yorks Restaurants geschrieben und ist heute fast ebenso bekannt für seine Artikel über Graphik wie für seine eigenen graphischen Arbeiten. Seine gründliche Kenntnis des Stoffes wird durch seine vielen Interessen und eine wahrhaft kosmopolitische Weltanschauung sehr bereichert.

Lorsque JEROME SNYDER prend la plume pour nous faire part de ses réflexions en matière d'art graphique, nous pouvons être assurés qu'il ne s'attache pas au seul aspect visible des choses, mais les explicite en les reliant à l'histoire de l'art et en les insérant dans le contexte général de notre époque multiforme, soumise à d'incessantes transformations dans les domaines social et scientifique. Jerome Snyder n'est pas un observateur extérieur, c'est un enfant de la balle qui s'est imposé à l'attention du monde de design comme lauréat de divers concours de compositions murales et d'affiches, puis comme directeur artistique de SPORTS ILLUSTRATED et du SCIENTIFIC AMERICAN. On lui doit également un guide des restaurants newyorkais (en collaboration avec Milton Glaser) et un grand nombre d'écrits critiques et théoriques sur l'art graphique. La connaissance spécialisée du sujet s'allie chez lui à une curiosité insatiable pour les sujets les plus divers et à un esprit authentiquement cosmopolite.

As in past years, the Editor's problem in compiling this volume was not to gather sufficient good material, but to find room for as much as possible of the striking work submitted. In thanking all contributors, whether represented in the final selection or not, he looks forward to receiving an equally gratifying selection of their work in the coming year.

Wie in vergangenen Jahren war es für den Herausgeber kein Problem, für diesen Band genügend gutes Material zu sammeln, sondern für möglichst viele der eingereichten brillanten Arbeiten Platz zu finden. Mit dem Dank an alle Einsender, ob in der letzten Auswahl vertreten oder nicht, verbindet sich seine Hoffnung auf eine ebenso befriedigende Auswahl ihrer Arbeit im kommenden Jahr.

Comme les années précédentes, l'Editeur a dû solutionner cette année encore le problème qui consiste non pas à réunir des travaux de qualité satisfaisante, mais à accommoder dans un seul volume la foule des excellentes productions qui lui ont été soumises. Il tient à remercier chaleureusement tous ceux qui lui ont fait tenir leurs travaux, qu'ils soient inclus ou non dans la sélection finale, et espère recevoir l'année prochaine un choix aussi remarquable du meilleur de leur production courante.

Introduction

Appropriately, the ancient Greek observation that 'we cannot step into the same stream twice' comes to mind when one assesses a collection of a year's effort in the graphic arts. The idea of continuing change is particularly relevant when we consider that the flow of creativity does not begin promptly on the first day of every year, and terminate conveniently on the last. A visual anthology such as this annual enjoys special value because it offers the observer of the graphic milieu a reflective moment to study its tides and movements at closer range. In that focus, one can pick out in detail the larger and smaller elements that make up its diversity.

Visual language, more so than other languages, is in a constant state of flux. While a formal or written tongue is confined largely to its national enclave and customs, graphic and visual concepts are exported and imported with little or no hindrance from national barriers or cultural tariffs. Trading of graphic styles, techniques, visual idioms, colloquialisms, is dependent primarily on the accessibility and easy exchange of information. An annual compilation such as this bears its own *laissez-passer*, so to speak.

By now, the geophysical notion of continental drifts is well accepted. Interestingly enough, while the continental land masses drift apart slowly, the distance of communication between nations, at least in the graphic sense, is being shortened at a rapid pace. If technology is reshaping life-styles throughout the world, it also has made differing societies more adaptable to new modes of graphic expression. To be sure, the graphic stream does not flow evenly, untrammelled, or at the same speed in all parts of the world. Necessity does not quite exercise the same motherhood in all places at all times. Graphic invention and ingenuity are not spawned equally or universally. But the printed page, the poster, the film, television, wherever the artist/designer lays a graphically ingenious hand, all are the bearers of cross-breeding ideas and styles.

Graphic forms, as with all earthly things, are subject to the laws of gravity. Despite the transcendent, creative flight of concepts, the ultimate measurement of success is on the ground level and depends on how the lives of people are affected. No ancient percipient philosopher, in all his wisdom, seeing the imperative of change, could have predicted the torrent of change we experience each day with seeming imperturbability. The all-important task of the contemporary graphics practitioner is to judge how to anticipate, to manipulate and bring about change. Today's designer and artist is something of a social engineer who not only is forging newer and richer ways of expression, but has the parallel responsibility of elevating the popular standard.

A noted American humorist commented plaintively that laughter comes harder these days because 'life has eclipsed comedy'. The American schoolchild is taught reverentially about the discovery of America by Columbus, yet will see a living American hero, the first man to have set foot on the moon, selling a commercial product on the television screen. The daily barrage of commercialism, whose brilliant form often exceeds its banal content, has bred a new cynicism. The rapidity of change, the consumption of human and natural resources, the ruthless exhaustion of talent, present an unrelenting moral challenge for those involved in the myriad aspects of graphic communication. In order to keep pace, one finds it not only impossible to step into the same creative stream twice, but ofttimes barely possible to dip a toe in just one.

In the search for new idioms, those countries with a richer background and more affluent larder of obsolete styles, in rummaging through these stockpiles, have found a new method of aesthetic recycling. In some countries, particularly in the United States, there has been a nostalgic wave. Earlier twentieth-century graphic ways and attitudes have been resurrected and modernized by being placed in the context of the feverish seventies. Whether the return to the past is our chance to gain a breathing space, or is a signal that perhaps the current pace is too vertiginous, one can only guess.

We have seen also the revival of realist and surrealist techniques, with their precise detailing of elements and a concomitant emphasis on ideological rather than narrative interplay. This approach may suggest that the artist is sending up his flare, calling attention to optical or intellectual probity as the needed order of the day. Humanism is evinced in the revival of the caricature of portrait dimension, a hint that we have not been totally engulfed in a faceless, numbered society. Typography, too, has taken on a more opulent mien, and the words and ideas spelled out are more layered in meaning, and colloquially brighter and wittier. All of which suggests that the spirit of confidence and optimism is not easily smothered.

This is an age when national governments are shuffled quicker than the sets of a theatrical mise-en-scène; when a closed pipeline valve in the Middle East can send greater-than-earthquake tremors throughout the world. It is a curious age, when physical survival depends on the mad engines of extinction being kept in rational balance. What we see between the covers of this annual is not only the irridescent reflection of our turbulent times. We find an oasis that shows where the best of the human spirit has prospered. What we see is the filtered part of that previously mentioned stream, free of pollution and detritus, and rich with a wealth of thought and skill. In brief, it is the best of artistic endeavour in our graphic world, a rewarding stream for all to step into not once, but again and again.

Jerome Snyder

Vorwort

Bewertet man eine Zusammenstellung dessen, was in den graphischen Künsten im Ablauf eines Jahres geleistet worden ist, fällt einem die treffende Feststellung der alten Griechen ein, man könne nicht zweimal in denselben Strom steigen. Das Bild vom steten Wandel passt insbesondere, wenn man bedenkt, dass der Fluss der Kreativität nicht einfach am ersten Tag des Jahres einsetzt und am letzten endet. Eine visuelle Anthologie, wie sie dieses Jahrbuch darstellt, erfreut sich besonderen Wertes, weil sie dem Beobachter des graphischen Bereichs einen bedächtigen, genauen Blick auf seine Strömungen und Gezeiten erlaubt. Man kann sich dabei im einzelnen die grösseren und kleineren Elemente heraussuchen, die seine Vielfalt ausmachen.

Die Bildsprache ist mehr als andere Sprachen stets im Fluss. Während eine formale oder geschriebene Sprache grösstenteils auf ihre nationalen Räume und Gebräuche beschränkt ist, überschreiten graphische und visuelle Konzepte fast ungehindert nationale und kulturelle Schranken. Der Austausch graphischer Stile, Techniken und visueller Eigenheiten hängt hauptsächlich von der Zugänglichkeit und leichtem Informationsaustausch ab. Eine jährliche Zusammenstellung wie diese hat sozusagen ihren eigenen Passierschein.

Heutzutage ist die geophysikalische Theorie der Kontinentalverschiebung weithin anerkannt. Während sich jedoch die Kontinente langsam voneinander entfernen, nimmt vergleichsweise die kommunikative Distanz zwischen den Nationen, zumindest bildlich gesprochen, rapide ab. Wiewohl die Technologie in aller Welt die Lebensart verändert, hat sie auch unterschiedliche Gesellschaftsformen für neue Arten graphischer Ausdrucksformen anpassungsfähig gemacht. Gewiss, der graphische Strom fliesst nicht in allen Teilen der Welt gleichmässig, unbehindert oder gar gleich schnell. Bedarf erzeugt nicht überall und allezeit dieselben Ergebnisse. Graphische Erfindungen und Einfälle werden weder gleich noch universell hervorgebracht. Aber das Druckgewerbe, das Plakat, Film und Fernsehen, alle Medien, in denen Künstler und Designer graphisch einfallsreich Hand anlegen, sind Informationsträger für die Kreuzung von Ideen und Stilrichtungen.

Graphische Formen sind, wie alles Irdische, den Gesetzen der Schwerkraft unterworfen. Trotz transzendentem, kreativem Flug von Konzepten, wird das Ausmass des Erfolges letztendlich auf dem Boden der Tatsachen gemessen, und es hängt davon ab, wie es auf das Leben der Menschen eingewirkt hat. Kein Philosoph der Antike, der auf den Imperativ des Wandels gestossen wäre, hätte bei all seiner Weisheit den reissenden Strom des Wandels vorhersagen können, dem wir tagtäglich mit scheinbarer Gelassenheit begegnen. Die wichtigste Aufgabe des Graphikers von heute ist es, zu beurteilen, wie Wandel vorausgesehen, manipuliert und herbeigeführt werden kann. Der Designer und Künstler von heute ist eine Art Soziotechniker, der nicht nur neuere und reichere Ausdrucksmöglichkeiten schmiedet, sondern daneben auch für das Anheben des allgemeinen Niveaus verantwortlich ist.

Ein bekannter amerikanischer Humorist hat beklagt, dass das Lachen heutzutage schwerer fällt, denn «das Leben hat die Komödie in den Schatten gestellt». Dem amerikanischen Schulkind wird ehrfurchtsvoll die Entdeckung Amerikas durch Kolumbus beigebracht, doch daneben sieht es einen lebenden amerikanischen Helden, den ersten Mann, der je seinen Fuss auf den Mond setzte, wie er im Fernsehen für irgendein Produkt wirbt. Das tägliche Bombardement der Werbung, deren brillante Form oft bei weitem den banalen Inhalt übersteigt, hat einen neuen Zynismus gezüchtet. Die Schnelle des Wandels, der Verbrauch menschlicher und natürlicher Quellen, der unerbittliche Talentverschleiss sind eine stete moralische Herausforderung für alle, die in den vielfältigen Bereichen graphischer Kommunikation tätig sind. Um Schritt zu halten, ist es einem nicht nur nicht möglich, zweimal in denselben kreativen Strom zu steigen, sondern auch oft kaum möglich, auch nur eine Zehe darin zu benetzen.

Auf der Suche nach neuen Ausdrucksmöglich-

keiten haben Länder mit grösserer Vergangenheit und einem reicheren Vorrat ausgedienter
Stilarten eine neue Methode ästhetischer Neu-
aufbereitung entdeckt. In einigen Ländern, insbesondere in den Vereinigten Staaten, hat es eine
Welle der Nostalgie gegeben. Die Graphik des
frühen 20. Jahrhunderts ist wiederbelebt und
modernisiert worden, indem sie in den Bezugs-
rahmen der fiebernden siebziger Jahre gestellt
worden ist. Ob der Rekurs auf die Vergangenheit
uns Gelegenheit bietet, Luft zu holen, oder ob er
ein Zeichen dafür ist, dass vielleicht das gegen-
wärtige Tempo zu schwindelerregend ist, darüber
lassen sich nur Vermutungen anstellen.

Zu beobachten war auch eine Wiederbelebung
von Realismus und Surrealismus, bei denen die
präzise Detaildarstellung mit einer Betonung der
ideologischen statt der erzählerischen Interaktion
einhergeht. Das könnte darauf hinweisen, dass
der Künstler ein Signal gibt, um die Aufmerksamkeit auf optische und intellektuelle Recht-
schaffenheit als Tagesnotwendigkeit zu lenken.
Durch die Wiederbelebung der Karikatur von
Porträtausmass wird Humanismus kundgetan,
ein Hinweis darauf, dass wir noch nicht in einer
gesichtslosen, numerierten Gesellschaft unter-

gegangen sind. Auch die Typographie hat ein
opulenteres Gebaren an den Tag gelegt, und die
vorbuchstabierten Worte und Ideen sind von
vielschichtigerer Bedeutung, sind klarer und
geistvoller. All das deutet an, dass der Geist des
Vertrauens und des Optimismus nicht so leicht
unterzukriegen ist.

Wir leben in einem Zeitalter, in dem Regierun-
gen schneller wechseln als Bühnenbilder und eine
abgedrehte Öl-Pipeline im Nahen Osten die Welt
stärker erschüttert als jedes Erdbeben. Es ist ein
merkwürdiges Zeitalter, in dem das Überleben
von den Wahnsinnsmaschinen der Vernichtung
abhängig ist, die in vernunftbedingtem Gleich-
gewicht gewahrt werden. Was auf den Seiten
dieses Jahrbuches zu sehen ist, ist nicht nur ein
schillernder Spiegel unserer turbulenten Zeit.
Wir finden auch eine Oase, die das Beste der
Blüte menschlichen Geistes zeigt. Frei von Ver-
unreinigung und Schutt und reich an Ideen und
Einfällen, zeigt sich hier der gesiebte Teil des
eingangs erwähnten Stroms. Es sind dies, kurz
gesagt, die besten künstlerischen Leistungen unserer graphischen Welt, ein lohnender Strom, in
den wir nicht nur einmal, sondern wieder und
wieder steigen sollten.

Jerome Snyder

Préface

A prendre la mesure d'une année d'efforts dans le domaine des arts graphiques, l'observateur quelque peu philosophe ne peut s'empêcher de songer au «panta rhei» d'Héraclite, à ce fleuve du temps qui s'écoule et dans l'eau duquel on ne peut jamais se baigner deux fois. Ce phénomène de changement continuel est d'autant plus évident que les manifestations toujours renouvelées de la créativité ne s'ordonnent pas selon une période annuelle enserrée entre deux dates fixes. Une anthologie visuelle telle que cet annuaire revêt une valeur particulière du fait qu'elle assure à l'observateur un point fixe d'où juger la succession des marées dans tout le détail souhaitable. C'est ainsi que les multiples éléments kaléidoscopiques s'ordonnent en cette unité changeante qu'est la production graphique d'une année.

Bien plus que d'autres, le langage visuel est en constante transformation. Qui plus est, il dépasse aisément le cadre forcément national d'une langue formelle ou écrite. Ses conceptions s'importent et s'exportent sans grand risque de méprise, une fois franchies les barrières nationales et culturelles consacrées. La circulation des styles et techniques graphiques, des codes visuels et des systèmes populaires de signes dépend en premier lieu de la facilité d'accès à l'information et des possibilités d'échange. Une compilation annuelle comme celle-ci est pourvue de son propre laissez-passer, si l'on peut dire.

De nos jours, la notion géophysique de la dérive des continents semble acquise. Mais alors que les continents s'éloignent insensiblement l'un de l'autre, les distances qui les séparent sont de plus en plus raccourcies au fur et à mesure que les moyens de communication s'améliorent. Ceci vaut également pour le domaine graphique. La technologie a bouleversé les modes de vie dans le monde entier; elle a aussi préparé des sociétés de structure fort diverse à accepter de nouveaux modes d'expression graphique. Le fleuve graphique ne déroule pas partout ses méandres sans entraves, et l'eau n'y circule pas à la même vitesse dans toutes les régions du globe. Nécessité ne fait pas loi dans tous les pays, pas plus que l'inven-

tivité et l'ingéniosité ne se donnent libre cours partout. Pourtant, la page imprimée, l'affiche, le cinéma, la télévision, tous les supports de l'imagination créatrice de l'artiste et du designer assurent la diffusion et la greffe constantes d'idées et de styles nouveaux.

Comme toutes choses sur Terre, les formes graphiques sont assujetties à la pesanteur. Les concepts ont beau prendre leur envol dans toute la splendeur d'une créativité transcendante, force leur est de considérer le succès final, qui se mesure humblement au sol, d'après leur impact sur la qualité de vie des hommes qui y vivent. «Panta rhei» – certes, beaucoup de sagesse pour un vieux sage présocratique, mais il ne croyait pas si bien dire ni n'aurait prévu le flot tumultueux, toujours renouvelé qui envahit notre vie quotidienne à l'âge des mutations. La tâche essentielle de l'artiste graphique engagé dans cette vie quotidienne est précisément de prévoir l'axe préférentiel de ce mouvement, de peser de tout son poids sur l'orientation du changement et d'y contribuer. Le designer, l'artiste d'aujourd'hui joue en quelque sorte le rôle d'un ingénieur des relations sociales chargé non seulement d'élaborer des modes d'expression nouveaux et plus riches, mais assumant aussi la responsabilité d'élever le niveau général de la qualité de vie.

Un humoriste américain bien connu se plaignait de voir le rire se raréfier de nos jours où «la vie éclipse la comédie». L'écolier américain apprend, suspendu aux lèvres de son maître, l'histoire de la découverte de l'Amérique par Christophe Colomb. Le soir venu, il voit un autre héros, bien vivant celui-là, le premier homme à avoir foulé le sol de la Lune, vendre un produit commercial sur le petit écran. Le feu roulant de la publicité, dont la forme brillante est souvent supérieure au contenu plutôt banal, engendre une nouvelle forme de cynisme. La rapidité du changement universel, l'épuisement des ressources humaines et naturelles, l'exploitation impitoyable du talent, tous ces facteurs se conjuguent pour lancer un défi moral des plus sérieux à tous ceux qui œuvrent dans l'immense domaine des communications graphiques. Si l'on veut suivre le mouvement, il paraît non seulement impossible de se tremper deux fois dans le même fleuve, mais aussi souvent de tremper ne serait-ce qu'un orteil rien qu'une fois.

A la recherche de langages nouveaux, les pays à la tradition plus riche et au garde-manger mieux pourvu de styles surannés ont découvert une nouvelle méthode de recyclage des trésors poussiéreux qui sommeillent dans leurs greniers: la vague rétro, qui a envahi certains pays, et tout particulièrement les Etats-Unis. C'est ainsi que des moyens d'expression et attitudes graphiques du début du siècle ont été exhumés et mis au goût du jour, c'est-à-dire adaptés au rythme lancinant des années 70. Il reste à voir si ce retour aux sources va nous permettre d'avoir les coudées plus franches ou s'il exprime simplement le besoin de souffler un peu, la course se faisant par trop effrénée.

Nous assistons également au renouveau des techniques réalistes et surréalistes avec leur amour du détail précis et l'importance qu'elles accordent à l'idéologie au détriment de la narration. Cette approche pourrait signifier que l'artiste se décide à illuminer le paysage graphique d'une fusée éclairante propre à attirer l'attention sur la nécessité d'une probité visuelle ou intellectuelle plus prononcée. La tendance humaniste s'affirme dans le nouvel essor de la caricature au grand format, qui nous avertit que nous résistons vigoureusement à l'absorption par une masse anonyme d'où les visages auraient été éliminés au profit de numéros. La typographie affiche, elle aussi, un air plus opulent, et les mots et idées qui s'y expriment ont une signification plus complexe en même temps qu'ils s'avèrent plus familiers, brillants et spirituels. Tout cela atteste que la confiance et l'optimisme restent intacts.

Nous vivons à une époque où les gouvernements sont renversés plus vite que nous y ont habitués les changements de décors au théâtre; où la fermeture d'un pipeline au Proche-Orient peut provoquer des séismes politiques dans le monde entier. C'est une bien curieuse époque où notre survie physique dépend de l'équilibre que la raison est en mesure de maintenir entre des engins de destruction terrifiants. Ce que nous voyons entre la première et la dernière page de couverture de cet annuaire n'est pas seulement la réflexion irisante de notre âge troublé. Nous y trouvons aussi une oasis de fraîcheur qui nous rassure sur les potentialités de l'esprit humain. Nous y voyons la portion filtrée du fleuve dont il était question, la portion libre de déchets, de pollution, et riche d'un immense talent et d'une forte pensée. Bref, il s'agit du meilleur qu'ait produit l'effort des artistes dans notre univers graphique. Ce fleuve-là est purifié et accueillant, et c'est un plaisir de s'y tremper non pas une seule fois, mais aussi souvent que possible.

Jerome Snyder

Index to Designers and Artists
Verzeichnis der Entwerfer und Künstler
Index des maquettistes et artistes

14

Index to Art Directors
Verzeichnis der Künstlerischen Leiter
Index des directeurs artistiques

Index to Agencies and Studios
Verzeichnis der Agenturen und Studios
Index des agences et studios

Index to Publishers
Verzeichnis der Verleger
Index des éditeurs

Index to Advertisers
Verzeichnis der Auftraggeber
Index des clients

■ Entry instructions will be mailed to anyone interested in
submitting samples of outstanding graphics or photography
for possible inclusion in our annuals. No fees involved. Closing dates
for entries:
GRAPHIS ANNUAL (Advertising and editorial art): 15 December
PHOTOGRAPHIS (Advertising and editorial photography): 30 June
GRAPHIS POSTERS (A new annual on poster art): 30 March
Write to: The Graphis Press, Dufourstr. 107, 8008 Zurich, Switzerland.

■ Einsendebedingungen können von jedermann angefordert werden,
der uns Beispiele hervorragender Graphik oder Photographie zur
Auswahl für unsere Jahrbücher unterbreiten möchte. Es werden keine
Gebühren erhoben. Einsendetermine:
GRAPHIS ANNUAL (Werbe- und redaktionelle Graphik): 15. Dezember
PHOTOGRAPHIS (Werbe- und redaktionelle Photographie): 30. Juni
GRAPHIS POSTERS (ein neues Jahrbuch der Plakatkunst): 30. März
Adresse: Graphis Verlag, Dufourstr. 107, 8008 Zürich, Schweiz.

■ Tout intéressé à la soumission d'excellents travaux graphiques et
photographiques peut obtenir les informations nécessaires. Sans charge
de participation. Dates limites:
GRAPHIS ANNUAL (art graphique publicitaire et rédactionnel): 15 décembre
PHOTOGRAPHIS (photographie publicitaire et rédactionnelle): 30 juin
GRAPHIS POSTERS (nouvel annuaire sur l'art de l'affiche): 30 mars
S'adresser à: Editions Graphis, Dufourstr. 107, 8008 Zurich, Suisse.

Editor, Art Director, Designer: Walter Herdeg
Assistant Editor: Stanley Mason
Project Manager: Charlotte Moine
Art Assistants: Sonja Barth, Wilfried Maret, Klaus Schröder, Peter Wittwer

1

Magazine Advertisements

Newspaper Advertisements

Zeitschriften-Inserate

Zeitungs-Inserate

Annonces de revues

Annonces de presse

1) 2) Full-page magazine advertisements printed in four colours from a series for *Kotobuki* confectionery and chocolates. (JPN)
3) Magazine advertisement for a burgundy made by the Italian Swiss Colony Winery in California and based on a long tradition. Bottle, roots and vignettes in colour. (USA)
4) Advertisement from an alcohol moderation campaign launched by Seagram Distillers Co. The handwriting (blue) deteriorates with the number of drinks. (USA)
5) Magazine advertisement inviting readers to a sweet-corn-eating festival in the home town of *Green Giant* canned vegetables. Illustration in green shades. (USA)
6) 'Put *Pepsi* on the table, it has more taste.' Double-spread magazine advertisement in full colour marking the 75th anniversary of *Pepsi-Cola*. (ITA)

1) 2) Ganzseitige Zeitschrifteninserate aus einer Serie für *Kotobuki* Konfektwaren und Schokoladen. Mehrfarbig. (JPN)
3) Zeitschrifteninserat für einen Burgunderwein aus Kalifornien. Flasche, Wurzel und Vignetten mehrfarbig. (USA)
4) Inserat aus einer Kampagne einer Branntweinbrennerei mit einem Aufruf zur Mässigung beim Alkoholkonsum. Die Handschrift verschlechtert sich mit der Anzahl Getränke. (USA)
5) Zeitschrifteninserat mit der Einladung, am Sweet-Corn-Festival in der Heimatstadt der *Green Giant* Gemüsekonserven teilzunehmen. Illustration in Grüntönen. (USA)
6) «Stell *Pepsi* auf den Tisch, es hat mehr Geschmack.» Doppelseitiges, mehrfarbiges Zeitschrifteninserat anlässlich des 75. Jubiläums von *Pepsi-Cola*. (ITA)

1) 2) Annonces de magazine, pleine page, quatre couleurs, figurant dans une série réalisée pour la confiserie et les chocolats *Kotobuki*. (JPN)
3) Annonce de magazine pour un bourgogne de l'Italian Swiss Colony Winery (Californie) incarnant une longue tradition. Bouteille, racines et vignettes en couleur. (USA)
4) Annonce de la Seagram Distillers Co. invoquant les bienfaits d'une consommation modérée d'alcool. L'écriture (en bleu) se dégrade avec le nombre de verres ingurgités. (USA)
5) Annonce de magazine invitant les lecteurs à participer à un festin de maïs organisé dans la ville des conserves de légumes *Green Giant*. Illustration aux tons verts. (USA)
6) «Mettez du *Pepsi* sur la table, il a meilleur goût.» Annonce de magazine, double page, en polychromie, pour le 75e anniversaire de *Pepsi-Cola*. (ITA)

Advertisements / Inserate / Annonces

Artist / Künstler / Artiste:

1) 2) NORIKO UENO / MITSUO KIHARA
3) BRUCE WOLFE / JACK MCKEE
4) CHUCK KINTZING
5) JOHN FAULKNER /
6) JOHN ALCORN / ELVEZIO GHIDOLI

Art Director / Directeur artistique:

1) 2) YASUO MATSUDA
3) JACK MCKEE
4) CHUCK KINTZING
5) THEO ANEMA
6) ELVEZIO GHIDOLI

Agency / Agentur / Agence – Studio:

1) 2) FUJI ADVERTISING SYSTEM
3) HONIG-COOPER & HARRINGTON
4) WARWICK, WELSH & MILLER
5) LEO BURNETT CO., INC.
6) MASIUS

Artist | Künstler | Artiste:
7)–13) TADASHI OHASHI

Art Director | Directeur artistique:
7)–13) TADASHI OHASHI

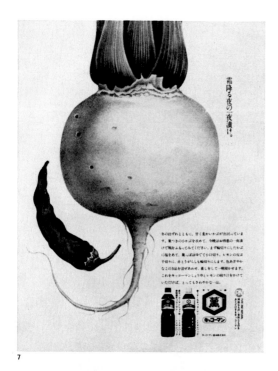

7

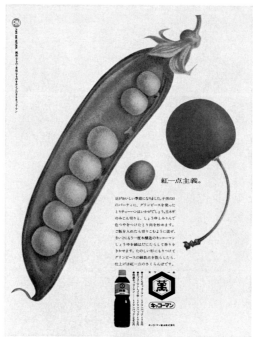

8

9

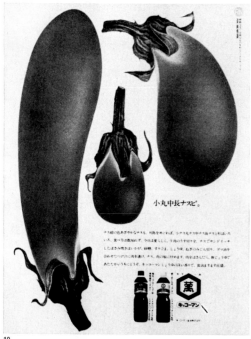

10

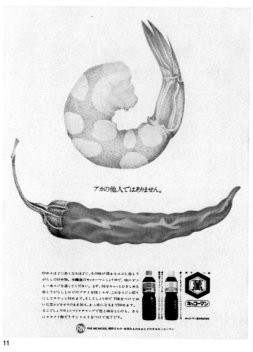

11

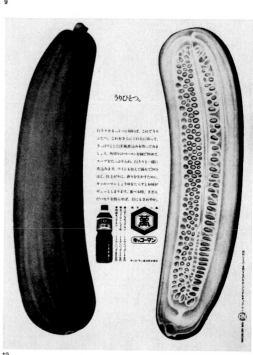

12

7)–13) Examples of full-page magazine advertisements from a long and continuing series for soy sauces made by Kikkoman Shoyu Co. Ltd. Vegetables and bottles in full colour. Tadashi Ohashi's advertising for *Kikkoman* products has now attained the status of a classic. The humorous advertisement in fig. 13 is reproduced in actual size. (JPN)

7)–13) Sieben Beispiele ganzseitiger Zeitschrifteninserate aus einer langen und weiterlaufenden Serie für die Soya-Saucen von Kikkoman Shoyu Co. Ltd. Gemüse und Flaschen sind mehrfarbig. Tadashi Ohashi's Werbung für *Kikkoman*-Produkte kann fast als klassisch bezeichnet werden. Das Inserat in Abb. 13 ist in Originalgrösse wiedergegeben. (JPN)

7)–13) Exemples d'une longue série d'annonces de magazine, pleine page, qui sera poursuivie, pour les sauces soya de la Kikkoman Shoyu Co. Ltd. Légumes et bouteilles en polychromie. Les annonces de Tadashi Ohashi pour les produits *Kikkoman* sont entre-temps devenues un classique. Fig. 13 en grandeur originale. (JPN)

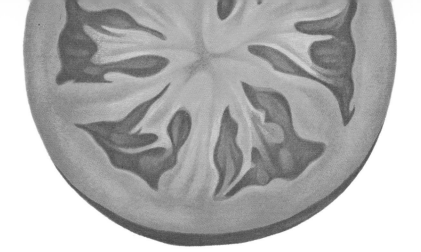

STOP夏バテ

CAUTION歯

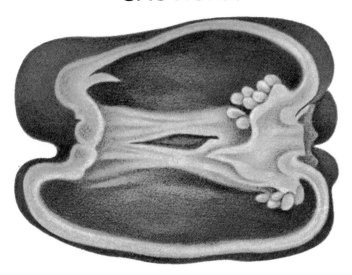

GO食欲

夏の終わり、秋風が立つころにおすすめしたい色あざやかな
バーベキュー。トマトはトマト、トウモロコシはトウモロコシ、
ピーマンはピーマン……とそれぞれを串にさして、炭火で軽
くあぶります。そしてキッコーマンしょうゆをベースに、みり
ん・トマトケチャップ・ワイン・ウスターソースを好み
の量で合わせたタレにつけ、ジュージューと焼きあげます。
しょうゆの焼ける香りはやっぱり最良のアペタイザーです。

●特選キッコーマン……→マンパック220円
●キッコーマンしょうゆ……→マンパック175円
●うすくちキッコーマン……→マンパック175円

天 下 一 品

萬

キッコーマン

キッコーマン醤油株式会社

Artist | Künstler | Artiste:

14) 15) PETER MAX
16) JÖRG HERMLE
17) JEAN MULATIER /
CARL HORN
18) PAUL DAVIS /
BILL BARNES
19) PAUL DAVIS / FRANK
BIANCALANA

New Datsun 1200 Sport Coupe.
An original portrait by Peter Max.

Own a Datsun Original.

15

Art Director | Directeur artistique:

14) 15) PETER MAX
16) JÖRG HERMLE
17) CARL HORN
18) CLIFF PROBST / DAVE PFISTER
19) FRANK BIANCALANA

Agency | Agentur | Agence – Studio:

14) 15) PETER MAX ENTERPRISES, INC.
16) SNAP
17) H. K. MCCANN CO.
18) HARMON & CROOK, INC.
19) LEE KING & PARTNERS

14) 15) Illustration in actual size and complete magazine advertisement for a *Datsun* sports model, which is claimed to be as modern as the colourful visions of Peter Max. (USA)
16) Black-and-white advertisement for *Pont-à-Mousson* steel pipes for oil and gas. (FRA)
17) 'Berlin is worth while.' Full-page magazine advertisement in colour for Berlin. (GER)
18) Magazine advertisement for General Transportation Services. Full colour. (USA)
19) Double-spread magazine advertisement in full colour for the shipping services of General American Transportation Corp. (USA)

14) 15) Illustration in Originalgrösse und vollständiges Zeitschrifteninserat für einen Sportwagen der Marke *Datsun*, welcher so modern wie die farbenprächtigen Phantasiebilder von Peter Max sein soll. (USA)
16) Schwarzweisses Inserat für *Pont-à-Mousson* Stahlrohre für Öl und Gas. (FRA)
17) Ganzseitiges, mehrfarbiges Zeitschrifteninserat für die Stadt Berlin. (GER)
18) Mehrfarbiges Zeitschrifteninserat für ein Transportunternehmen. (USA)
19) Doppelseitiges, mehrfarbiges Zeitschrifteninserat für die Schiffahrtsdienstleistungen der General American Transportation Corp. (USA)

14) 15) Illustration grandeur nature et annonce complète de magazine pour une voiture de sport *Datsun*, aussi moderne que les créations hautes en couleur de Peter Max. (USA)
16) Annonce noir-blanc pour les pipe-lines en acier de *Pont-à-Mousson*. (FRA)
17) «Berlin en vaut la peine.» Annonce de magazine, pleine page, en couleur, pour Berlin. (GER)
18) Annonce de magazine pour General Transportation Services. En polychromie. (USA)
19) Annonce polychrome de magazine, sur double page, pour les services de fret de la General American Transportation Corporation. (USA)

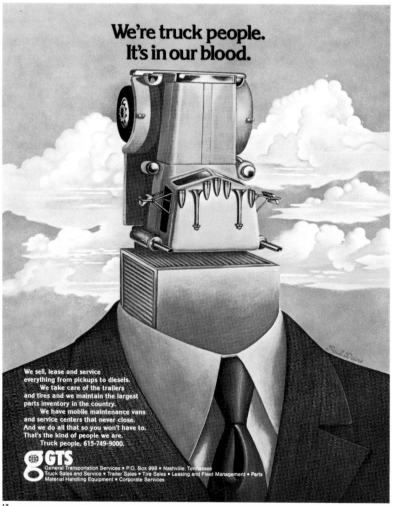

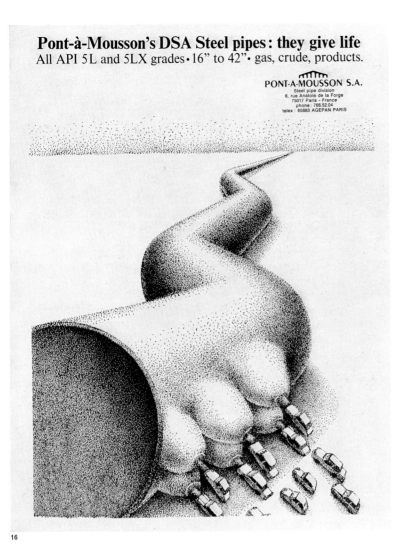

20

21

23

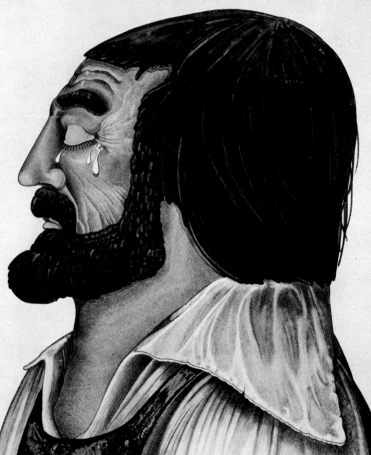

32

Acier et fer

Puissant trait d'union
vers l'industrie suisse
de la construction

acifer

Münchenstein	Landquart
Regensdorf	Buchs SG
Thayngen	Lengwil TG
Rothenburg	Visp
Lausanne	Martigny

22

A bedtime story for builders.

Once upon a time, there were three little pigs who decided to make their fortunes building and selling houses.

The first little pig, whose name was Posey, was very artistic. He thought looks were everything, so he designed a beautiful stick house and hired a lot of help and began to build. For a long, long time, Posey and his crew measured and sawed and hammered and nailed. Until finally, the house was finished.

And it was very beautiful.

So Posey had no trouble selling it to a little old lady from Connecticut. But alas! When Posey paid for all his help and all the materials and all the fancy trim, he sadly realized that he had made very little profit.

So, disenchanted, he got out of the building business and became a used-car salesman, specializing in Porkpaes, Thunderpigs and Hogswagens.

The second little pig's name was Pokey, and he was a bit lazy. So he decided to build a modular house, because it was mostly pre-built

and he wouldn't have as much to do.

Which meant Pokey could take a lot of naps in the mud and munch on peopled pick's feet while his helpers did the work. But alas! When the modular house was complete, it wasn't very pretty or practical.

And by the time poor Pokey had paid his help, and the high cost of the materials and transportation, he didn't have a poke left to pig in. For Pokey, it was Chapter Eleven.

So he moved to the Poorhouse. Where he lives this very day.

The third little pig was very perceptive. Which is why everyone called him Percy.

He wisely decided to build a panelized Mayhill Home. It arrived one morning on a single truck, and a short time later, when it was finished, it was just as beautiful as Posey's house. And far more practical.

Percy quickly sold his Mayhill house. And when he paid all his

costs, including the complete Mayhill Package, he danced a jig Pig-style. Because he discovered he had made an extra thousand dollars profit. So Percy, being a very practical pig, bought and built more panelized Mayhill homes. To his delight, they were sold almost as fast as they were finished.

And Percy made about 5% extra profit on each one.

Today, Percy is a very successful pig. He owns a huge development with hundreds of happy Mayhill homes. He calls it Hog Heaven.

And that's just what Percy is in.

MORAL: When you're building homes, hog yourself some extra profit. Call or write Tommy Young, Dept. A, Mayhill Homes Corporation, P.O. Box 1778, Gainesville, Ga. 30501. Telephone 404/536-9871. He'll show you how to build the Mayhill panelized way. So you can sell more houses. And make more on each house you sell.

Which can certainly keep the wolf away from your door.

24

20) 21) Magazine advertisements with full-colour illustrations from a series for *Marantz* distortion-free stereo sets. (USA)

22) Full-page newspaper advertisement for an iron and steel supplier. Black and blue. (SWI)

23) Double-spread magazine advertisement, with a parody of a Longfellow poem, for *Ornade* capsules against allergies. Illustrations in colour. (USA)

24) Advertisement for *Mayhill* homes placed in a builders' magazine. Illustrations in bright colours. (USA)

25) Magazine advertisement for a *United Artists* record entitled *Roll over, Beethoven*, who is posthumously portrayed. Black and white. (USA)

20) 21) Zeitschrifteninserat mit mehrfarbigen Illustrationen aus einer Serie für *Marantz*-Stereoanlagen. (USA)

22) Ganzseitiges Zeitungsinserat für das Stahl- und Eisenunternehmen *acifer*. Schwarz und blau. (SWI)

23) Doppelseitiges Zeitschrifteninserat, mit einer Parodie auf ein Gedicht von Longfellow, für *Ornade*-Kapseln gegen Allergien. Mehrfarbige Illustrationen. (USA)

24) «Eine Gute-Nacht-Geschichte für Bauunternehmer.» Fachzeitschrifteninserat für *Mayhill* vorfabrizierte Häuser. Farbig. (USA)

25) Zeitschrifteninserat für eine *United Artists*-Schallplatte mit dem Titel *Roll over, Beethoven*, der hier entsprechend portraitiert ist. Schwarzweiss. (USA)

20) 21) Annonces de magazine, avec illustrations polychromes; série en faveur des équipements stéréo *Marantz* exempts de distorsion. (USA)

22) Annonce de journal, pleine page, pour un fournisseur de produits sidérurgiques. Noir et bleu. (SWI)

23) Annonce de magazine, double page, avec un pastiche d'un poème de Longfellow. Publicité pour les capsules *Ornade* qui combattent les allergies. Illustrations couleur. (USA)

24) Annonce de magazine pour les maisons préfabriquées *Mayhill*. Illustrations en polychromie. (USA)

25) Annonce de magazine pour un disque édité par *United Artists* et intitulé *Roll over, Beethoven*, avec un «portrait» du grand musicien. Noir et blanc. (USA)

TELL TCHAIKOVSKY THE NEWS: ELECTRIC LIGHT ORCHESTRA II

There aren't many records that knock you over the first time with their sheer, boundless brilliance. Very, very few, in fact. Yet Jeff Lynne has been making such records for years, with the Idle Race and the Move, and now with the Electric Light Orchestra. His finest effort to date is *Roll Over Beethoven*, a magnificent single that has enjoyed a lengthy reign over the British charts and is now breaking out like crazy within days of its U.S. release.

The record is an astonishing mixture of classical instrumentation and hard rock, molded by the advanced structural concepts of Lynne, Bev Bevan and other group members. There are so many things happening in this record that you'll never tire of hearing it. It's one of the classics.

The eight-minute version of *Roll Over Beethoven* can be heard on the Electric Light Orchestra's second album, ELO II. It follows NO ANSWER, a chart album that was one of the critical favorites of 1972, but it represents such an advancement of the original ELO concept that there is really no comparison. The response to the album has been immediate and ecstatic; it's being played everywhere, and causing widespread mania. There aren't many albums as startlingly innovative as this one, or groups as remarkable as the Electric Light Orchestra. They're one of the few groups that are trying to bring rock & roll back to life, without robbing any graves.

Roll over, Beethoven.

On United Artists Records & Tapes

ROLL OVER BEETHOVEN/UA-XW173-W ELOII-UA-LA040-F

UA

25

26) Double-spread trade press advertisement for *Sylvania* bulbs, which are designed to repel night-flying insects. (USA)
27) Colour advertisement for a *Pfizer* psychotropic drug recommended for use in old age. (GBR)
28) Newspaper advertisement for a sale of men's and women's clothing. (SWI)
29) Advertisement for the Rainier Brewing Co., Seattle. (USA)
30) Black-and-white magazine advertisement for *Pioneer-Moss*, photoengravers, with a list of the advertising agencies they work for. (USA)
31) 32) Detail of the illustration (recalling more spacious days of food enjoyment) and complete full-colour magazine advertisement for *Sharwood's* peach chutney. (GBR)

26) Doppelseitiges Fachzeitschrifteninserat für *Sylvania*-Glühbirnen, die eine insektenabstossende Wirkung haben. (USA)
27) Mehrfarbiges Inserat für ein pharmazeutisches Produkt von *Pfizer* gegen Depressionen und Angstzustände bei älteren Leuten. (GBR)
28) Zeitungsinserat für einen Sonderverkauf von Damen- und Herrenbekleidung. (SWI)
29) Anzeige der Brauerei Rainier Brewing Co. in Seattle. (USA)
30) Schwarzweisses Zeitschrifteninserat für eine photolithographische Anstalt, mit einer Liste der Werbeagenturen, die zu ihren Kunden zählen. (USA)
31) 32) Detail der Illustration (die an die Gaumenfreuden vergangener Zeiten erinnert) und vollständiges mehrfarbiges Zeitschrifteninserat für Pfirsich-Würztunke. (GBR)

26) Annonce de revue professionnelle, double page, pour les ampoules *Sylvania* destinées à écarter les insectes nocturnes. (USA)
27) Annonce en couleur pour une drogue psychotrope *Pfizer* propre à soulager les maux du troisième âge. (GBR)
28) Annonce de journal pour une vente de vêtements de dames et messieurs. (SWI)
29) Annonce pour la brasserie Rainier Brewing Co. à Seattle. (USA)
30) Annonce de magazine noir-blanc pour l'atelier de photogravure *Pioneer-Moss*, avec une liste des agences publicitaires qui comptent parmi la clientèle de cette entreprise. (USA)
31) 32) Détail de l'illustration (rappelant les délices gastronomiques du passé) et annonce complète de magazine, en polychromie, pour du chutney aux pêches. (GBR)

Advertisements / Inserate / Annonces

26

27

28

29

34

31

30

32

Artist | Künstler | Artiste:

26) ROGER HANE

27) ANTHONY BENSTED / JOHN FOAT

28) ULRICH KEMMNER

29) PAT MALONEY / MAXWELL ARNOLD

30) HERB LUBALIN

31) 32) BARRY CRADDOCK

Art Director | Directeur artistique:

26) ROSARIO ARNONE

27) ANTHONY BENSTED

30) IRWIN ROTHMAN

31) 32) PAUL LEEVES

Agency | Agentur | Agence – Studio:

26) DOYLE DANE BERNBACH, INC.

27) THE PFIZER GROUP

29) THE MAXWELL ARNOLD AGENCY

31) 32) THE RH KIRKWOOD CO. LTD.

35

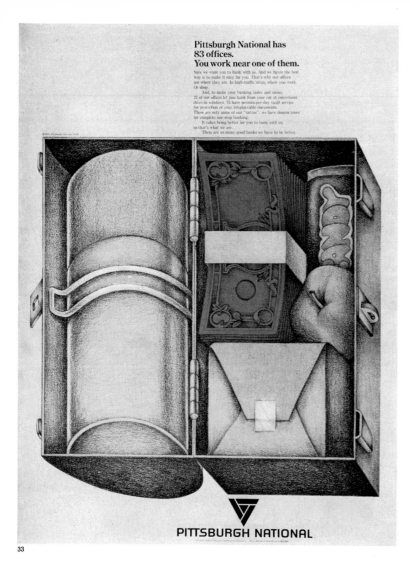

34

38

39

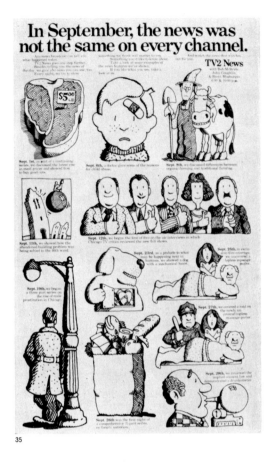

In September, the news was not the same on every channel.

35

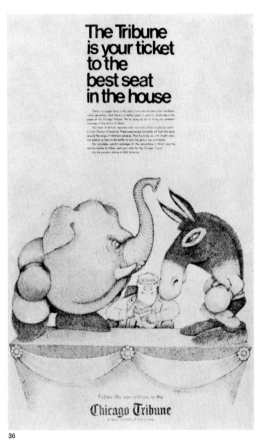

The Tribune is your ticket to the best seat in the house

Follow the conventions in the
Chicago Tribune

36

This is what you pay for: **This is what you get:**

Northridge Lakes
Apartments from $179 to $370 a month
Condominiums from $23,900 to $38,900

37

WHAT TO DO IF YOU RECEIVE A MALICIOUS OR ANNOYING CALL.

Just hang up immediately.
In most instances that's enough to stop the caller from calling again. Too often, though, people unwittingly encourage the caller by talking back.
You can't argue with a sick mind, so don't try.
If hanging up quickly doesn't work, don't panic. You're still not helpless. Call our business office. You'll find the number in the front of your telephone directory.
In persistent cases, our Annoyance Call Bureau takes over to try and trap the offender.
Working with the police, our bureau has been responsible for 844

arrests.
And offenders have learned that a 10 cent phone call can cost them as much as $1,000 and a year in prison under state law.
We know being on the receiving end of any obscene phone call is an upsetting experience.
But if you know how to handle it, it can turn out alright.
New York Telephone is in business to give you service. And part of our obligation is to see to it that no one abuses that service.
Because we know...

You judge us every time you use the phone.

New York Telephone

40

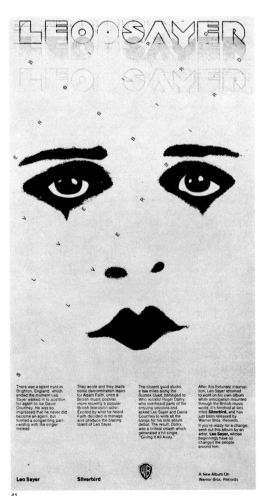

Leo Sayer   Silverbird   A New Album On Warner Bros. Records

41

33) Newspaper advertisement about the centrally situated branches of the Pittsburgh National Bank. (USA)
34) Newspaper advertisement announcing a programme with Cannonball Adderley on a KNBC television channel. (USA)
35) Full-page newspaper ad for WBBM television. (USA)
36) Full-page newspaper advertisement about the political reporting of the CHICAGO TRIBUNE. (USA)
37) Full-page newspaper advertisement about apartments offered by Wisconsin Condominium Sales. (USA)
38) 39) Double-spread trade press advertisements for Mace Marketing Services Ltd. Full-colour illustrations. (USA)
40) Full-page newspaper ad for New York Telephone. (USA)
41) Newspaper ad for a *Warner Bros.* record by Leo Sayer. (USA)

33) Zeitungsinserat, das auf die leichte Erreichbarkeit der vielen Filialen einer Bank aufmerksam macht. (USA)
34) Zeitungsinserat als Ankündigung eines KNCB-Fernsehprogramms mit Cannonball Adderley. (USA)
35) Ganzseitiges Zeitungsinserat für einen Fernsehsender. (USA)
36) Ganzseitiges Zeitungsinserat über die politischen Reportagen in der CHICAGO TRIBUNE. (USA)
37) Ganzseitiges Zeitschrifteninserat für die Eigentumswohnungen einer Immobiliengesellschaft. (USA)
38) 39) Doppelseitige Fachzeitschrifteninserate für eine Vertriebsorganisation. Farbig. (USA)
40) Zeitungsinserat für eine Telephongesellschaft. (USA)
41) Zeitungsinserat für eine *Warner Bros.* Schallplatte. (USA)

33) Annonce de journal mettant en relief la position centrale des guichets de la Pittsburgh National Bank. (USA)
34) Annonce de journal présentant un programme télévisé KNBC avec Cannonball Adderley en vedette. (USA)
35) Annonce de journal pleine page pour une chaîne TV. (USA)
36) Annonce de journal pleine page sur la qualité des reportages politiques du CHICAGO TRIBUNE. (USA)
37) Annonce de journal pleine page présentant les appartements mis en vente par Wisconsin Condominium Sales. (USA)
38) 39) Annonces de revues professionnelles, double page, pour Mace Marketing Services Ltd. En polychromie. (USA)
40) Annonce pour une compagnie de téléphone. (USA)
41) Annonce de journal pour un disque *Warner Bros.* (USA)

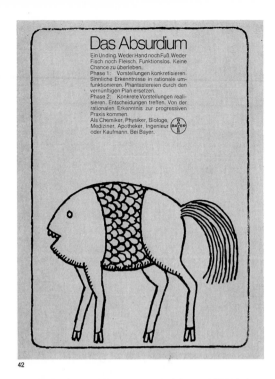

Das Absurdium

Ein Unding. Weder Hand noch Fuß. Weder Fisch noch Fleisch. Funktionslos. Keine Chance zu überleben.
Phase 1: Vorstellungen konkretisieren. Sinnliche Erkenntnisse in rationale um-funktionieren. Phantastereien durch den vernünftigen Plan ersetzen.
Phase 2: Konkrete Vorstellungen reali-sieren. Entscheidungen treffen. Von der rationalen Erkenntnis zur progressiven Praxis kommen.
Als Chemiker, Physiker, Biologe, Mediziner, Apotheker, Ingenieur oder Kaufmann. Bei Bayer.

42

DIENTEROL
o antidiarréico total

43

"New England Life? Capital company, old boy. Mutual funds, investment counseling, and something else that eludes me right now."

"Well, that's life."

44

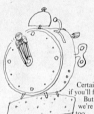

Some folks just don't know what makes us tick

Time and again, international businessmen turn to the UBS for practical financial solutions.

Certainly we're famous for our timepieces. And, if you'll forgive the immodesty, with some justification. But in certain (especially business) quarters, we're famous for quite a number of other things, too.

Such as our banking services. As offered by the Union Bank of Switzerland: with our international approach to financial matters, the well-grounded assistance we provide concerning every facet of trade with our export-minded country (remember those watches?), our experience in every aspect of import/export financing.

And our habit of neglecting to watch the clock when grappling with client problems, whatever their size.

All wound up to assist you on all continents.

Union Bank of Switzerland

Zurich (Head Office), Basle, Berne, Geneva, Lucerne, Lugano, St. Gall and over 180 branches elsewhere in Switzerland. Branch Offices in London and Tokyo. Representative Offices in Bahrain – Beirut – Bogotá – Buenos Aires – Caracas – Chicago – Hong Kong – Johannesburg – Melbourne – Mexico City – Montreal – New York – Rio de Janeiro – San Francisco – São Paulo – Singapore – Sydney – Tokyo.
London EC 2N 1AJ: 118 Old Broad Street – Beirut: Starco South 1001-4 – Johannesburg: 37, Sauer Street – Bahrain: POB 795

45

You can't keep us in gnome·man's·land

The UBS is very much out-and-about, tending client interests on all continents.

Certain respected members of the aristocracy notwithstanding, no bank grows if its staff fiddles around in the vaults all day.

As witness the giant strides made by the Union Bank of Switzerland. Today, we have the largest number of branches of any Bank in Switzerland, 18 representative offices overseas, branches in London and Tokyo and a network of no fewer than 10000 correspondent banks. The dynamism inspired by our young, though experienced, management is known and appreciated on all continents.

As is the fact that, in spite of our size, we know there's no such thing as a little financial problem.

Every man's idea of a great Swiss bank.

Union Bank of Switzerland

Zurich (Head Office), Basle, Berne, Geneva, Lucerne, Lugano, St. Gall and over 180 branches elsewhere in Switzerland. Branch Offices in London and Tokyo. Representative Offices in Bahrain – Beirut – Bogotá – Buenos Aires – Caracas – Chicago – Hong Kong – Johannesburg – Melbourne – Mexico City – Montreal – New York – Rio de Janeiro – San Francisco – São Paulo – Singapore – Sydney – Tokyo.
London EC 2N 1AJ: 118 Old Broad Street – Beirut: Starco South 1001-4 – Johannesburg: 37, Sauer Street – Bahrain: POB 795

46

Vi direbbe volentieri a viva voce quali sono le vernici sottomarine che preferisce – cioè quelle a base di VERSADUCT 460 o di resina epossidica. Vi direbbe inoltre quanto questo sottosmalto costituito di resina epossidica e di indurente, epossidica e d'indurente, sott'acqua e come possa essere applicato facilmente. Vantaggio rilevanti anche per chi usa questo sistema – sopr'acqua –.

Il VERSADUCT 460 è un indurente modificato a base di poliammino-imidazolina per resine epossidiche a bassa viscosità, come ad esempio l'EUREPOX 780 (Schering AG).
Il VERSADUCT 460 unito alla resina epossidica indurisce senza lasciare superfici appiccicose. Esso conferisce un elevato grado di lucentezza anche ad un'umidità relativa del 95% senza pre-reazione, aderisce inoltre anche su superfici umide.

Questo indurente è indicato soprattutto per la produzione di vernici prive o contenenti una minima parte di solventi, stucchi e malte a base di resina sintetica. Forniamo alle industrie delle vernici, degli inchiostri da stampa, di materiali per la protezione di metalli, agenti anti-fouling, resine poliammin-anfoteriche che de la tissotropizza-zione di resine alchidiche.
VERSAMID®, VERSADUCT®, TRIHAEDUR®, GM, composti stagno-organici.

SCHERING SpA
Divisione Chimica Industriale
Via Mancinelli, 7/11
20131 Milano
Telefono 26 78 72
Telex: 33 259 Schering

Schering AG

100 ANNI SCHERING
100 ANNI DI PROGRESSO

Peccato che sia muto.

47

42) Recruitment advertisement for *Bayer* placed in students' magazines. Black and white. (GER)
43) Colour advertisement for a cure for diarrhoea. (BRA)
44) Colour ad for New England Mutual Life Insurance Co. (USA)
45) 46) From a series of international advertisements for the Union Bank of Switzerland. Black and white. (SWI)
47) Trade magazine advertisement for underwater paints made by Schering AG. Red brush, blue ground. (ITA)
48) 49) Double-spread advertisement for *Benadryl,* an antiallergic drug, with its colour illustration. (USA)

42) Aus einer Anzeigenserie für Studentenzeitschriften mit Hin-weis auf Berufsmöglichkeiten bei *Bayer.* Schwarzweiss. (GER)
43) Farbiges Inserat für eine Arznei gegen Diarrhöe. (BRA)
44) Mehrfarbiges Inserat einer Versicherungsgesellschaft. (USA)
45) 46) Aus einer Serie von Zeitschrifteninseraten der Schwei-zerischen Bankgesellschaft. Schwarzweiss. (SWI)
47) Fachzeitschrifteninserat für Unterwasserfarben von Schering AG. Roter Pinsel, blauer Grund. (ITA)
48) 49) Doppelseitiges Fachzeitschrifteninserat für *Benadryl* ge-gen Allergien, mit Detail der Farbillustration. (USA)

42) Annonce de recrutement de *Bayer* publiée dans des revues estudiantines. Noir et blanc. (GER)
43) Annonce couleur pour une cure antidiarrhéique. (BRA)
44) Annonce couleur pour une compagnie d'assurances. (USA)
45) 46) Exemples d'une série d'annonces internationales pour l'Union de Banques Suisses. Noir et blanc. (SWI)
47) Annonce de revue professionnelle pour les peintures sous-marines de la Schering SA. Pinceau rouge, fond bleu. (ITA)
48) 49) Annonce double page et illustration couleur qui y figure. Publicité pour l'antiallergique *Benadryl.* (USA)

Artist | Künstler | Artiste:

42) BARBARA + HANNES GEISSLER
43) ZIRALDO PINTO
44) ROWLAND B. WILSON
45) 46) RENÉ FEHR
47) CLAUS-DIETER ALEX
48) 49) ROY CARRUTHERS / JIM MCFARLAND

Art Director | Directeur artistique:

43) ENOK SACRAMENTO
44) STAVROS COSMOPULOS / DICK PANTANO
45) 46) RUEDI KÜLLING
47) GERHARD MARX
48) 49) JIM MCFARLAND

Agency | Agentur | Agence – Studio:

43) RHODIA-PROPAGANDA
44) HILL, HOLLIDAY, CONNORS, COSMOPULOS, INC.
45) 46) ADVICO-DELPIRE AG
48) 49) SUDLER & HENNESSEY

Advertisements / Inserate / Annonces

AFTER THE FLOOD CAME THE POLLEN

THAT'S WHY MAN INVENTED
BENADRYL
(diphenhydramine HCl)
PARKE-DAVIS

48

50)–52) 'Catch me, I'm your red (yellow, blue).' From a series of magazine advertisements for colours for the packaging trade made by a printing-ink manufacturer. (GER)

53) 54) Black-and-white advertisements from a campaign for Cousins Mortgage and Equity Investments—here about their flexibility and unprecedented success. (USA)

55) 56) Magazine advertisements from a campaign for the Package and Container Environment programme launched by the Container Corporation of America. (USA)

57) 59) Local identity advertisements for the Container Corporation. Black and white, red print. (USA)

58) CCA ad for an athletic event. Black and white. (USA)

50)–52) Aus einer Serie Zeitschrifteninserate der Druckfarbenfabrik Gebr. Schmidt GmbH für die Greif-Farben, die für die Packungsindustrie bestimmt sind. (GER)

53) 54) Schwarzweisse Inserate aus einer Kampagne für ein Investmentunternehmen – hier über dessen Flexibilität und beispiellosen Erfolg. (USA)

55) 56) Zeitschrifteninserate aus einer Kampagne für ein Programm der Container Corporation für Packungen und Behälter, die gegen alle äusseren Einflüsse schützen. (USA)

57) 59) Inserate für die Container Corporation of America. Schwarzweiss, mit roter Schrift. (USA)

58) CCA Inserat für eine sportliche Veranstaltung. (USA)

50)–52) «Attrape-moi, je suis ton rouge (jaune, bleu).» Série d'annonces de magazines pour des encres d'imprimerie utilisées dans l'industrie de l'emballage. (GER)

53) 54) Annonces noir-blanc figurant dans une campagne de Cousins Mortgage and Equity Investments et mettant ici en relief la souplesse et le succès de cette compagnie. (USA)

55) 56) Annonces de magazine figurant dans une campagne de la Container Corporation of America en faveur de son programme favorable à l'environnement. (USA)

57) 59) Annonces de prestige pour la Container Corporation. Noir-blanc, caractères rouges. (USA)

58) Annonce CCA pour une rencontre d'athlétisme. (USA)

50

51

52

55

56

57

Artist | Künstler | Artiste:

50)–52) JOSSE GOFFIN/OLAF LEU
53) 54) RICK MEYEROWITZ/RICHARD HENDERSON
55) 56) DAVID WILCOX
57) 59) BILL BONNELL III
58) DAVID ANDERSON

Art Director | Directeur artistique:

50)–52) OLAF LEU
53) 54) RICHARD HENDERSON
55) 56) JOHN MASSEY
57)–59) BILL BONNELL III

Agency | Agentur | Agence – Studio:

50)–52) OLAF LEU DESIGN
53) 54) COLE, HENDERSON, DRAKE, INC.
55) 56) N.W. AYER & SON, INC.
57)–59) CONTAINER CORPORATION OF AMERICA

**Advertisements / Inserate
Annonces**

How flexible should a REIT be?

We're Cousins Mortgage and Equity Investments, a publicly-owned real estate investment trust listed on the New York Stock Exchange. And we think a real estate investment trust should be flexible in two large areas.

First, we don't believe a REIT should specialize in just one or two kinds of loans. Because today's financial real estate market is so inter-locking and fast-moving that specialization means painting yourself into a corner. And then getting stuck there.

That's why we've got all kinds of different loans in our portfolio. Everything from short-term condominium financing to intermediate standing second mortgages to a permanent loan on a coliseum.

And there's another side to flexibility—the customer's side. A good REIT should be willing to stretch and bend to get its loan requirements and all of your money needs together. *Fast.*

Judging from our growth, our philosophy of double flexibility seems to be what the industry was looking for. Last year, it helped us generate $138,000,000 worth of new business—and double in size. This year, we've already got over $350,000,000 in total loan commitments.

If you're in the market for any kind of real estate financing, give Jim Drais a call at (404) 432-0671. Or write him at 300 Interstate North, Atlanta, Georgia 30339. He'll bend over backwards to work with you.

Cousins Mortgage and Equity Investments

53

The trouble is, our story sounds almost too good to be true.

Cousins Mortgage and Equity Investments is a publicly-owned real estate investment trust (REIT) listed on the New York Stock Exchange. We look for real estate investments that offer a high fixed return, and/or additional return based on how well such an investment does financially.

By law, we have to return 90% of our profits to our shareholders—but we've been returning 100%. And by any standards, we've had some excellent profits.

When we opened in 1970, we had an asset base of $40,000,000. By the end of 1971, we had grown to $85,000,000. A year later we had doubled in size again, while generating $138,000,000 in new business. And paying a dividend of $1.95 per share—a 16% increase over 1971.

All in only 2 years. We realize that it sounds unbelievable, but we've got some very believable reasons behind our unprecedented success.

We're advised by Cousins Properties Incorporated—one of the most successful diversified real estate companies in the Southeast. Their experience gives us in-depth knowledge of today's real estate market. And a lot of stability in the industry.

We've got $265,000,000 available to lend, and that includes one of the largest shareholders' equity bases in the business—over $80,000,000.

And we have an Automatic Dividend Investment Plan that's unique in the industry—an arrangement so attractive that over half of our outstanding shares participated in it last year.

If you'd like to take a firsthand look at just how good and true our story is, we invite you to visit us or write for our annual report. All you have to do is give Tarlton Pittard a call at (404) 432-0671. Or write him at Cousins Mortgage and Equity Investments, 300 Interstate North, Atlanta, Ga. 30339.

Cousins Mortgage and Equity Investments

54

Here is the beginning of philosophy; a recognition of the conflicts between men, a search for their causes, a condemnation of mere opinion . . . and the discovery of a standard of judgment.

Epictetus   Discourses   1st Century A.D.

Container Corporation of America

58

What can a leading international packaging organization do for the folks here at home?

Everything.

Everything, that is, relating to paperboard, package design and research, shipping containers, folding cartons, plastic packaging, composite cans, corporate identity programs, point-of-purchase displays, exhibition displays. With ten major facilities in the Chicago area—plus our corporate headquarters, we are simply equipped to do everything. Test us.

Container Corporation of America

59

-41

62

63

Artist / Künstler / Artiste:

60) ELAINE WOZNIAK
61) ELWYN MEHLMAN
62) 63) GIANVITTORE CALVI
64) RAY DOMINGO
65) JON LOPEZ
66) JOE SAFFOLD / PETE COUTROULIS

Art Director / Directeur artistique:

60) 61) LARRY W. PILLOT
62) 63) GIANVITTORE CALVI
64) HARLAN MILLER
65) JON LOPEZ
66) PETE COUTROULIS

Agency / Agentur / Agence – Studio:

60) 61) LANG, FISHER & STASHOWER, INC.
62) 63) AROLDO ARAUJO PROPAGANDA
64) SHARP ADVERTISING / E & R GRAPHICS
65) JON LOPEZ
66) JIM WELLER & PARTNERS

66

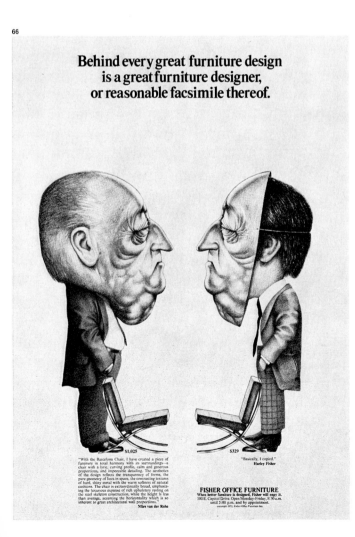

Behind every great furniture design is a great furniture designer, or reasonable facsimile thereof.

FISHER OFFICE FURNITURE

60) 61) Magazine advertisements from a campaign for Cleveland Trust, here offering help in handling money and forecasts of company development. Illustrations in colour. (USA)
62) 63) Complete magazine advertisement for a financing system that is "armed to the teeth" and detail of the colour illustration. (BRA)
64) Advertisement in pastel shades for a television channel. (USA)
65) Black-and-white advertisement for the film *Raven's End*. (USA)
66) Full-page newspaper advertisement for *Fisher,* who "copied" a piece of Mies van der Rohe furniture—at one third the price. Black and white. (USA)

60) 61) Zeitschrifteninserat aus einer Kampagne für Cleveland Trust, die ihren Beistand in Geldangelegenheiten und Entwicklungsvoraussagen anbietet. Mehrfarbig. (USA)
62) 63) Vollständiges Zeitschrifteninserat für ein Finanzierungssystem, das «bis auf die Zähne bewaffnet» ist, mit Detail der Farbillustration. (BRA)
64) Inserat in Pastellfarben für eine Fernsehgesellschaft. (USA)
65) Schwarzweisses Inserat für den Film *Raven's End*. (USA)
66) Ganzseitiges Zeitungsinserat für einen nach einem Modell von Mies van der Rohe kopierten Stuhl, der nur einen Drittel dessen Preises kostet. Schwarzweiss. (USA)

60) 61) Annonces de magazine figurant dans une campagne en faveur de Cleveland Trust, qui offre ici son concours pour la gestion prospective et financière des entreprises. Illustrations couleur. (USA)
62) 63) Annonce complète de magazine pour un système financier «armé jusqu'aux dents», et détail de l'illustration couleur. (BRA)
64) Annonce aux tons pastels pour une chaîne de télévision. (USA)
65) Annonce noir et blanc pour le film *Raven's End*. (USA)
66) Annonce de journal, pleine page, pour *Fisher,* qui s'est ingénié à «copier» un meuble de Mies van der Rohe – pour un tiers du prix de l'original. Noir et blanc. (USA)

Advertisements / Inserate / Annonces

69

68

72

67) 68) Magazine advertisement donated by Time for a Salvation Army
appeal, with detail of illustration. Black and white. (AUL)
69) Double-spread, full-colour advertisement in trade magazines for *Levi's*
slacks and tops. (USA)
70) Full-page newspaper advertisement announcing a toy exhibition in a
department store. Black and white. (SWI)
71) "If you ask your computer for formulations, it'll tell you nothing about
quality." Black-and-white advertisement for a chemical firm. (GER)
72) Institutional magazine advertisement for the Atlantic Richfield Company
on how cultures can help each other. Full colour. (USA)
73) Full-page newspaper advertisement announcing an exhibition of Japanese
goods in a Bernese department store. Red sun. (SWI)
74) Magazine advertisement for luxury apartments in Atlanta. (USA)

70

71

73

74

67) 68) Von TIME gespendetes Zeitschrifteninserat mit einem Aufruf der Heilsarmee, mit Detail der Illustration. Schwarzweiss. (AUL)
69) Doppelseitiges, mehrfarbiges Fachzeitschrifteninserat für Jeans und Jacken von *Levi's*. (USA)
70) Ganzseitiges Zeitschrifteninserat für eine Spielwarenausstellung im Kaufhaus Loeb in Bern. Schwarzweiss. (SWI)
71) Inserat der Chemischen Fabrik Kalk GmbH. (GER)
72) Mehrfarbiges, institutionelles Zeitschrifteninserat der Atlantic Richfield Company, das zeigt, wie die verschiedenen Kulturen einander von Nutzen sein können. (USA)
73) Ganzseitiges Zeitungsinserat als Ankündigung einer japanischen Ausstellung im Kaufhaus Loeb, Bern. Rote Sonne. (SWI)
74) Zeitschrifteninserat für Luxuswohnungen. Schwarzweiss. (USA)

67) 68) Annonce de magazine payée par TIME: appel de l'Armée du Salut, et détail de l'illustration. Noir et blanc. (AUL)
69) Annonce de revue professionnelle, double page, en polychromie, pour les ensembles *Levi's* (pantalons et vestes). (USA)
70) Annonce de journal, pleine page, annonçant une exposition de jouets dans un grand magasin. Noir et blanc. (SWI)
71) «Si vous demandez des formules à votre ordinateur, il vous les donnera, mais ne dira rien de la qualité.» Annonce chimique noir-blanc. (GER)
72) Annonce de magazine de prestige pour l'Atlantic Richfield Company sur l'entraide entre civilisations différentes. En polychromie. (USA)
73) Annonce de journal, pleine page, annonçant une exposition de produits japonais dans un grand magasin de Berne. Soleil rouge. (SWI)
74) Annonce de magazine pour des appartements de luxe à Atlanta. (USA)

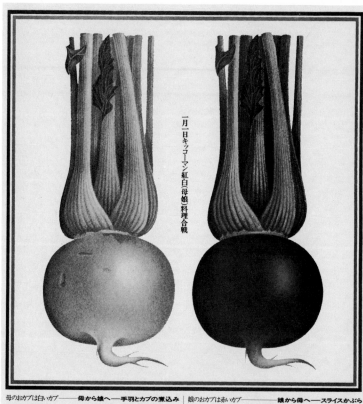

75) Newspaper advertisement for the soy sauces of Kikkoman Shoyu Co. Ltd. (JPN)
76)–78) Full-page newspaper advertisements, with illustrations in full colour (see fig. 78), for *Kikkoman* soy sauces. For other examples of advertising for this company, which comprises many different campaigns by the same artist, see figs. 7–13. (JPN)

75) Zeitungsinserat für die Soya-Saucen von Kikkoman Shoyu Co. Ltd. (JPN)
76)–78) Ganzseitige Zeitungsanzeigen, mit mehrfarbigen Illustrationen (siehe Abb. 78), für *Kikkoman* Soya-Saucen. Andere Beispiele der Werbung dieses Herstellers, die verschiedene Kampagnen des gleichen Künstlers umfasst, sind in Abb. 7 bis 13 zu finden. (JPN)

75) Annonce de journal pour les sauces soya de la Kikkoman Shoyu Co. Ltd. (JPN)
76)–78) Annonces de journal, pleine page, avec illustrations en polychromie (cf. la fig. 78), pour les sauces soya *Kikkoman*. Pour d'autres exemples de la publicité de cette entreprise, qui comprend un grand nombre de campagnes très diverses de la main du même artiste, voir les fig. 7 à 13. (JPN)

76

75

77

Artist | Künstler | Artiste:
75)–78) TADASHI OHASHI

Art Director | Directeur artistique:
75)–78) TADASHI OHASHI

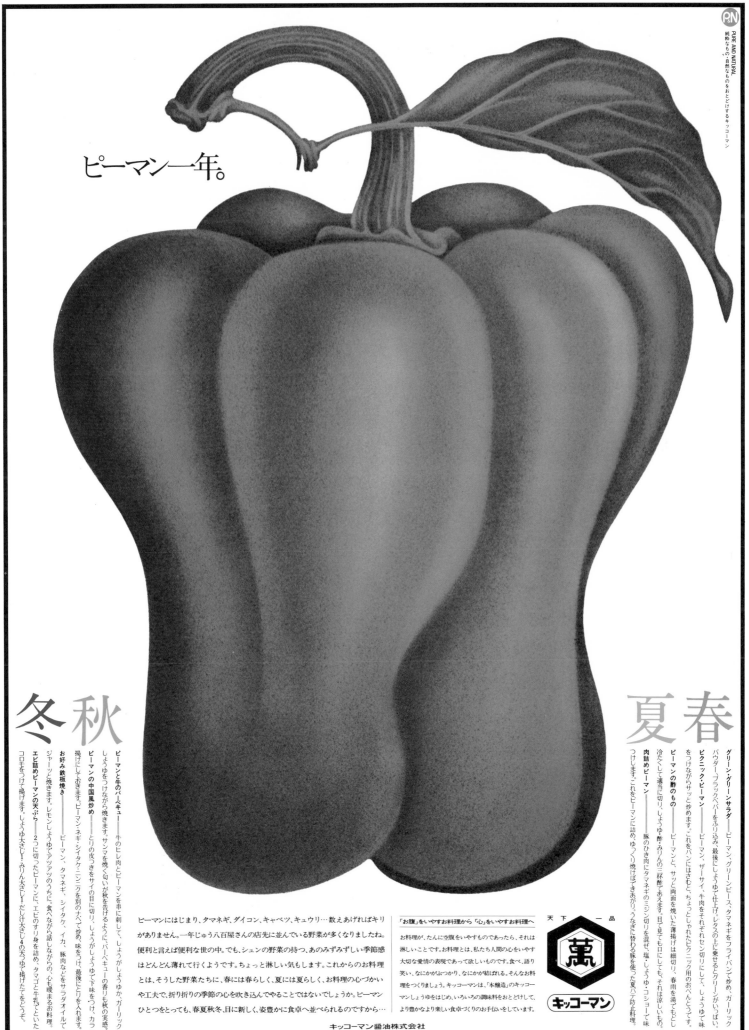

79

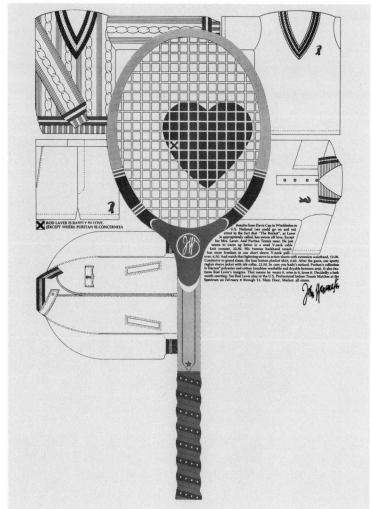

80

79)–82) Examples of full-page newspaper advertisements for the *John Wanamaker* department stores. Fig. 79 is for Western jeans and jackets, fig. 80 for tennis clothing bearing Rod Laver's insignia, fig. 81 for Christmas displays in the traditional spirit, fig. 82 for *Manhattan* shirts, with a reference to the sale of Manhattan to the United States by the Red Indians for 24 dollars in 1626. (USA)

79)–82) Beispiele ganzseitiger Zeitungsanzeigen für die *John Wanamaker* Kaufhäuser. Abb. 79 wirbt für Western Jeans und Jacken, Abb. 80 für Tenniskleider mit dem Rod Laver Abzeichen, Abb. 81 für eine Weihnachtsausstellung im herkömmlichen Geiste und Abb. 82 für *Manhattan* Hemden, dessen Preis an den Verkauf von Manhattan durch die Indianer im Jahre 1626 für 24 Dollar erinnert. (USA)

79)–82) Exemples d'annonces de journal, pleine page, pour les grands magasins *John Wanamaker:* 79) jeans et vestes de style western, 80) tenues de tennis aux insignes de Rod Laver, 81) décorations de Noël traditionnelles, 82) chemises *Manhattan,* avec rappel de l'origine de Manhattan, vendue en 1626 pour 24 dollars aux Etats-Unis par les Indiens. (USA)

Agency / Agentur / Agence – Studio:
79)–82) JOHN WANAMAKER ADVERTISING DEPT.

Advertisements / Inserate / Annonces

81

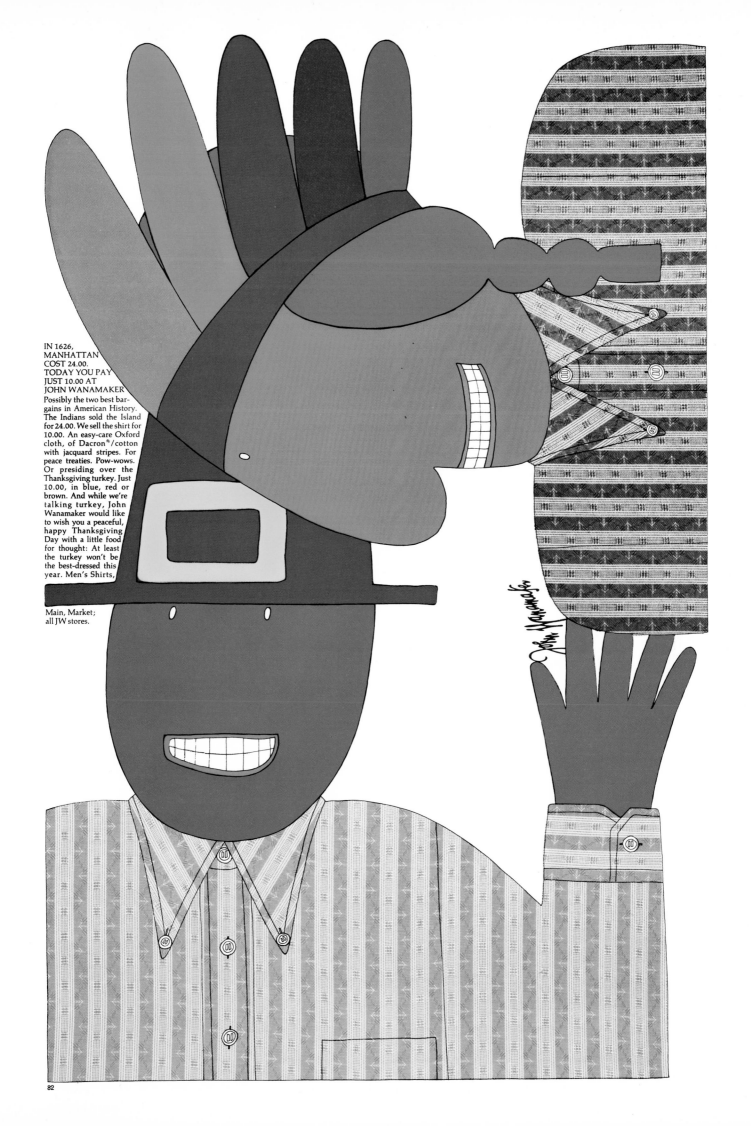

IN 1626,
MANHATTAN
COST 24.00.
TODAY YOU PAY
JUST 10.00 AT
JOHN WANAMAKER
Possibly the two best bargains in American History. The Indians sold the Island for 24.00. We sell the shirt for 10.00. An easy-care Oxford cloth, of Dacron®/cotton with jacquard stripes. For peace treaties. Pow-wows. Or presiding over the Thanksgiving turkey. Just 10.00, in blue, red or brown. And while we're talking turkey, John Wanamaker would like to wish you a peaceful, happy Thanksgiving Day with a little food for thought: At least the turkey won't be the best-dressed this year. Men's Shirts,

Main, Market; all JW stores.

How to open a $1000 savings account. With our money.

We've come to the conclusion that saving money, regularly, is one of the toughest tasks anyone faces; somehow there's always something financially "more important" at the moment than adding to your savings account.

So we've come up with a *guaranteed* savings plan—a new service we think you'll find unusual. And unusually helpful. Here's how it works:

Just stop by our main office or one of our branch offices listed below. We'll give you a one-year loan for any amount you wish up to $1000. That money will then be placed immediately in a new or existing Regular Savings Account.

Your loan will be paid—like other loans—by monthly installments. And at the end of one year it will have been paid in full.

In other words, you'll be *forcing* yourself to save, rather than depending on a wishful-thinking, hit-or-miss plan. And at any time you can withdraw any amount from your savings account, except the balance due on your loan.

So if you have trouble saving your money, see us. We'll help you with *our* money.

For further information, call 746-0511. Or stop by The Georgia Bank office nearest you: Main Office, 515 Mulberry Street; Pio Nono Branch, Pio Nono Plaza; Riverside Branch, 2930 Riverside Drive; Northeast Plaza Branch, Northeast Plaza. Member FDIC.

THE GEORGIA BANK
Maybe you should get to know us.

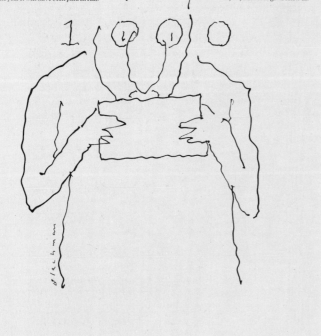

83

Next time your bank gets to you, maybe you should get to know us.

We don't think you should have to put up with so-so service from a bank, any more than you would from any other business. In other words, if you're not getting accurate records, a lot of financial help and friendly day-to-day service—then maybe you should come talk with us.

We're not the biggest bank in town, but we're not the littlest, either. Which means we're large enough to offer you complete Full Service banking—and small enough to know you by name.

We've got four excellent locations, with quick drive-in windows at each. And we're coming up with some new approaches to banking that we think you'll like. For instance: Your own personal banker. A bank-wide policy that gives women the credit they deserve. An early bird drive-in window

that opens at 8:15 a.m. And the highest interest rates ever on all six of our savings plans.

One more thing: if you're afraid that changing banks will be too much trouble—don't be. We'll handle every bit of the paper work. All you have to do is sign your name; we'll close out your old accounts and open new ones at our bank. It's that simple.

So just keep this thought in mind: now there's no reason to stay with a bank that's getting to you.

Because we want you to get to know us.
Main Office, 515 Mulberry Street;
Pio Nono Branch, Pio Nono Plaza;
Riverside Branch, 2930 Riverside
Drive; Northeast Plaza Branch,
Northeast Plaza. Member FDIC.

THE GEORGIA BANK
Maybe you should get to know us.

84

EATON'S

The Cherry Blossom — Flower of the Mysterious Orient.

Decorate your home with the delicate freshness of cherry blossoms. Evoking the mystique of the East, they are life-like plastic in dainty shades of pink or yellow. **32" long: 1.00 branch; 44" long: 2.05 branch.** Visit Eaton's garden of artificial flowers and choose from the abundance of beautiful blooms and greenery. Downtown Only ('Gift Shop', Sixth Floor and 'Trouvailles', Main Floor) Dept. 216. Personal Shopping Only.

85

EATON'S

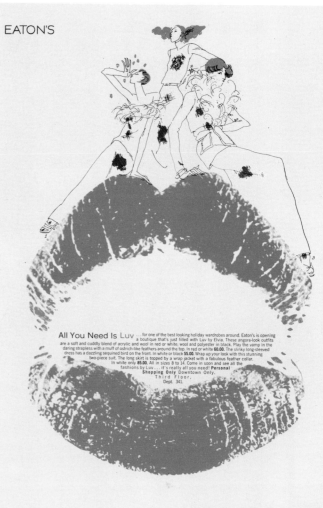

All You Need Is Luv ... for one of the best looking holiday wardrobes around. Eaton's is opening a boutique that's just filled with Luv by Elvia. These angora-look outfits are a soft and cuddly blend of acrylic and wool in red or white; wool and polyester in black. Play the vamp in the daring strapless with a muff of ostrich-like feathers around the top. In red or white **60.00.** The slinky long-sleeved dress has a dazzling sequined bird on the front. In white or black **55.00.** Wrap up your look with this stunning two-piece suit. The long skirt is topped by a wrap jacket with a fabulous feather collar. In white only **85.00.** All in sizes 8 to 14. Come in soon and see all the fashions by Luv ... it's really all you need! **Personal Shopping Only Downtown Only.**
Third Floor, Dept. 341.

86

83) 84) Full-page newspaper advertisements about a savings plan and the services offered by The Georgia Bank. Black and white. (USA)

85) 86) Full-page newspaper advertisements for *Eaton's* department stores. Fig. 85 offers artificial flowers, fig. 86 a fashion range. (CAN)

87) Newspaper advertisement with colour illustration for a magazine. The text says that the man who lives in his shell will never like LE NOUVEL OBSERVATEUR. (FRA)

88) Newspaper ad announcing a programme on *The Mind of Man* on TV Channel 13. (USA)

89) 90) Black-and-white space promotion advertisements for THE NEW YORK TIMES. (USA)

83) 84) Ganzseitige Zeitungsinserate für einen Sparplan und die Dienste der Georgia Bank. Schwarzweiss. (USA)

85) 86) Ganzseitige Zeitungsinserate für *Eaton's* Kaufhäuser. Abb. 85 bietet künstliche Blumen an, Abb. 86 ein Modesortiment. (CAN)

87) Zeitungsinserat mit Farbillustration für eine Zeitschrift. Der Text besagt, dass der Mensch, der in sich zurückgezogen lebt, nie den NOUVEL OBSERVATEUR schätzen wird. (FRA)

88) Ankündigung eines Fernsehprogramms über den Geist des Menschen. (USA)

89) 90) Schwarzweisse Eigeninserate der NEW YORK TIMES als Inseratenwerbung. (USA)

83) 84) Annonces de journal, pleine page: plan d'épargne et services offerts par la Georgia Bank. Noir et blanc. (USA)

85) 86) Annonces de journal, pleine page, pour les grands magasins *Eaton's*: 85) pour des fleurs artificielles, 86) pour la mode. (CAN)

87) Annonce de journal, avec illustration couleur, pour le magazine LE NOUVEL OBSERVATEUR, honni de ceux qui vivent dans une tour d'ivoire ou repliés dans leur coquille. (FRA)

88) Annonce de journal pour un programme de la chaîne TV Channel 13 sur l'*Esprit humain*. (USA)

89) 90) Annonces noir-blanc du NEW YORK TIMES s'adressant aux annonceurs potentiels. (USA)

Homme en marche immobile
vers les nouvelles sociétés.
Homme crépusculaire, paupières pesantes
à se cacher l'évidence du jour.
Homme aux oreilles absentes,
pour s'épargner d'entendre les cris du monde.
Homme en forme de coquille,
de cocon, de carapace.
Jamais tu n'aimeras LE 1 NOUVEL
obsevateur

87

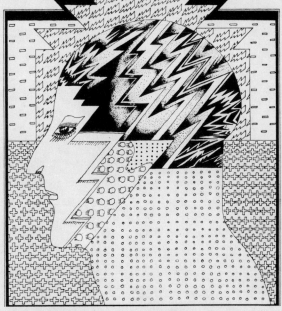

The Electric Organ

The human brain!
It generates and consumes electricity.
It receives; it transmits.
It records, rewinds and plays back.
The Mind of Man is astounding:
A yogi sits in an airtight box and can survive on only 1/4 oxygen a human requires.

A man, using brain power only, can reduce his blood pressure until all his vital signs indicate death.

Brain power—the men who study it and the men who use it—is the subject of a two-hour special.

13 The Mind of Man. See it tonight at 7.

88

Artist / Künstler / Artiste:

83) R.O. BLECHMAN / JERRY SULLIVAN
84) JACK DAVIS / JERRY SULLIVAN
85) GERARD FRIGCHETEAU / ERIC CAPEL
86) GEORGINE STRATHY / CAROL SEDGEWICK
87) ANDRÉ FRANÇOIS / ROBERT SADOUX
88) JACK UNRUH
89) 90) GARY SOLIN / ANDREW KNER

Art Director / Directeur artistique:

83) 84) JERRY SULLIVAN / PERRY MITCHELL
85) 86) H. GOLFOS SANTROCH
87) ROBERT DELPIRE
88) MIKE STEEL
89) 90) ANDREW KNER

Agency / Agentur / Agence – Studio:

83) 84) COLE, HENDERSON, DRAKE
85) 86) EATON'S ADVERTISING DEPT.
87) DELPIRE-ADVICO S.A.
88) HOUSTON RITZ & ASSOC.

89

More New Yorkers with professional/managerial jobs read The New York Times than read both other New York newspapers combined.

90

As many New Yorkers with household incomes of $25,000 or more read The New York Times as read both other New York newspapers combined.

TAKE YOUR TASTEBUDS ON A TRIP TO SWITZERLAND!

Come to Eaton's and discover Switzerland. Learn why Swiss cuisine is so well known. Enjoy new taste experiences. From October 22 through October 27, Switzerland will be featured in Eaton's Fine Food Shop, Blue Cake Counter and Ninth Floor Restaurant. There will even be a contest . . . you may win a Saint Bernard stuffed dog. Read

on . . . find out what's happening . . . then come down to Eaton's and join in on the fun. Eaton's Downtown Only. Main Floor, Dept. 379.

Cheese 'n Chocolates

Swiss cheese can help you create a very interesting meal. Start off with raclette — a special kind of cheese that you melt and serve with

tiny boiled potatoes. Then try a cheese fondue — so delicious and satisfying. For an unusual dessert, how about a chocolate fondue. You can use milk chocolate by

TOBLER or SUCHARD . . . two great names in chocolate. You will also find a tempting assortment of bars with all kinds of fillings. See demonstrations of Knorr Swiss soups, Oulevay biscuits and Lutin Muesli bars, too. And this will be a one-stop dinner — you can get all the fixings at Eaton's Fine Food Shop.

Chocolate Cake and Swiss Menu

Eaton's Blue Cake Counter will have a special Swiss Chocolate cake availabe during this promotion. Luscious chocolate and whipped cream are combined to make a delightful dessert. The 6" cake will be 2.00. The Ninth Floor Restaurant will be in on the fun too. There will be a special Swiss menu to tempt you all week long. It will include Onion Soup Baloise,

Mushrooms on Toast à l'Emmenthal, plat Bernoise and Crème de Marrons Chantilly. It's sure to be delicious!

You Could Win a Saint Bernard Toy

Wouldn't you like to have a beautiful Saint Bernard plush toy? All you have to do is come in to the Fine Food Shop and fill out the entry form. No purchase is necessary. The prizes, provided by Tobler and Suchard, will be: 5 large toy dogs, approx. 36" high; 50 small toy dogs, approx. 15" high. The contest lasts now through Saturday, October 27. The drawing will take place on Monday, October 29. Come in and give it a try! Downtown Only, Main Floor. Dept. 379.

EATON'S

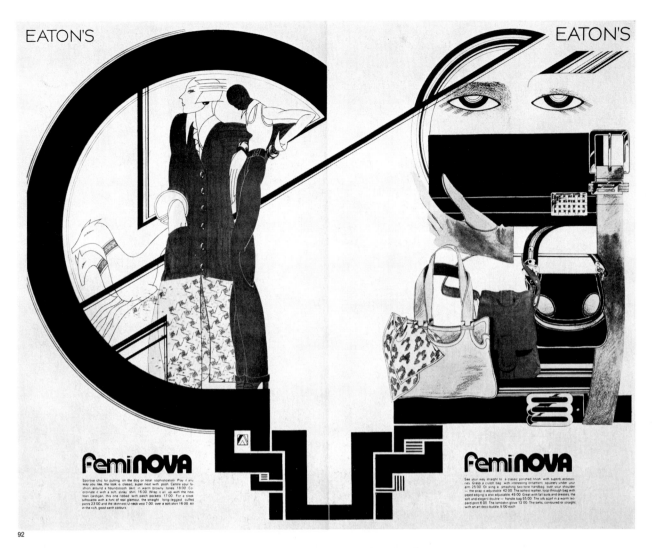

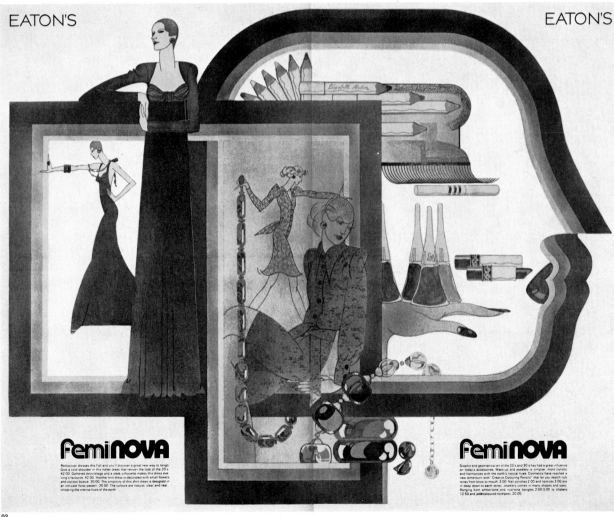

91) Full-page newspaper advertisement about Swiss foods sold by *Eaton's* department stores. Black and white. (CAN)

92) 93) Double spreads from a newspaper supplement about new fashion styles in clothing and accessories offered by *Eaton's* department stores. (CAN)

91) Ganzseitiges Zeitungsinserat über kulinarische Spezialitäten der Schweiz, die bei *Eaton's* erhältlich sind. (CAN)

92) 93) Doppelseiten aus einer Zeitungsbeilage für *Eaton's* Kaufhäuser über den neuen Modetrend bei Kleidern und Accessoires. (CAN)

91) Annonce de journal, pleine page, pour spécialités alimentaires suisses vendues dans les grands magasins *Eaton's*. (CAN)

92) 93) Doubles pages d'un supplément de journal présentant la mode nouvelle (vêtements et accessoires) mise en vente chez *Eaton's*. (CAN)

Artist | Künstler | Artiste:
91) AL WARUNKIW /
MARK FORDHAM
92) 93) GEORGINE STRATHY /
CAROL SEDGEWICK /
CLAUDIA MILNE

Art Director | Directeur artistique:
91)-93) H. GOLFOS SANTROCH

Agency | Agentur | Agence – Studio:
91)-93) EATON'S ADVERTISING
DEPT.

53

2

Booklets
Folders
Catalogues
Invitations
Programmes

Broschüren
Faltprospekte
Kataloge
Einladungen
Programme

Brochures
Dépliants
Catalogues
Invitations
Programmes

94)-100) Full-page illustrations (all in colour) and spreads from a large booklet on career development issued by *L'Oréal*. In the spreads, the individual appears on a transparent sheet between text and picture. In the pictures, a maze gives place to a clear profile. (FRA)

94)-100) Ganzseitige Illustrationen (alle mehrfarbig) und Doppelseiten aus einer grossen Broschüre von *L'Oréal* über Aufstiegsmöglichkeiten. Bei den Doppelseiten erscheint der Einzelmensch auf einem durchsichtigen Blatt zwischen Text und Illustration. (FRA)

94)-100) Illustrations pleine page, en couleur, et doubles pages d'une brochure au grand format sur les possibilités de carrière chez *L'Oréal*. Les personnages des doubles pages apparaissent sur une feuille transparente intercalée entre le texte et l'image. (FRA)

Artist | Künstler | Artiste:
94)-100) JEAN LAGARRIGUE

Agency | Agentur | Agence –Studio:
94)-100) QUADRANT CAMPBELL-EWALD

94

95

96
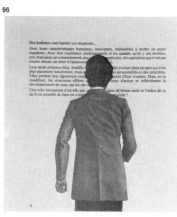

97

98

99

100

Booklets / Broschüren / Prospectus

Tandearil®
in obstetrics and
gynecology

101

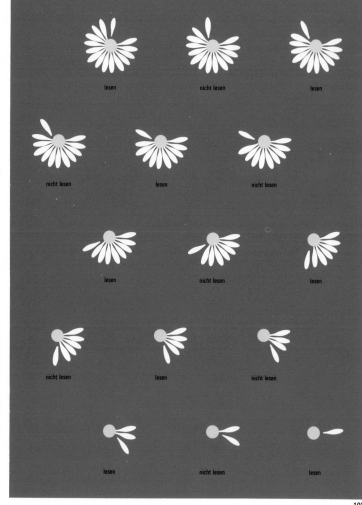

lesen   nicht lesen   lesen

nicht lesen   lesen   nicht lesen

lesen   nicht lesen   lesen

nicht lesen   lesen   nicht lesen

lesen   nicht lesen   lesen

102

Booklets / Broschüren
Prospectus

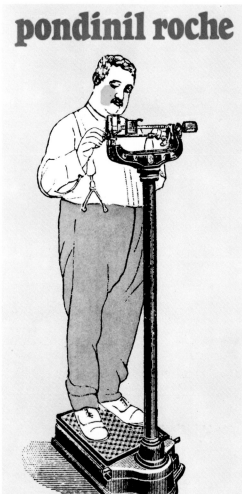

pondinil roche

103

101) Cover of a folder about the uses of a *Ciba-Geigy* drug in gynaecology. (CAN)
102) Cover of a folder about the tranquillizer *Nobrium*. (SWI)
103) Cover of a folder about a *Roche* medicament against obesity. Red, brown and black on pale beige ground. (BEL)
104) 105) From a portfolio of large black-and-white drawings on the subject of aging persons, commissioned by *Sandoz*. (SWI)
106) Cover of a folder about *Lomudal,* a preparation against asthma. (FRA)
107) 108) Double spread about the combination of therapeutic agents in pharmaceuticals (strands in orange, yellow and green), and double gatefold spread illustrating the genesis of a medicine (in full colour), for a German pharmaceutical association. (GER)

101) Umschlag eines Faltprospekts über die Anwendungsmöglichkeiten eines *Ciba-Geigy*-Medikamentes in der Gynäkologie. (CAN)
102) Umschlag eines Prospekts über das Beruhigungsmittel *Nobrium*. (SWI)
103) Umschlag eines Prospekts über ein *Roche*-Medikament gegen Fettleibigkeit. Rot, braun und schwarz auf hellbeigem Grund. (BEL)
104) 105) Aus einer im Auftrag von *Sandoz* verfertigten Mappe mit grossen Zeichnungen zum Thema der alternden Menschen. (SWI)
106) Umschlag eines Prospekts über *Lomudal,* ein Präparat gegen Asthma. (FRA)
107) 108) Doppelseite (Stränge in Orange, Gelb und Grün) und dreiseitiger Ausleger mit einer Darstellung der Entstehung einer Arzneispezialität, aus der Broschüre *Vom Wirkstoff zum Arzneimittel,* die vom Bundesverband der Pharmazeutischen Industrie e.V., Frankfurt/M., zusammengestellt wurde. (GER)

101) Couverture d'un dépliant; emploi d'un médicament *Ciba-Geigy* en gynécologie. (CAN)
102) Couverture d'un dépliant consacré au tranquillisant *Nobrium*. (SWI)
103) Couverture d'un dépliant consacré à un médicament *Roche* de l'obésité. Rouge, brun, noir sur fond beige pâle. (BEL)
104) 105) Exemples des dessins noir-blanc au grand format sur le thème du troisième âge figurant dans un album publié par *Sandoz*. (SWI)
106) Couverture d'un dépliant présentant l'antiasthmatique *Lomudal*. (FRA)
107) 108) Double page sur la combinaison d'agents thérapeutiques dans les remèdes (cordelettes orange, jaunes, vertes), et encart sur double page illustrant la genèse d'un médicament (en polychromie), tirés d'une brochure pour une association pharmaceutique allemande. (GER)

104

105

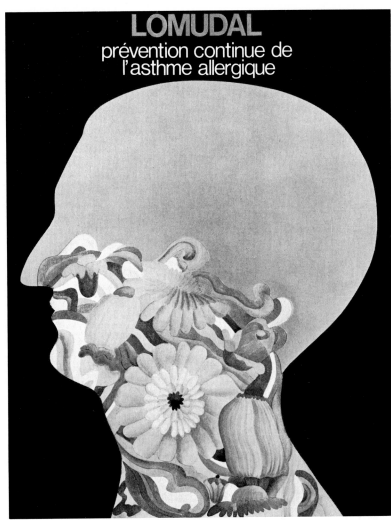

LOMUDAL
prévention continue de l'asthme allergique

106

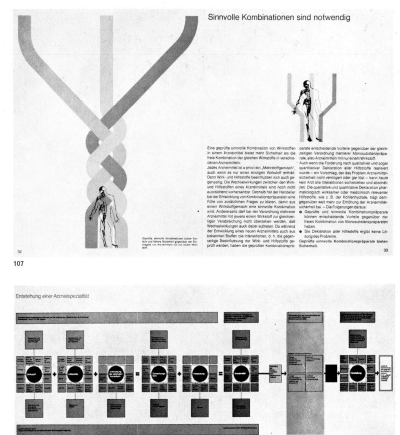

Sinnvolle Kombinationen sind notwendig

Eine geprüfte sinnvolle Kombination von Wirkstoffen in einem Arzneimittel bietet mehr Sicherheit als die freie Kombination der gleichen Wirkstoffe in verschiedenen Arzneimitteln.

Jedes Arzneimittel ist a priori ein „Mehrstoffgemisch", auch wenn es nur einen einzigen Wirkstoff enthält. Denn Wirk- und Hilfsstoffe beeinflussen sich auch gegenseitig. Die Wechselwirkungen zwischen den Wirk- und Hilfsstoffen eines Arzneimittels sind noch nicht ausreichend vorhersehbar. Deshalb hat der Hersteller bei der Entwicklung von Kombinationspräparaten eine Fülle von zusätzlichen Fragen zu klären, damit aus einem Wirkstoffgemisch eine sinnvolle Kombination wird. Andererseits darf bei der Verordnung mehrerer Arzneimittel mit jeweils einem Wirkstoff zur gleichzeitigen Verabreichung nicht übersehen werden, daß Wechselwirkungen auch dabei auftreten. Da während der Entwicklung eines neuen Arzneimittels auch aus bekannten Stoffen die Interaktionen, d. h. die gegenseitige Beeinflussung der Wirk- und Hilfsstoffe geprüft werden, haben die geprüften Kombinations-

parate entscheidende Vorteile gegenüber der gleichzeitigen Verordnung mehrerer Monosubstanzpräparate, also Arzneimittel mit nur einem Wirkstoff.
- Auch wenn die Forderung nach qualitativer und sogar quantitativer Deklaration aller Hilfsstoffe realisiert würde – ein Vorschlag, der das Problem Arzneimittelsicherheit nicht verringert oder gar löst – kann heute kein Arzt alle Interaktionen vorhersehen und abschätzen. Die qualitative und quantitative Deklaration pharmakologisch wirksamer oder medizinisch relevanter Hilfsstoffe, wie z. B. der Kohlenhydrate, trägt damit gegenüber weit mehr zur Erhöhung der Arzneimittelsicherheit bei. – Die Folgerungen daraus:
  ● Geprüfte und sinnvolle Kombinationspräparate können entscheidende Vorteile gegenüber der freien Kombination von Monosubstanzpräparaten haben.
  ● Die Deklaration aller Hilfsstoffe ergibt keine Lösung des Problems.

Geprüfte sinnvolle Kombinationspräparate bieten Sicherheit.

Geprüfte, sinnvolle Kombinationen bieten Vorteile und höhere Sicherheit gegenüber der Einzelgabe von Arzneimitteln mit nur einem Wirkstoff.

32

33

107

Entstehung einer Arzneispezialität

108

109

110

111

112

Artist / Künstler / Artiste:

109)-111) ZIRALDO PINTO
112) EWALD BECKER/GRIT VON FRANSECKY
113) PIERRE BUISSERET
114) 115) ROGER HUMBERT/ERIKA FRANKE

Booklets / Prospekte / Prospectus

109) 110) Two sides of a folder about *A.H.Robins* cures for colds. Full colour. (BRA)
111) From a series of folder covers using collage for a *Merck* product for the treatment of sciatica, stiff neck, etc. (BRA)
112) Colour illustration from a folder about mediaeval beds, for a sleep-inducing drug. (GER)
113) Card (pink/magenta/grey/black) for a *Boehringer* cough cure. (BEL)
114) 115) Full-colour covers from a series of folders for *Roche* psychotropic drugs, here for use in heart and skin disorders. (SWI)

109) 110) Zwei Seiten aus einem Prospekt über ein pharmazeutisches Produkt von *A.H.Robins* gegen Erkältungen. Mehrfarbig. (BRA)
111) Aus einer Serie Collage-Prospektumschläge für ein *Merck*-Produkt zur Behandlung von Ischias, Nackenstarre, etc. (BRA)
112) Farbillustration aus einem Prospekt über mittelalterliche Schlafgewohnheiten, für das Schlafmittel *Mandrax*. (GER)
113) Karte (mehrfarbig) für eine Arznei gegen Halsschmerzen. (BEL)
114) 115) Farbige Umschläge aus einer Serie *Roche*-Prospekte über Beruhigungsmittel, hier gegen Herz- und Hautbeschwerden. (SWI)

109) 110) Deux côtés d'un dépliant vantant les mérites des cures anti-rhumes *A.H.Robins*. En polychromie. (BRA)
111) D'une série de couvertures de dépliants *Merck* exécutées sous forme de collages (remèdes de la sciatique, du torticolis, etc.). (BRA)
112) Dépliant pour un somnifère: les lits du Moyen Age. (GER)
113) Carte rose, magenta, gris, noir pour un béchique *Boehringer*. (BEL)
114) 115) Exemples d'une série publicitaire pour les drogues psychotropes *Roche*. Couvertures polychromes: troubles cardiaques et dermatologiques. (SWI)

Art Director | Directeur artistique:

113) PIERRE BUISSERET
114) 115) JACQUES HAUSER

Agency | Agentur | Agence – Studio:

109) 110) ROBINS-DEP. PUBLICIDADE
111) MERCK-DIV. PROPAGANDA

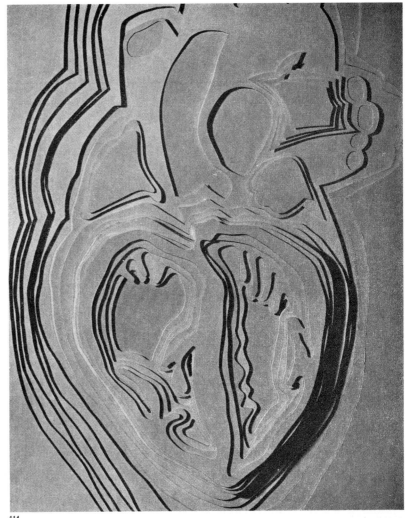

114

Silomat®
se coupe en 4
pour calmer la toux
de l'**enfant,**
l'adulte,
le vieillard
et l'opéré.

113

115

What is cholesterol? Cholesterol is a fat-like sub-stance found in all animal fats.

What is the source of cholesterol? Some cholesterol is manufactured naturally in the body, and some comes from the foods we eat. Two types of foods—those high in cholesterol and those high in saturated fats—are the main dietary source. In the body they undergo chemical changes and eventually are converted to fatty cholesterol deposits that may build up on the blood vessel walls. Other foods can be converted to cholesterol, but the two types mentioned are the most significant.

What are saturated fats? Saturated fats are generally the ones that are solid in the natural state. Animal fats and some vegetable oils, such as coconut and olive oils, are highly saturated.

What are polyunsaturated fats? Polyunsaturated fats are generally the ones that are oils in the natural state. Most vegetable oils, such as safflower and corn oils, are highly polyunsaturated.

What is the most important difference between saturated and polyunsaturated fats? The most important difference between saturated fats and poly-unsaturated fats is the way in which they are handled by the body—the way in which they affect the body

chemistry, especially cholesterol.

How can cholesterol affect my heart? Cholesterol can gradually build up on the walls of the coronary arteries. These are the blood vessels of the heart. They branch off into smaller and smaller arteries deep throughout the heart, supplying the blood and oxygen needed for the enormous pumping task—70 to 75 times a minute all day every day of life.

Because the passageway through the coronary

Artist's representation of gradual build-up of fatty substances, including cholesterol, in a coronary artery. Each segment represents a different time sequence.

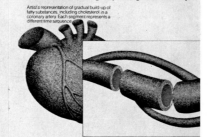

arteries is so narrow, cholesterol and other fatty substances can build up and cause blockage more easily than in larger arteries.

How long does this build-up take? The accumulation of cholesterol on the artery walls is a very slow process that takes many years. In some people it can start very early in life. This build-up is called atherosclerosis, a form of hardening of the arteries.

What happens when the coronary arteries become

partially clogged? When partial clogging of the coronary arteries occurs, the heart may not always get the amounts of oxygen and blood it needs for the work it has to do. When this happens, there may be pain in the chest, which is called angina.

Can this build-up process be stopped? There are indications that the build-up of cholesterol can be stopped, or even reversed, if the proper steps are taken at any time while the build-up is taking place.

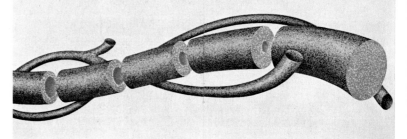

116) 117) Double spreads from a booklet to promote *Promise* margarine. The figures (in brown and yellow) illustrate the build-up of cholesterol in coronary passages. (USA)
118) Colour sheet tipped to the front of a folder on the *Pfizer* calming agent *Vistaril*. It illustrates a dictum on pain by Seneca. (USA)
119) Cover of a *Roche* booklet about quinine promoting the hypnotic *Noludar*. Mustard background, white lettering. (USA)
120) 121) Folder and actual-size detail of the illustration for a *Roche* psychotropic drug. (ITA)
122) Cover of a *Beecham* folder on a treatment for skin infections. Bright hues on black. (AUL)

116) 117) Doubles pages d'une brochure publicitaire pour la margarine *Promise*. Les dessins bruns et jaunes illustrent l'accumulation du cholestérol dans les coronaires. (USA)
118) Feuillet de couleur encollé au recto d'un dépliant *Pfizer* sur l'analgésique *Vistaril*. On y voit l'illustration d'une maxime de Sénèque sur la douleur. (USA)
119) Couverture d'une brochure *Roche* consacrée à la quinine et recommandant l'usage de l'hypnotique *Noludar*. Fond moutarde, lettres blanches. (CAN)
120) 121) Dépliant et détail grandeur nature de l'illustration pour un psychotrope *Roche*. (ITA)
122) Couverture d'un dépliant *Beecham*: traitement des infections de la peau. Couleurs vives. (AUL)

116) 117) Zwei Doppelseiten aus einer Broschüre für Margarine. Die Abbildungen (in Braun und Gelb) illustrieren die Ablagerung von Cholesterin in den Herzgefässen. (USA)
118) Auf den Umschlag eines Prospekts aufgeklebte Farbillustration zu einem Spruch von Seneca über Schmerzen, für das Beruhigungsmittel *Vistaril* von *Pfizer*. (USA)
119) Umschlag einer Broschüre von *Roche* über den Weg vom Chinin zum Schlafmittel *Noludar*. Weisse Schrift auf senffarbenem Grund. (CAN)
120) 121) Prospekt und Illustration in Orignalgrösse, für ein Beruhigungsmittel von *Roche*. (ITA)
122) Umschlag eines *Beecham*-Prospekts über ein Mittel zur Behandlung von Hautinfektionen. (AUL)

"SCORN PAIN: EITHER IT WILL GO AWAY OR YOU WILL." SENECA

3. In search of the fever tree

From Herb to Hypnotic

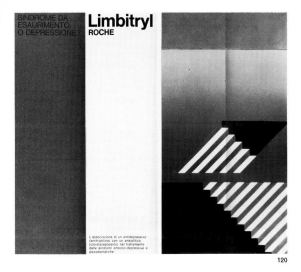

120

Artist | Künstler | Artiste:

116) 117) ROGER MUSICH
118) MARK ENGLISH / FRANK WAGNER
119) ROLF HARDER
120) 121) UFFICIO PUBBLICITÀ ROCHE
122) JO ANNE HOOK / LYNDON WHAITE

Art Director | Directeur artistique:

116) 117) ROGER MUSICH
118) FRANK WAGNER
119) ROLF HARDER / JOHN MALOUGH
120) 121) UFFICIO PUBBLICITÀ ROCHE
122) LYNDON WHAITE

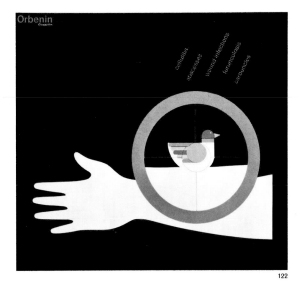

122

Agency | Agentur | Agence – Studio:

116)–118) SUDLER & HENNESSEY
119) DESIGN COLLABORATIVE
120) 121) UFFICIO PUBBLICITÀ ROCHE
122) KENT BEARD ADVERTISING

121

Booklets / Broschüren / Prospectus

Artist / Künstler / Artiste:

124) 125) DON IVAN PUNCHATZ / A. NEAL SIEGEL
126) 127) ETIENNE DELESSERT / A. NEAL SIEGEL
128) DAVID PALLADINI
129) 130) WALTER LIENERT

Art Director / Directeur artistique:

124)–127) A. NEAL SIEGEL
128) JOSEPH FAZIO
129) 130) WALTER LIENERT

Agency / Agentur / Agence – Studio:

123) R.I.T. S.A., DEPT. PUBLICITÉ
124)–127) SMITH KLINE & FRENCH
128) GEIGY PHARMACEUTICALS
129) 130) CIBA-GEIGY, ZENTRALE WERBUNG

Ornade® Rewrites History: The Raven

Each Spansule® capsule contains 8 mg. Teldrin®
(brand of chlorpheniramine maleate);
50 mg. phenylpropanolamine hydrochloride;
2.5 mg. isopropamide, as the iodide.

124

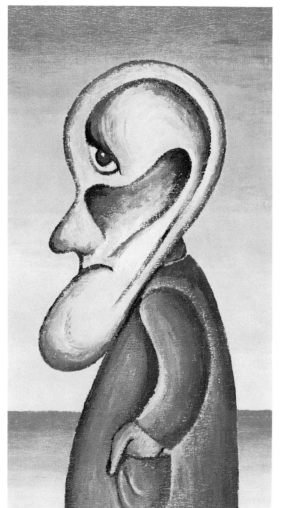

123

Ornade® Rewrites History:

Each Spansule® capsule contains 8 mg. Teldrin®
(brand of chlorpheniramine maleate);
50 mg. phenylpropanolamine hydrochloride;
2.5 mg. isopropamide, as the iodide.

The Midnight Ride of Paul Revere

126

The hazardous hibachi

128

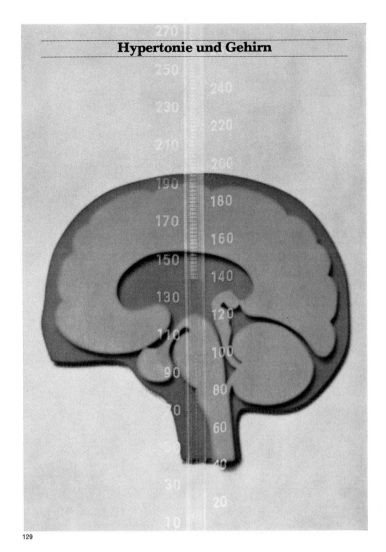

129

Ornade Rewrites History: The Raven

Ornade: To Relieve Nasal Allergies

125

Ornade Rewrites History:

The Midnight Ride of Paul Revere

Ornade: To Relieve Cold Symptoms

127

123) Card describing *Stapolidex* ear drops. Full colour. (FRA)
124)-127) Covers and three-panel spreads from two folders in a series in which historical incidents are rewritten in rhyme to include the effects of the antiallergic drug *Ornade*. (USA)
128) Cover of a folder designed to contain a *Geigy* series of medical reports. Full colour. (USA)
129) 130) From a series of *Ciba* folders on a remedy for high blood pressure. Red on grey. (SWI)

123) Vorderseite einer Karte über *Stapolidex*-Ohrentropfen. Mehrfarbig. (FRA)
124)-127) Vorderseiten und dreiteilige Prospekte aus einer Serie über das Antiallergicum *Ornade*, das im Zusammenhang mit geschichtlichen Begebenheiten gezeigt wird. (USA)
128) Umschlag einer Sammelmappe für eine Serie medizinischer Berichte von *Geigy*. Farbig. (USA)
129) 130) Aus einer Serie *Ciba*-Prospekte über *Adelphan-Esidrex* für die Blutdrucksenkung. (SWI)

123) Carte descriptive pour les gouttes *Stapolidex* pour les oreilles. En polychromie. (FRA)
124)-127) Couvertures et triples pages de deux dépliants d'une série parodiant des événements historiques en vers de manière à mentionner l'effet de l'antiallergique *Ornade*. (USA)
128) Couverture d'un dépliant pour classer divers rapports médicaux *Geigy*. En polychromie. (USA)
129) 130) Exemples de dépliants *Ciba* présentant un hypotenseur. Rouge sur gris. (SWI)

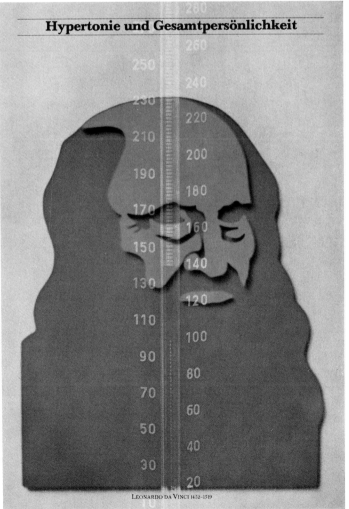

LEONARDO DA VINCI 1452–1519

130

ne pas tousser: **nétux**

131

ne pas tousser: **nétux**

132

136

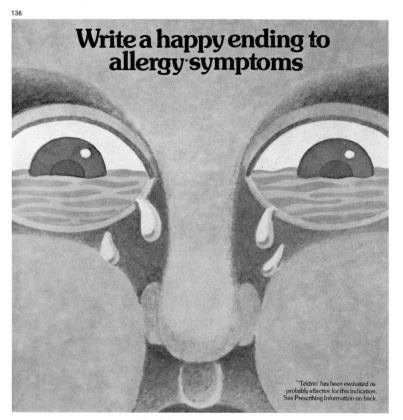

Write a happy ending to allergy symptoms

"Teldrin' has been evaluated as probably effective for this indication. See Prescribing Information on back.

131)-133) From a series of cards for a *Roussel* cough mixture, in which a famous French cartoonist has introduced a cough into various well-known paintings, here by Manet and Toulouse-Lautrec. Pen drawings, coloured borders. (FRA)

134) 135) Full-colour artwork illustrating drug dependence, and complete sleeve with removable card, for a product of Smith Kline & French Labs. against chronic neurotic anxiety. The picture is uncovered when the card is withdrawn. (USA)

136) Cover of a folder about *Teldrin*, a pharmaceutical that combats watering of the eyes in nasal allergies. Pink face, greenish eyes in blue waters. (USA)

137) 138) Cover and double spread from a large booklet about the opening of the Meyer L. Prentis Cancer Centre in Detroit. Cover and inside illustration in full colour. (USA)

131)-133) Aus einer Serie Karten für ein *Roussel*-Präparat gegen Husten. Ein bekannter französischer Karikaturist stellt Figuren aus berühmten Gemälden – hier von Manet und Toulouse-Lautrec – hustend dar. Federzeichnung, farbige Umrandung. (FRA)

134) 135) Mehrfarbige Illustration, die die Abhängigkeit von Medikamenten darstellt, und vollständiger Schieber mit ausziehbarer Karte, für ein Produkt von Smith Kline & French Labs. gegen chronische, neurotische Angstzustände. (USA)

136) Umschlag eines Faltprospekts über *Teldrin*, ein pharmazeutisches Produkt zur Bekämpfung von tränenden Augen bei Allergien. Rosa Gesicht, grüne Augen in blauem Wasser. (USA)

137) 138) Umschlag und Doppelseite aus einer grossformatigen Broschüre über die Eröffnung des Meyer L. Prentis Instituts für Krebsforschung in Detroit. Umschlag und Illustration mehrfarbig. (USA)

131)-133) Cartes figurant dans une série publicitaire pour un béchique *Roussel:* un dessinateur d'humour bien connu y fait tousser les personnages de divers tableaux de maître (ici deux Manet et un Toulouse-Lautrec). Dessins à la plume, bord coloré. (FRA)

134) 135) Composition polychrome illustrant la dépendance à l'égard des drogues, et pochette complète avec la carte qui y est insérée, pour un produit des Laboratoires Smith Kline & French calmant l'angoisse névrotique chronique. Illustration visible à carte retirée. (USA)

136) Couverture d'un dépliant consacré au *Teldrin*, un médicament qui tient les yeux secs dans les cas d'allergie nasale. Visage rose, yeux verdâtres, eaux bleues. (USA)

137) 138) Couverture et double page d'une brochure au grand format informant sur l'inauguration du Centre Meyer L. Prentis de Recherches sur le Cancer à Detroit. Couverture et illustration intérieure en polychromie. (USA)

ne pas tousser: nétux

133

134

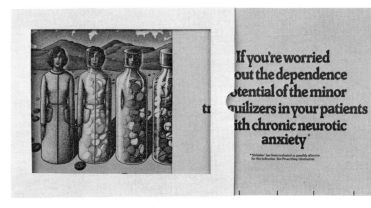

135

Artist | Künstler | Artiste:

131)-133) TIM
134) 135) ROGER HANE / MARGARET HAWLEY / ALAN J. KLAWANS
136) BOB FROST / MONOGRAM, INC.
137) KEN GRANNING
138) DIANE & JIM JEFFERIES / PETER NOTHSTEIN

137

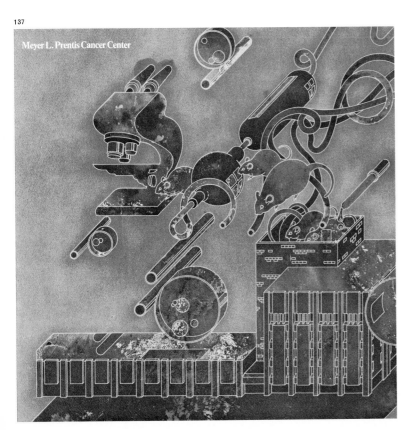

Meyer L. Prentis Cancer Center

138

Art Director | Directeur artistique:

131)-133) MAURICE LANTIEZ
134) 135) ALAN J. KLAWANS
136) WILLIAM A. SCHILLING
137) 138) PETER NOTHSTEIN

Agency | Agentur | Agence – Studio:

131)-133) PROTEA
134)-136) SMITH KLINE & FRENCH

**Booklets
Prospekte
Prospectus**

139

140

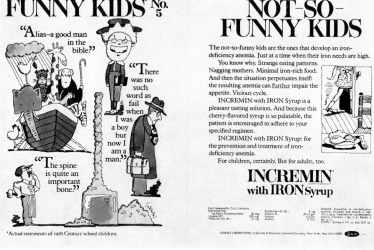

141

Booklets / Prospekte / Prospectus

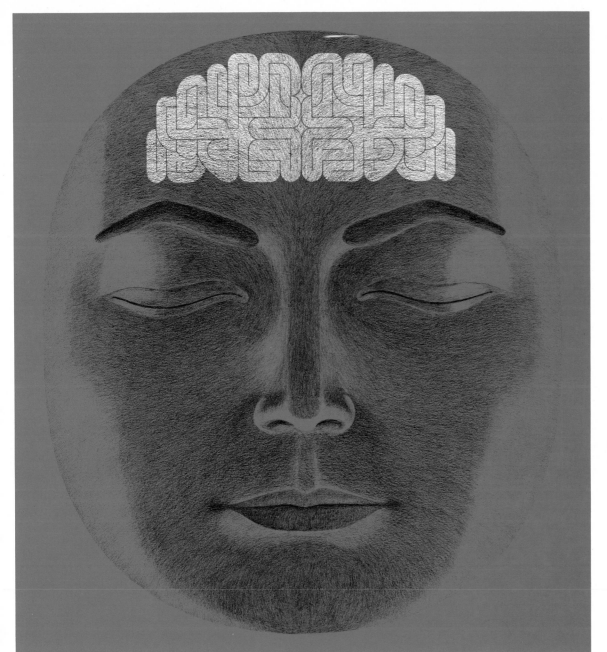

Artist | Künstler | Artiste:

139)–141) SIMMS TABACK/DAVID BARBA
142) 143) ROLF HARDER
144) 145) DIETMAR WINKLER

Art Director | Directeur artistique:

139)–141) DAVID BARBA
142) 143) ROLF HARDER/JOHN MALOUGH

Agency | Agentur | Agence – Studio:

139)–141) NAIMARK & BARBA, INC.
142) 143) DESIGN COLLABORATIVE
144) 145) MIT DESIGN SERVICES

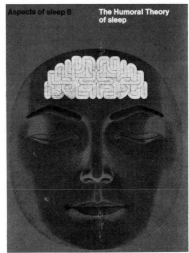

Aspects of sleep 8   The Humoral Theory of sleep

142

143

Massachusetts
Institute of
Technology

Special Summer
Programs 1967

144

An important element of the continuous process of education is the opportunity for professional men and women to keep pace with new developments in their fields. M.I.T. seeks to provide this opportunity by offering a series of intensive Programs that review current trends and introduce new ideas and approaches to problems in the physical and social sciences, in engineering and in management.

These Programs of one or two weeks' duration are offered as a part of the Institute's Summer Session, which includes regular subjects for M.I.T. undergraduate and graduate students and other degree candidates. Participants in the Special Programs include representatives from industrial companies, government agencies, and educational institutions. The residential and recreational facilities of the Institute will be available to registrants of the Special Summer Programs during their stay at M.I.T.

On behalf of the Institute, I extend a warm welcome to those of you who will join us next summer; we hope you will find your participation and visit to M.I.T. a stimulating experience.

Howard W. Johnson
President

The Summer Session of 1967 will be the eighteenth in which M.I.T. has presented Special Summer Programs of the type announced in this folder. In past years, registrants for this series have come from industrial companies, government agencies, and research and educational institutions throughout this nation and overseas. The Programs thus promise interesting associations with professional colleagues of varied experience.

The 1967 series will include the 39 Programs described in this folder, all on subjects of current technological importance. We confidently assure participants of a stimulating intellectual and professional experience — coupled with the recreational advantages of summer in New England.

A limited number of Special Summer Program Scholarships are available to defray in part the Program tuition of members of teaching staffs (rank of instructor or higher) of other educational institutions. Requests for such scholarships should accompany applications for admission.

James M. Austin
Director of the Summer Session

145

69

146) 147) Paintings by an Austrian artist of a 'loaded heart' and the 'affluent heart' inserted in a series of folders promoting pharmaceuticals made by Heilmittelwerke Wien GmbH. (AUS)

148) Cover of an enrolment card for membership of the J.B. Speed Art Museum, Louisville. Yellow nib and print on deep orange ground. (USA)

149) Envelope (tan and greenish blue) mailed to dentists offering free toys for children buying *Lactona* toothbrushes. The toys are designed to incorporate the old toothbrush. (USA)

150) Cartoon strip in full colour on a folder about an R.I.T. sulphonamide against diseases of cattle. The strip illustrates the method of administration. (BEL)

151) Full-colour design on the package for a tongue-depresser given to doctors as part of a promotion campaign for a *Beecham* broad-spectrum antibiotic. (AUL)

146) 147) Gemälde eines österreichischen Künstlers von «Belastungsherz» und «Wohlstandsherz», als Einlage zu einer Serie Prospekte über ein Herzpräparat der Heilmittelwerke Wien. (AUS)

148) Umschlag zu einer Anmeldekarte für die Mitgliedschaft eines Kunstmuseums in Louisville. Feder und Schrift gelb auf orangem Grund. (USA)

149) An Zahnärzte verschickter Umschlag (ocker und türkis). Es werden beim Kauf von *Lactona*-Zahnbürsten zusammensetzbare Spielzeuge gratis angeboten. (USA)

150) Mehrfarbiger Cartoon-Strip auf einem Prospekt über ein pharmazeutisches Produkt gegen Krankheiten des Viehs. Der Strip zeigt, wie dem Tier die Arznei eingegeben wird. (BEL)

151) Mehrfarbige Illustration auf einer Packung für ein Geschenk an Ärzte als Teil einer Werbekampagne für ein Breitspektrum-Antibiotikum von *Beecham*. (AUL)

146

146) 147) Représentations peintes d'un « cœur chargé » et d'un « cœur typique de la société d'abondance », par un artiste autrichien. Dépliants des Heilmittelwerke Wien S. à r.l. (AUS)
148) Couverture d'une carte de cotisant du Musée d'Art J.B. Speed à Louisville. Bec de plume et caractères jaunes sur fond orange foncé. (USA)
149) Enveloppe (brun roux et bleu verdâtre) expédiée aux dentistes et offrant des jouets gratuits
aux enfants achetant une brosse à dents *Lactona*. Les jouets sont conçus de façon à incorporer
les vieilles brosses. (USA)
150) Bande dessinée polychrome sur un dépliant présentant un sulfamide R.I.T. employé en
médecine vétérinaire. On y voit la méthode recommandée pour l'administration. (BEL)
151) Dessin polychrome sur l'emballage d'un abaisse-langue cadeau. Produits *Beecham*. (AUL)

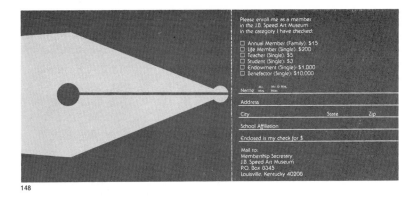

148

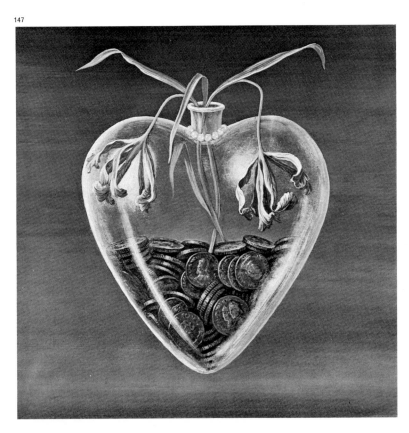

147

149

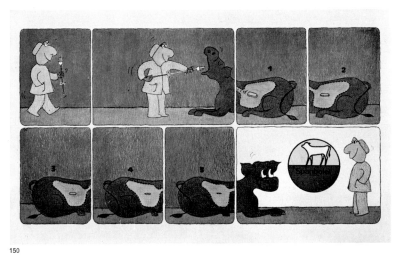

150

151

Artist | Künstler | Artiste:

146) 147) LUDWIG SCHWARZER / HANS MÜLLER
148) HARRIET WINNER / DAN STEWART
149) BILL FINELLI
151) LYNDON WHAITE

Art Director | Directeur artistique:

146) 147) G. FORSTHUBER
148) DAN STEWART / HARRIET WINNER
149) BILL FINELLI
151) LYNDON WHAITE

Agency | Agentur | Agence – Studio:

146) 147) CHEMIE LINZ AG, WERBEABTEILUNG
148) DESIGNERS STEWART & WINNER, INC.
150) R.I.T. S.A., DÉPT PUBLICITÉ
151) LYNDON WHAITE GRAPHIC DESIGN

152

153

152) Cover of a booklet about the services of The Mile Square Health Centre, Chicago. Black design on grey ground. (USA)

153)-155) Cover (in yellow and white on grey-beige ground) and two black-and-white spreads from a guide for patients issued by the Rush-Presbyterian-St. Luke's Medical Centre in Chicago. Fig. 155 shows newspapers as one of the services to patients. (USA)

156) 'One day, in the woods of Sauvabelin, the animals took counsel ...'. Cover in actual size of a folder about a residential development at the edge of the woods in which care is being taken to preserve the rural environment. (SWI)

152) Umschlag einer Broschüre über die Dienstleistungen des Mile Square Health Center in Chicago. Schwarz auf grauem Grund, weisse Schrift. (USA)

153)-155) Umschlag (in Gelb und Weiss auf grau-beigem Grund) und zwei schwarzweisse Doppelseiten aus dem Leitfaden für Patienten eines Krankenhauses in Chicago. Abb. 155 zeigt Zeitungen als eine der Dienstleistungen an die Patienten. (USA)

156) «Eines Tages, in den Wäldern von Sauvabelin, berieten sich die Tiere ... ». Umschlag in Originalgrösse eines Faltprospekts über die Planung einer Wohnsiedlung in der Nähe eines Waldes, wobei der Erhaltung der landschaftlichen Umgebung viel Aufmerksamkeit geschenkt wird. (SWI)

152) Couverture d'une brochure présentant les services du Mile Square Health Center de Chicago. Dessin noir sur fond gris. (USA)

153)-155) Couverture jaune et blanc sur fond gris-beige et deux doubles pages noir-blanc d'un guide distribué aux malades par l'hôpital Rush-Presbyterian-St. Luke's Medical Center de Chicago. 155) Le service de périodiques. (USA)

156) «Un jour, dans les bois de Sauvabelin, les animaux tinrent conseil ... ». Couverture grandeur nature d'un dépliant consacré à un projet de construction – une résidence à l'orée du bois tenant compte de toutes les exigences de l'écologie. (SWI)

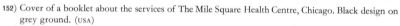

154

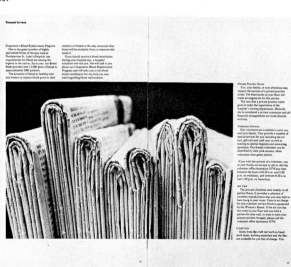

Booklets / Prospekte / Prospectus

155

156

Artist | Künstler | Artiste:

152) MICHAEL REID

153)—155) HALINA J. LOGAY/MICHAEL REID

Art Director | Directeur artistique:

152)—155) MICHAEL REID

156) CHRISTIAN SCHMUTZ

Agency | Agentur | Agence – Studio:

152)—155) MICHAEL REID DESIGN

156) CREATION 3 S.A.

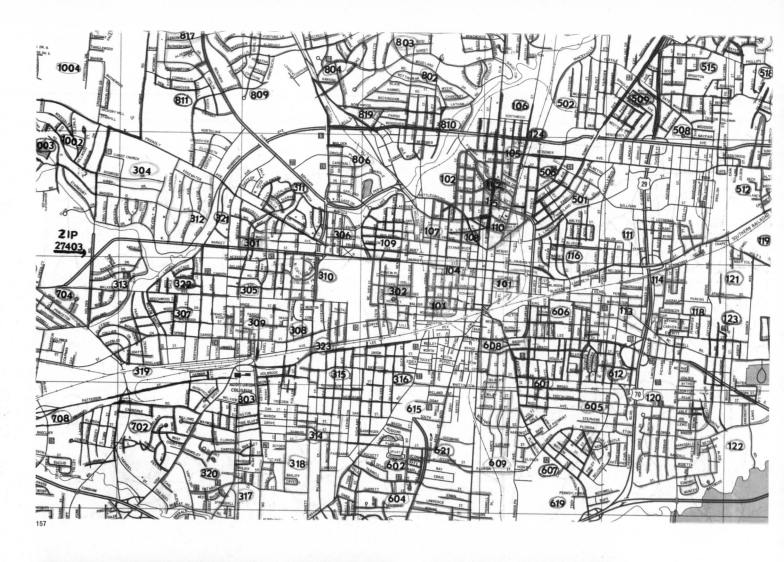

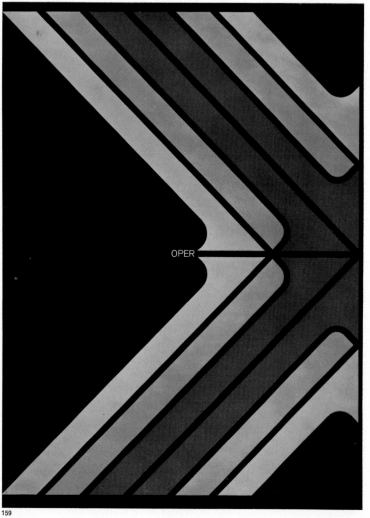

CORNING   Automatic Dividend
Reinvestment
Service and
Optional Cash
Investment

Artist | Künstler | Artiste:

157) 158) WALTER EINSEL/
CLARK L. ROBINSON
159) CHRISTIAN SCHMUTZ/
LAURENT CEPPI
160) FRANK ROCKWELL
161) FRANÇOIS REQUIEN
162) LOU MYERS
163) ROGER HANE/
ED RUGGLES
164) HANS KNÖPFLI

Art Director | Directeur artistique:

157) 158) CLARK L. ROBINSON
159) CHRISTIAN SCHMUTZ
160) ROBERT L. IVERS
161) FRANÇOIS REQUIEN
162) VIC GIALLEONARDO
163) ED RUGGLES
164) HANS KNÖPFLI

Agency | Agentur | Agence – Studio:

157) 158) CLARK L. ROBINSON,
INC.
159) CREATION 3 S.A.
160) CORNING DESIGN
161) AGENCE RHODANIENNE
162) DOREMUS & CO.
163) YOUNG & RUBICAM, INC.
164) HANS KNÖPFLI

162

158

163

161

164

75

How not to blow a job interview.

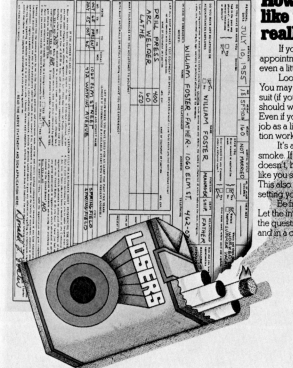

How to look like you're really looking.

If you already have an appointment, be on time. Or even a little ahead.

Look as sharp as you can. You may not want to wear a suit (if you're a guy), but you should wear a tie and jacket. Even if you're applying for a job as a lifeguard or construction work.

It's also a good idea not to smoke. If the interviewer doesn't, he probably won't like you smelling up his office. This also avoids accidents like setting your application on fire.

Be friendly and courteous. Let the interviewer ask most of the questions. Answer honestly and in a clear voice.

165

166

How to keep the big day from becoming a nightmare.
The most important thing you can do when you go for an interview is be yourself.

You probably have more to offer than you realize. But you should consider your strong points before you get there. Ask yourself what you're best at, what your interests are, and what you want out of life.

Try seeing yourself as others see you. A mirror will help. No joke.

If you're not yourself during an interview, they might hire the wrong person. Or turn down the wrong person. The one you're trying to be.

Don't be discouraged if you don't get the first job you apply for. Or the second. Or the third. The fourth one or the fourteenth one may turn out to be a lifetime career.

167

168

First off, make sure you really want the job.
Some people go looking for a job because (a) everyone else is out looking, so there's nobody to hang around with, (b) school's out and they just want someplace to go every day, and (c), their parents are putting on the heat. Reasons like these make you do strange things when you go for an interview. Like slouch on the couch, mumble when spoken to, and say dumb things.

So when you go out to look for a job, make sure that's really what you're looking for.

169

165)-170) Cover, pages and double spreads, all in full colour, with tips on how to behave at a job interview, from a large recruitment brochure issued by the US Army, which points out that it has 300 different jobs to choose from. (USA)

171) 172) Page and one of the many inserts from a large and lavish booklet issued by the US Army and giving advice and instructions to recruiting officers. (USA)

165)-170) Umschlag, Seiten und Doppelseiten, alle mehrfarbig, aus einer Broschüre zur Personalwerbung der Armee, die 300 Stellen zum Aussuchen hat. Es werden Ratschläge gegeben, wie man sich beim Vorstellen verhalten sollte. (USA)

171) 172) Seite und eine der vielen Einlagen aus einer grossen und aufwendigen Broschüre der Armee mit Ratschlägen und Instruktionen an Personal-Offiziere. (USA)

165)-170) Couverture, pages et doubles pages en polychromie d'une brochure de recrutement grand format publiée par l'Armée américaine, qui offre 300 emplois différents; on y enseigne la tactique à appliquer lors de la première présentation chez l'employeur. (USA)

171) 172) Page et encart figurant dans une luxueuse brochure au grand format publiée par l'Armée américaine: conseils et instructions destinés aux officiers recruteurs. (USA)

How to find employers who might be looking for you. Try putting together a list of all the people and places you might work for.

Make it a big list. The more places you go, or send a resume (we'll explain that later), the better your chances.

Look in the Yellow Pages and the Classified Section of your local newspaper for hints.

Ask your Guidance Counselor, parents, relatives and friends for leads.

Check with your state's Department of Labor or Employment Service.

Now that you know yourself, get to know them. Before you go for a job interview, read up on the company you'll be visiting.

If it's an insurance company, for example, find out what makes an insurance company tick. Or a bank. Or a department store.

You will come off better if you're interested in a company's overall work as well as the particular job you're applying for.

170

171

172

Artist | Künstler | Artiste:

165)-172) MABEY TROUSDELL, INC.

Art Director | Directeur artistique:

165)-172) MABEY TROUSDELL, INC.

Agency | Agentur | Agence – Studio:

165)-172) MABEY TROUSDELL, INC.

Booklets / Prospekte / Prospectus

173

174

Booklets / Prospekte / Prospectus

179

THROUGH THE SKY

"Welcome aboard our flight! Here is a headset and program so you can enjoy music. Dinner will be served soon."

The stewardesses do all they can to make the trip safe and comfortable. They show how to use emergency oxygen and the location of exits. They help care for children and they serve the meals.

"Would you like a magazine or a pillow? We will be flying at 30,000 feet and should arrive on time."

175

173)-176) Cover (in pastel shades), page and double spreads (showing the narrow interleaved texts) from a colouring booklet presented by the City of Los Angeles to children who had been invited to visit an airport. (USA)

177) 178) Two double spreads from a calorie counting booklet issued by REDBOOK magazine. Red on blue print, figures in flat colours. (USA)

179) Cover of a *McGraw Hill* art film directory. Black on silver. (USA)

180)-182) Cover (dark blue ground, with die-cut window) and two double spreads from a booklet issued to mark the centenary of the *Zurich* insurance company. Fig. 181 is part of a historical retrospect, fig. 182 shows the distribution of business. (SWI)

180

Artist | Künstler | Artiste:

173)-176) THE COMPANY
177) 178) VALERIE KLECKNER
179) GILBERT LESSER
180)-182) RENATO FARINOLI

Art Director | Directeur artistique:

173)-176) THE COMPANY
179) GILBERT LESSER
180)-182) ADRIANO PFISTER

Agency | Agentur | Agence–Studio:

173)-176) THE COMPANY
180)-182) ADOLF WIRZ AG

The Zurich Group introduces itself

100 years...

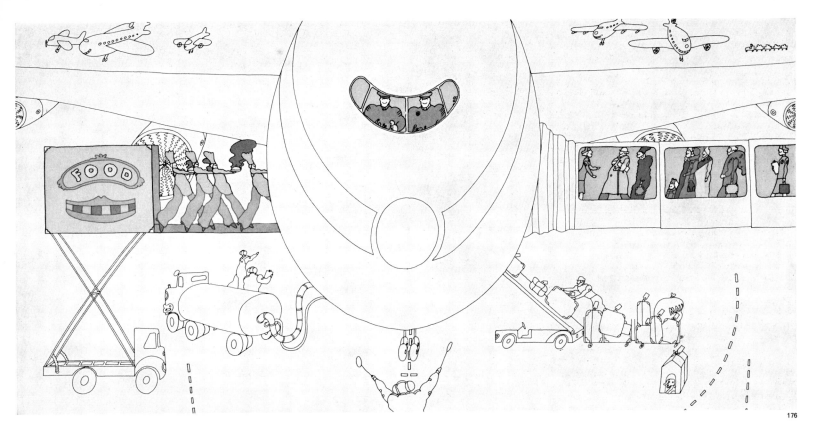

176

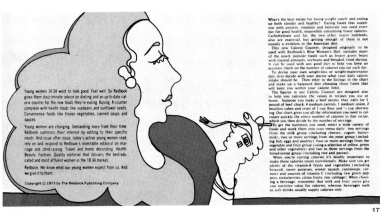

177

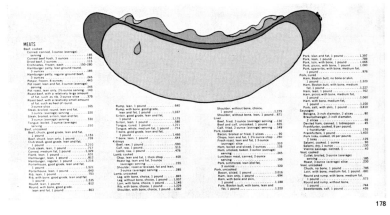

178

173)-176) Umschlag (in Pastellfarben), Seite und Doppelseiten (mit schmalen Textseiten) aus einem Malheft, das von der Stadt Los Angeles an Kinder verschenkt wurde, die zur Besichtigung eines Flughafens eingeladen wurden. (USA)

177) 178) Zwei Doppelseiten aus einem Kalorienzähler, der von der Zeitschrift REDBOOK herausgegeben wurde. Schrift rot und blau, Abbildungen in flach aufgetragenen Farben. (USA)

179) Umschlag eines Verzeichnisses über Kunstfilme. Schwarz auf Silber. (USA)

180)-182) Umschlag (dunkelblauer Grund mit ausgestanztem Fenster) und zwei Doppelseiten aus einer Broschüre der *Zurich*-Versicherungsgesellschaft. Abb. 181 ist Teil eines historischen Rückblicks, Abb. 182 zeigt eine Aufteilung der Geschäfte. (SWI)

173)-176) Couverture (tons pastels), page et doubles pages (montrant les textes intercalaires étroits) d'une brochure à colorier distribuée par la ville de Los Angeles aux enfants qui viennent visiter l'un de ses aéroports. (USA)

177) 178) Deux doubles pages d'une brochure publiée par le magazine REDBOOK et indiquant la teneur en calories de divers aliments. Caractères rouges et bleus, couleurs en à-plat. (USA)

179) Couverture d'un répertoire *McGraw Hill* du cinéma d'art. Noir sur argent. (USA)

180)-182) Couverture (fond bleu foncé, fenêtre en découpe) et deux doubles pages d'une brochure commémorant le centenaire de la compagnie d'assurances *Zurich*. La fig. 181 fait partie d'une rétrospective, la fig. 182 montre les activités du groupe. (SWI)

181

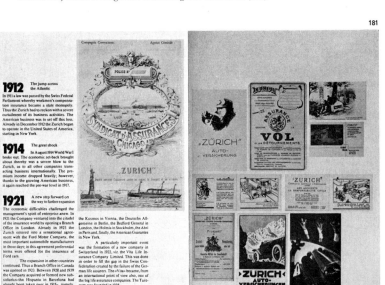

182

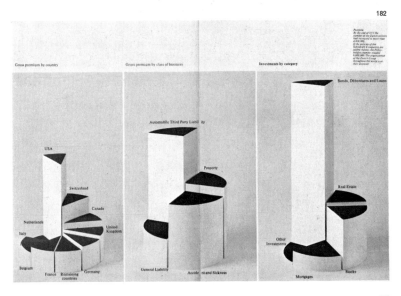

183)-186) Three pages and one corresponding spread – all in muted shades of beige and grey, with black – from a booklet explaining the household services (here cleaning, maintenance, maid) offered to home-owners by Big Canoe Corporation, a real estate enterprise. (USA)

187) Central spread of a booklet from a 'travel building-block' series issued by German Railways, here for a trip through Franconia. Chiefly red and brown shades. (GER)

188) One side of a large direct-mail folder sent out by Equitable Federal Savings and Loan Association, here listing their services, with full-colour illustrations. (USA)

189) Copy of a poster – showing the things formerly needful for a rural existence – enclosed in an invitation to the opening of a new building of Citizens National Bank. (USA)

183)-186) Drei Seiten und eine entsprechende Doppelseite – alle in grauen und beigen Tönen, mit Schwarz – aus einer Broschüre über die Haushaltdienste (hier Reinigung, Wartung, Spettfrau), die von einer Immobilienfirma an die Hauseigentümer angeboten werden. (USA)

187) Mittlere Doppelseite aus einer Broschüre der Deutschen Bundesbahnen aus der Serie «Reisebaukasten» – hier über eine Reise durch Franken. Vorwiegend rot und braun. (GER)

188) Rückseite eines grossen Direktwerbe-Faltprospekts einer Sparkasse. Es werden hier ihre Dienstleistungen aufgezählt. Mehrfarbige Illustrationen. (USA)

189) Kopie eines Plakats – gezeigt werden die Dinge, die früher als die Notwendigkeiten des Landlebens galten – als Beilage zur Einladung an die Eröffnung eines Bankgebäudes. (USA)

183)-186) Trois pages et double page correspondante ; tons beige et gris mat, plus noir. Brochure expliquant les services offerts aux propriétaires de maisons par l'agence immobilière Big Canoe Corp. Les illustrations se réfèrent au nettoyage, à l'entretien et à la femme de chambre. (USA)

187) Double page centrale d'une brochure présentant les services de voyage intégrés des Chemins de Fer Allemands: ici, lors d'un voyage en Franconie. Prédominance de tons rouges et bruns. (GER)

188) L'un des côtés d'un dépliant au grand format utilisé dans la publicité directe de l'Equitable Federal Savings & Loan Association. Illustrations en polychromie. (USA)

189) Affichette montrant les accessoires de la vie rurale d'autrefois, encartée dans une invitation pour l'inauguration d'un nouveau bâtiment de la Citizens National Bank. (USA)

183

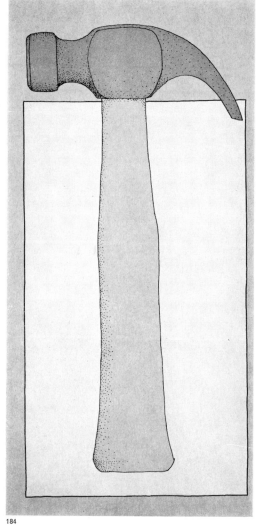

184

187

Booklets / Prospekte / Prospectus

185

The nitty-gritty facts about Equitable.

Your money works as hard as you do. Day in and day out. On passbook accounts we pay interest every day from deposit to withdrawal. You never lose a cent because of the calendar.

We pay you. We pay the highest passbook rate allowed by law: 5% per year, compounded quarterly. We also have three types of savings/investment certificates. (Early withdrawal can mean a loss of up to 90 days' interest.) There's a 5.25% certificate with a $3,000 minimum and a term of 6 months. A 5.75% certificate with a $10,000 minimum and a 1-year term. And a 6% certificate with a term of 2 years and a $15,000 minimum.

The roof over your head. An Equitable specialty. We make home loans so you can buy, build or refinance a house. We make available an Escrow Fund to take care of the taxes and insurance on your new home. And at Equitable there's no prepayment penalty.

Nothing's perfect. If your home isn't all it could be, or if it isn't all it should be, don't hesitate to call on us. We'll help you expand, repair or redecorate your home with an Equitable home improvement loan.

We want to be there when you need us. There's only one word to describe our office hours...convenient. Our offices are smack in the middle of the shopping and business districts of Lancaster (123 South Broad Street) and Circleville (159 East Main Street). If you can't get to our offices, you can make deposits and withdrawals with our handy Save-by-Mail postage-free envelopes. And, if our regular hours aren't your regular hours, there's always our 24-hour depository.

Equitable Federal
Savings and Loan Association

188

186

189

Artist | Künstler | Artiste:

183)-186) DAN PRUITT
187) EVA GRABMÜLLER
188) GRAPHICSGROUP
189) PAUL DAVIS / WILLIAM FINN

Art Director | Directeur artistique:

183)-186) TOM WOOD
187) HANS-JÜRGEN RAU
188) GRAPHICSGROUP
189) JAMES WILKINS

Agency | Agentur | Agence–Studio:

183)-186) CREATIVE SERVICES, INC.
187) STUDIO RAU
188) HAMEROFF & ASSOC.
189) WILLIAM FINN & ASSOC., INC.

190

191

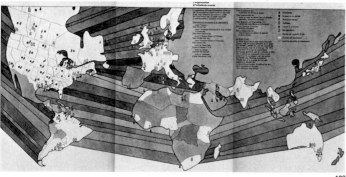

192

190)-194) Cover, pages and gatefold spread, all in colour, from a brochure on *Esso* in France. Fig. 191 refers to research and exploitation in France, fig. 192 to the worldwide organization, fig. 193 to company history and fig. 194 to information. (FRA)

190)-194) Umschlag, Seiten und Doppelseite mit Ausleger aus einer Broschüre über *Esso* Frankreich. Abb. 191 bezieht sich auf Forschung und Auswertung in Frankreich, Abb. 192 auf die weltweite Organisation, Abb. 193 auf die Geschichte der Firma, Abb. 194 auf Information. (FRA)

190)-194) Couverture, pages et encart sur double page, en polychromie; brochure d'*Esso* en France. 191) Recherche et exploitation en France; 192) l'organisation mondiale d'*Esso*; 193) histoire du groupe; 194) l'effort d'information. (FRA)

Artist / Künstler / Artiste:
190)-194) ANATOLE PASTENAK / BERNARD LONDINSKY

Art Director / Directeur artistique:
190)-194) JEAN-BENOIT BRUANT

Booklets / Prospekte / Prospectus

193

195

195) 196) Two flat prints from a series offered by *Essochem Europe* in advertisements in the trade press and showing renderings by various artists of the company's plants, here at Cologne and Port-Jérôme. (BEL)

197) Card with sliding scale for measuring density values, handed to clients by a manufacturer of printing inks. Green, yellow and orange on orange ground. (GER)

198) Inside of a *Letraset* folder about the *Pantone* colour mixing system. Eyes in various blue, green and red shades. (GER)

199) 200) Complete cover and opening double spread, both in full colour, of a *Fiat* brochure on a method of 'conquering rust' in cars. (ITA)

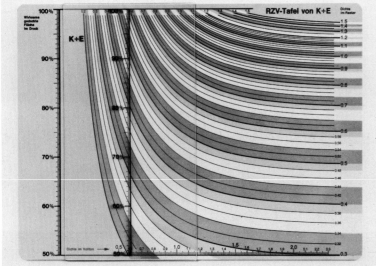

197

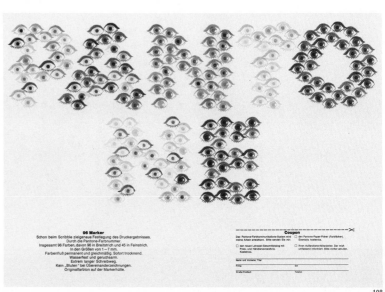

198

Port-Jérôme Plant: painting by Durie commissioned by Essochem.

Pierre Paul Durie

196

Booklets / Prospekte / Prospectus

195) 196) Zwei Drucke aus einer Serie, die in Inseraten der *Essochem Europa* in der Fachpresse angeboten werden und Darstellungen der Fabrikanlagen der Gesellschaft durch verschiedene Künstler zeigen, hier diejenigen in Köln und Port-Jérôme. (BEL)

197) RVZ-Tafel zur Ermittlung der Dichtewerte von Rasterstufen, die als Arbeitsmittel den Kunden der Druckfarbenfabrik Kast + Ehinger überreicht wurde. Grün, gelb und orange. (GER)

198) Innenseite eines *Letraset*-Faltprospekts über das *Pantone*-Farbmischsystem. Augen in verschiedenen Schattierungen von Blau, Grün und Rot. (GER)

199) 200) Vollständiger Umschlag und erste Doppelseite, beide mehrfarbig, aus einer Broschüre von *Fiat* über eine Methode, bei Automobilen den «Rost zu besiegen». (ITA)

195) 196) Deux estampes (imprimées à plat) figurant dans une série d'*Essochem Europe* offerte par voie d'annonces dans la presse spécialisée et représentant des vues artistiques des différentes usines du groupe, ici celles de Cologne et de Port-Jérôme. (BEL)

197) Carte avec curseur, pour la mesure des densités, offerte à ses clients par un fabricant d'encres d'imprimerie. Vert, jaune, orange sur fond orange. (GER)

198) Intérieur d'un dépliant *Letraset* sur le système *Pantone* de mixage de couleurs. Yeux en divers bleus, verts et rouges. (GER)

199) 200) Couverture complète et double page initiale, en polychromie, d'une brochure *Fiat* enseignant comment tenir en échec la rouille qui s'attaque aux carrosseries. (ITA)

199

200

85

201

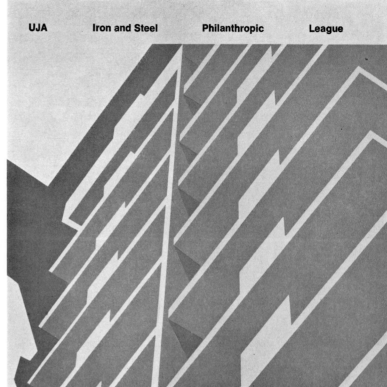

202

203

201) Cover of a booklet for International Harvester giving advice on heavy-duty truck operations. Black print, embossed design on silver. (USA)

202) Invitation to a testimonial dinner issued by the United Jewish Appeal. Vermilion and orange on pale beige paper. (USA)

203) 204) Double spread, showing a tapestry and a hand-embroidered picture, and cover of a booklet issued by the Crafts Advisory Committee on the occasion of a crafts exhibition in the Victoria & Albert Museum. (GBR)

205) Illustration from a brochure about insurance (here on rising medical costs) issued by the Insurance Company of North America. (USA)

206) Page from a brochure about season subscriptions to the Goodman Theatre, Chicago. (USA)

207)-209) Cover with single and double panels of a large folder describing *Raychem* products and markets. Colour illustrations. (USA)

204

205

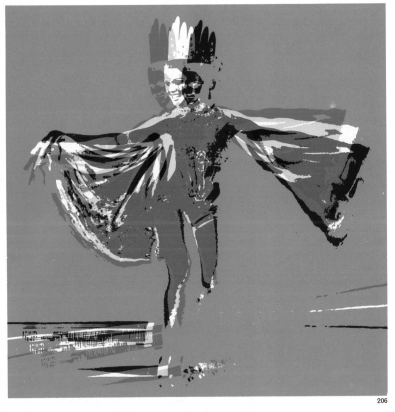

206

Raychem

207

201) Umschlag einer Broschüre von International Harvester mit Ratschlägen über den Einsatz von Lastwagen. Schwarze Schrift, geprägtes Design auf Silber. (USA)

202) Einladung zu einem Nachtessen des United Jewish Appeal. Zinnoberrot und Orange auf hellbeigem Grund. (USA)

203) 204) Doppelseite, die einen Wandteppich und ein handgesticktes Bild zeigt, und Umschlag einer Broschüre, die anlässlich einer Ausstellung von handwerklicher Kunst im Victoria-und-Albert-Museum herausgegeben wurde. (GBR)

205) Illustration aus einer von der Insurance Company of North America herausgegebenen Broschüre über Versicherungen (hier über die steigenden Spitalaufenthaltskosten). (USA)

206) Seite aus einem Prospekt über Saison-Abonnemente eines Theaters in Chicago. (USA)

207)–209) Umschlag mit einfachem und doppeltem Feld eines grossen Faltprospekts, der Produkte und Absatzgebiete von *Raychem* beschreibt. Mehrfarbige Illustrationen. (USA)

201) Couverture d'une brochure d'International Harvester donnant des conseils pour l'emploi de camions lourds. Noir, dessin gaufré sur argent. (USA)

202) Invitation à un banquet en faveur de l'action du United Jewish Appeal. Vermillon et orange sur papier beige pâle. (USA)

203) 204) Double page, avec la reproduction d'une tapisserie et d'une image brodée à la main, et couverture d'une brochure du Crafts Advisory Committee à l'occasion d'une exposition d'artisanat d'art au Musée Albert et Victoire de Londres. (GBR)

205) Illustration tirée d'une brochure d'assurance (sujet traité ici: l'augmentation des frais médicaux) publiée par l'Insurance Company of North America. (USA)

206) Page d'une brochure pour les abonnés du Goodman Theatre à Chicago. (USA)

207)–209) Couverture avec volets simple et double d'un dépliant au grand format présentant les produits et marchés *Raychem*. Illustrations couleurs. (USA)

Booklets / Prospekte
Prospectus

208

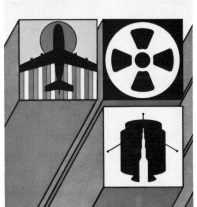

209

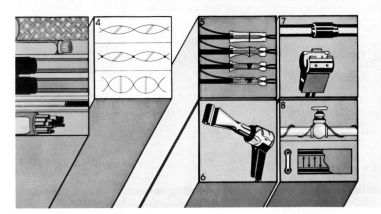

Artist | Künstler | Artiste:

201) JOHN DOLBY
202) ARLENE PACCHIANO
203) 204) COLIN FORBES
205) WALLY NEIBART/FORD, BRYNE & ASSOC.
206) LES HOLLOWAY
207)–209) MICHEL DATTEL

Art Director | Directeur artistique:

202) ARLENE PACCHIANO
205) FORD, BRYNE & ASSOC.
206) HAYWARD R. BLAKE
207)–209) J.K. FOGLEMAN

Agency | Agentur | Agence – Studio:

201) BBDM, INC.
202) UNITED JEWISH APPEAL
203) 204) PENTAGRAM DESIGN PARTNERSHIP
205) FORD, BRYNE & ASSOC.
206) THE DESIGN PARTNERSHIP, INC.
207)–209) RAYCHEM COMMUNICATIONS & DESIGN DIVISION

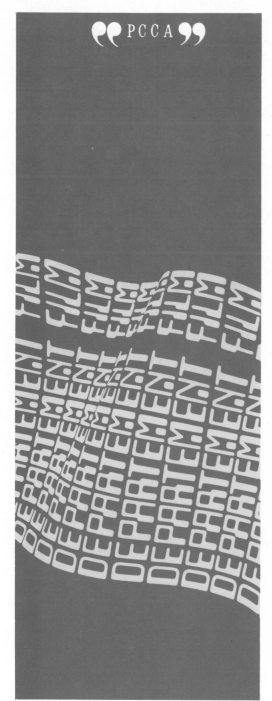

210

211

212

213

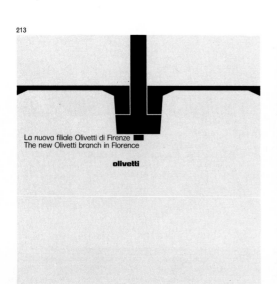

La nuova filiale Olivetti di Firenze
The new Olivetti branch in Florence

olivetti

214

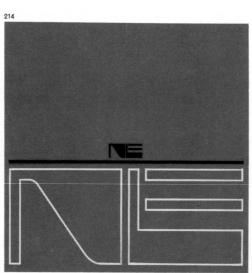

215

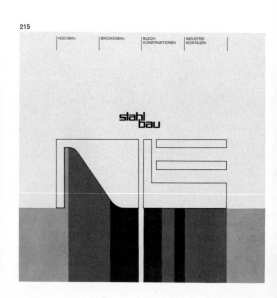

216

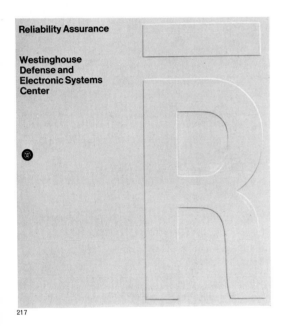

217

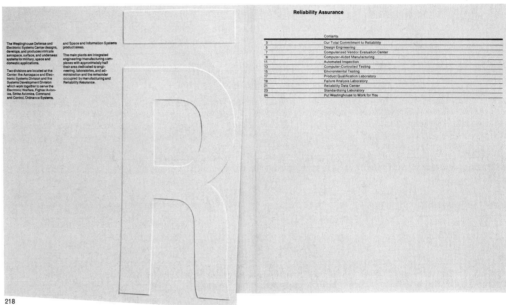

218

Artist | Künstler | Artiste:

210)-212) PIERRE COMTE
213) GIACOMO SALA
214) 215) HEINZ SCHAAF
216) MARIO GRASSO
217) 218) EDDIE BYRD

Art Director | Directeur artistique:

210)-212) PIERRE COMTE
213) FRANCO BASSI
214) 215) HEINZ SCHAAF
216) LUCIEN BRINGOLF
217) 218) EDDIE BYRD

Agency | Agentur | Agence – Studio:

213) OLIVETTI UFFICIO PUBBLICITÀ
214) 215) ATELIER HEINZ SCHAAF
216) ADESCAP ADVERTISING
217) 218) WESTINGHOUSE CORPORATE
DESIGN CENTER

210)-212) Three folders about the services of the *Pierre Comte* film studios. (FRA)
213) Cover of a large booklet about the new *Olivetti* building in Florence. Black and white. (ITA)
214) 215) Cover (in silver-blue, black and beige) and page from a brochure for a structural steel company. (GER)
216) Panel from a children's comic-strip poster issued by *incabloc*, makers of shockproof watch movements. (SWI)
217) 218) Blind-embossed white cover and opening spread of a *Westinghouse* brochure about reliability. (USA)

210)-212) Drei Faltprospekte über die Dienstleistungen der *Pierre Comte* Filmstudios. (FRA)
213) Umschlag einer grossen Broschüre über ein neues *Olivetti*-Gebäude in Florenz. Schwarzweiss. (ITA)
214) 215) Umschlag und Seite aus einer Prestige-Broschüre von Neusser Eisenbau Bleichert KG. (GER)
216) Spiel für Kinder, von *incabloc*, Hersteller von Stosssicherungen für Steinankeruhren, herausgegeben. (SWI)
217) 218) Blindgeprägter, weisser Umschlag und Doppelseite aus der *Westinghouse*-Broschüre über Zuverlässigkeit. (USA)

210)-212) Trois dépliants explicitant les services offerts par la société de production de films *Pierre Comte*. (FRA)
213) Couverture d'une brochure au grand format sur le nouvel immeuble *Olivetti* à Florence. Noir et blanc. (ITA)
214) 215) Couverture bleu argenté, noir et beige et page d'une brochure pour une société d'acier de construction. (GER)
216) Partie d'un poster en bandes dessinées pour enfants publié par *incabloc* (mouvements d'horlogerie antichocs). (SWI)
217) 218) Couverture blanche gaufrée et première double page d'une brochure *Westinghouse* sur la fiabilité. (USA)

Booklets / Prospekte / Prospectus

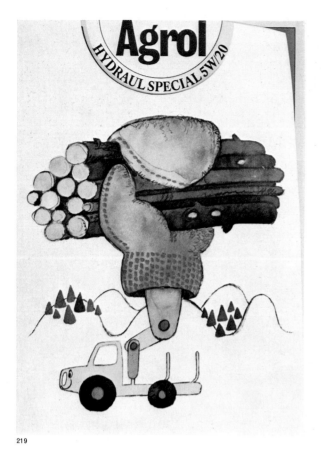

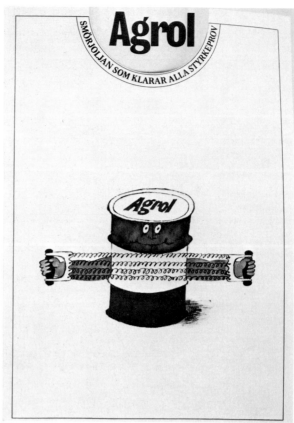

219

220

221

Booklets / Prospekte / Prospectus

223

222

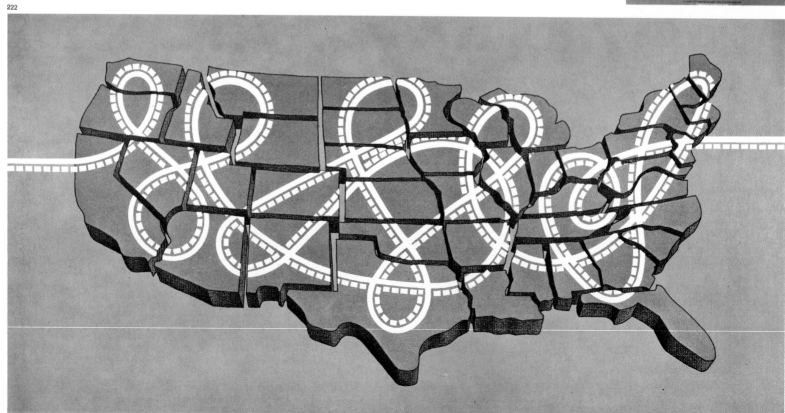

219) 220) Colour covers for folders, here for a winter oil and a complete list of "elastic" agricultural lubricants. (SWE)
221) Black-and-white label for a furniture testing office. (NOR)
222) 223) Cover design (grey and white map on blue-green ground) and complete cover of a brochure to promote imported car advertising in THE NEW YORK TIMES. (USA)
224) Mailing piece for the promotion of a series of *Time-Life* books, colour sheet illustrating the emergence of man. (USA)
225) Black embossed cover of a *Univac* book of signs, from ancient hieroglyphs to computer alphabets. (ITA)
226) Front of a colour folder about *Bonna* cross-country skis. (NOR)

219) 220) Farbige Umschläge für *Agrol*-Prospekte, hier über ein Winteröl und Schmiermittel für Landwirtschaftsmaschinen. (SWE)
221) Schwarzweisse Etikette einer Prüfungsstelle für Möbel. (NOR)
222) 223) Illustration (Karte grau und weiss, Grund blaugrün) und vollständiger Umschlag einer Broschüre als Inseratenwerbung der NEW YORK TIMES für importierte Automobile. (USA).
224) Direktwerbung zur Förderung einer neuen Buchreihe von *Time-Life*, über den Ursprung des Menschen, mit mehrfarbigen Illustrationen. (USA)
225) Geprägter schwarzer Umschlag eines *Univac*-Buches über Zeichen, von den alten Hieroglyphen bis zum Computer-Alphabet. (ITA)
226) Vorderseite eines Farbprospekts über *Bonna*-Langlaufskis. (NOR)

219) 220) Couvertures couleurs de dépliants, ici pour une huile d'hiver et une liste complète de lubrifiants agricoles. (SWE)
221) Etiquette noir-blanc pour un bureau de contrôle de meubles. (NOR)
222) 223) Motif de couverture (carte grise et blanche sur fond bleu-vert) et couverture complète d'une brochure destinée aux annonceurs de voitures d'importation dans le NEW YORK TIMES. (USA)
224) Element de publicité directe pour une série de livres *Time-Life*. Le feuillet en couleur illustre l'hominisation. (USA)
225) Couverture gaufrée noire d'un livre *Univac* consacré à l'histoire des signes, des hiéroglyphes aux langages machines. (ITA)
226) Recto d'un dépliant couleur sur les skis de fond *Bonna*. (NOR)

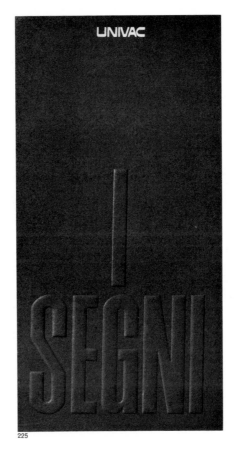

225

226

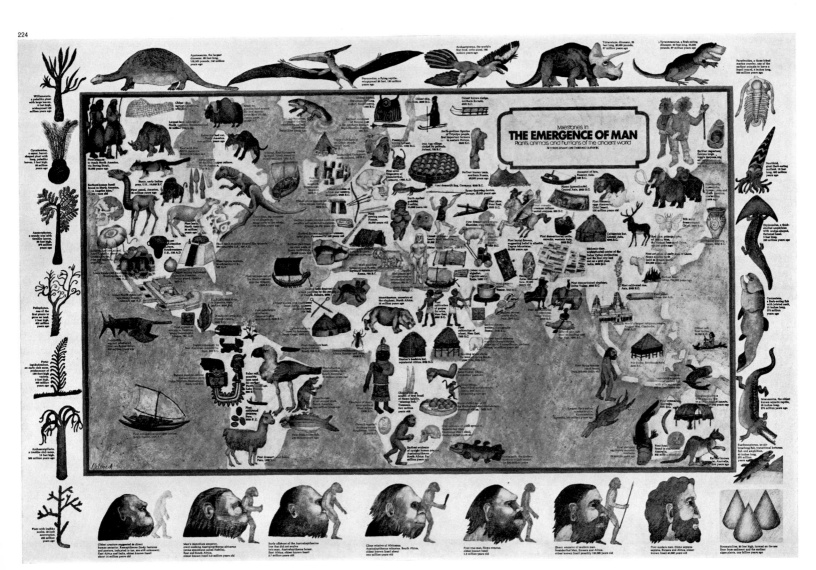

224

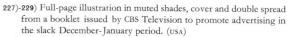

227

228

229

227)-229) Full-page illustration in muted shades, cover and double spread from a booklet issued by CBS Television to promote advertising in the slack December-January period. (USA)
230) 231) Cover and page of a folder to promote recruitment advertising (here for electrical or electronic engineers) in THE NEW YORK TIMES. Illustrations in flesh and grey shades. (USA)
232) Unfolded cover spread (the actual cover is at bottom right) for a booklet presenting *United Artists* film collections for campus showings. Bright colours. (USA)
233) 234) Illustrations from a prospectus for a book, here referring to a school for the prevention of hijacking. (AUS)

227)-229) Ganzseitige Illustration (in dumpfen Tönen), Umschlag und Doppelseite aus einer Broschüre der CBS zur Förderung der Fernsehwerbung während der flauen Periode Dezember–Januar. (USA)
230) 231) Umschlag und Seite aus einem Faltprospekt zur Förderung von Stelleninseraten in THE NEW YORK TIMES, hier für Elektroingenieure. Illustrationen in beigen und grauen Tönen. (USA)
232) Ungefalzte Umschlagseite (der eigentliche Umschlag ist unten rechts) einer Broschüre über eine Filmkollektion der *United Artists* zur Vorführung an Schulen. Mehrfarbig. (USA)
233) 234) Illustrationen aus einem Prospekt für ein Buch, hier in bezug auf eine Schule zur Verhinderung von Flugzeugentführungen. (AUS)

227)-229) Illustration pleine page aux tons mats, couverture et double page d'une brochure de CBS Television destinée aux annonceurs durant la morte-saison de décembre/janvier. (USA)
230) 231) Couverture et page d'un dépliant destiné aux entreprises offrant des emplois (ici: d'ingénieurs électriciens et électroniciens) dans le NEW YORK TIMES. Tons chair et gris. (USA)
232) Page de couverture dépliée (couverture visible en bas, à droite) d'une brochure présentant les collections de films *United Artists* à l'usage des universités. Couleurs vives. (USA)
233) 234) Illustrations tirées d'un prospectus pour un livre, traitant ici d'une école de prévention de la piraterie aérienne. (AUS)

Artist / Künstler / Artiste:

227)-229) MARTY NORMAN / IRA TEICHBERG
230) 231) DAVID PRESTONE / ANDREW KNER / PETER SCHAEFER
232) MILTON GLASER
233) 234) GEORG SCHMID

Art Director / Directeur artistique:

227)-229) LOU DORFSMAN / IRA TEICHBERG
230) 231) ANDREW KNER / PETER SCHAEFER
232) MILTON GLASER

Agency / Agentur / Agence-Studio:

227)-229) CBS / BROADCAST GROUP
232) NEW AUDIENCES, INC.

Booklets / Prospekte / Prospectus

230

231

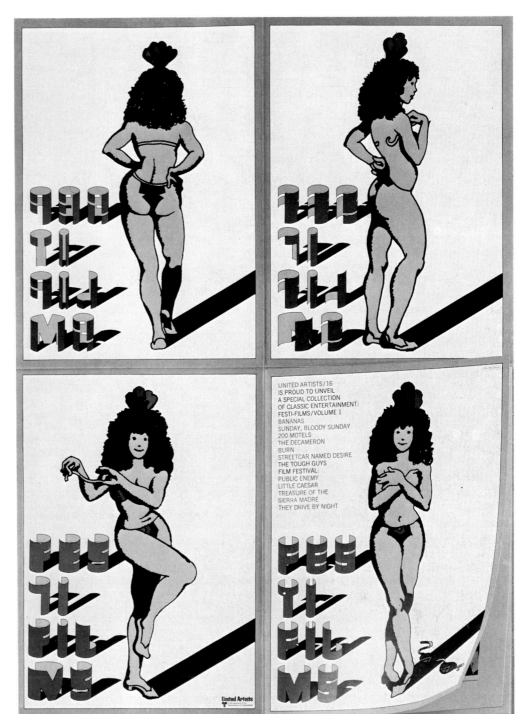

232

233

234

Bayerischer Rundfunk Sommerprogramm 1973

235

Jazz
Goes To
College

236

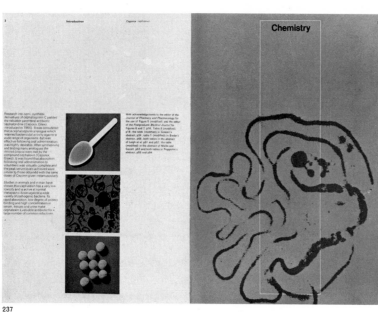

Chemistry

237

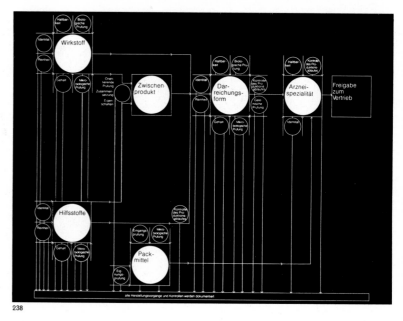

238

Booklets / Prospekte / Prospectus

235) Cover of a summer programme of the Bavarian radio and television authority. Butterflies and moths in full colour. (GER)

236) Promotion piece for jazz on CTI records. Black and white on pale blue. (USA)

237) Double spread from a *Glaxo* booklet about the antibiotic *Ceporex*. Inserts on left in colour, right-hand page blue-green on lime green. (GBR)

238) Diagram (on transparent paper) of a quality control system, from a booklet about the *Wülfing* pharmaceutical company. (GER)

239) Cover of a questionnaire booklet issued by The American Symphony Orchestra League. White on very pale beige, black print. (USA)

240) Page from a booklet announcing a talk to be given by the editor of a business magazine about the prospects for the coming year. The drawing illustrates crystal gazing as one way of forecasting the future. (USA)

241) 242) Cover and page, both in full colour, from a booklet about Old Montreal issued by the manufacturers of *Belvedere* cigarettes. (CAN)

235) Umschlag einer Broschüre mit dem Sommerprogramm 1973 des Bayerischen Rundfunks. Schmetterlinge und Nachtfalter mehrfarbig. (GER)

236) Werbung für Jazzaufnahmen auf CTI-Schallplatten. Schwarzweiss auf Hellblau. (USA)

237) Doppelseite aus einer *Glaxo*-Broschüre über das Antibiotikum *Ceporex*. Bilder auf der linken Seite mehrfarbig, rechte Seite blaugrün auf Lindengrün. (GBR)

238) Diagramm (auf durchsichtigem Papier) über die Qualitätskontrolle, aus einer Broschüre über Johann A. Wülfling-Bauer & Cie., Hersteller pharmazeutischer Präparate. (GER)

239) Umschlag einer Befragungsbroschüre der American Symphony Orchestra League. Weiss auf Hellbeige, schwarze Schrift. (USA)

240) Seite aus einer Broschüre als Ankündigung einer Rede des Herausgebers einer Fachzeitschrift über die Aussichten für das kommende Jahr. Die Zeichnung illustriert die Prophezeihung mittels Kristallkugel als einen der Wege, in die Zukunft zu schauen. (USA)

241) 242) Umschlag und Seite, beide mehrfarbig, aus einer Broschüre über Alt-Montreal, die vom Zigarettenhersteller *Belvedere* herausgegeben wurde. (CAN)

Survey Questionnaire

The American
Symphony Orchestra
League

Conducted by:
Smith, Bucklin &
Associates, Inc.

January 1973

239

Crystal ball gazing as a method of divination is
thought to have originated in Egypt six thousand
years before the Christian era.

Today crystal gazing is mostly practiced by old gypsy
women who have the power to look into your past,
present, future and pocket book.

240

Belvedere vous invite
à faire une
Promenade dans le
Vieux-Montréal

Belvedere invites you
for
A walk in
Old Montreal

241

19

242

235) Couverture d'un programme d'été de la Radio-Télévision Bavaroise. Papillons et mites poly-chromes. (GER)
236) Elément publicitaire pour les disques de jazz CTI. Noir, blanc sur bleu pâle. (USA)
237) Double page d'une brochure *Glaxo* consacrée à l'antibiotique *Ceporex*. Encarts de gauche en couleur, page de droite bleu-vert sur vert citron. (GBR)
238) Graphique (sur papier transparent) d'un système de contrôle de la qualité figurant dans une brochure de la société pharmaceutique *Wülfing*. (GER)
239) Couverture d'un questionnaire publié sous forme de brochure par l'American Symphony Orchestra League. Blanc sur beige très pâle, caractères noirs. (USA)
240) Page d'une brochure annonçant une conférence du rédacteur en chef d'un magazine d'affaires sur les perspectives de l'année. Le dessin se réfère à la boule de cristal, qui constitue l'un des moyens d'interroger l'avenir. (USA)
241) 242) Couverture et page polychromes d'une brochure consacrée au vieux Montréal et publiée par le fabricant des cigarettes *Belvedere*. (CAN)

Artist / Künstler / Artiste:
235) WALTER TAFELMAIER
236) GUY BILLOUT / BOB CIANO
237) ROGER O. DENNING
238) HANS-JÜRGEN RAU
239) DAVID M. SEAGER
240) L. SONS / W. PIRTLE /
R. SULLIVAN / G. BOOTH /
J. SUMMERFORD
241) WILLIAM CAMPBELL

Art Director / Directeur artistique:
236) BOB CIANO
237) ROGER O. DENNING
238) HANS-JÜRGEN RAU
239) BERNARD B. SANDERS
240) JACK SUMMERFORD
241) FRANK A. LIPARI

Agency / Agentur / Agence – Studio:
238) BROSE & PARTNER / BENTON & BOWLES
239) SANDERS & NOE, INC.
240) THE RICHARDS GROUP
241) GAZETTE CANADIAN PRINTING LTD.

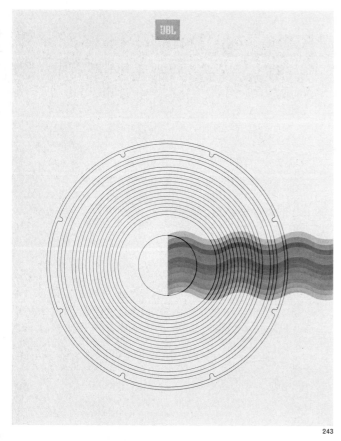

243) Cover of a catalogue of loud speakers made by James B. Lansing Sound, Inc. Black and white with waves in rainbow colours. (USA)
244) Invitation to a Calder retrospective, Maeght Gallery, Zurich. Red/black. (SWI)
245) Cover of a Hessian monthly television programme including a *Sesame Street* transmission for children. Black and white. (GER)
246) Page of a large booklet presenting the West German coalition cabinet in the form of a top-secret file with a seal that has to be broken by the reader. (GER)
247) Wine-coloured invitation to the opening of a restaurant in Turin. (ITA)
248) Cover of a folder about the 52nd Milan Trade Fair. Polychrome squares. (ITA)
249) Cover of a booklet about the American food industry issued by the Newspaper Advertising Bureau, Inc. (USA)
250) Large invitation to the preview of a products exhibition staged by Robert Benjamin Inc. Red and white. (USA)
251) 252) Two panels each of two monthly calendars of announcements issued by the San Francisco Museum of Art. (USA)

243) Umschlag eines Katalogs der von James B. Lansing Sound, Inc., hergestellten Lautsprecher. Schwarzweiss mit regenbogenfarbenen Wellen. (USA)
244) Einladung an eine Calder Retrospektive in der Galerie Maeght, Zürich. (SWI)
245) Umschlag eines Fernsehprogramms des Hessischen Rundfunks, mit einer *Sesamstrasse*-Übertragung für Kinder. Schwarzweiss. (GER)
246) Seite aus einer grossen Broschüre über das westdeutsche Bundeskanzleramt in der Form eines strenggeheimen Dokumentes. (GER)
247) Weinrote Einladung zur Eröffnung eines Restaurants in Turin. (ITA)
248) Umschlag eines Prospekts über die 52. Mailänder Messe. Farbige Quadrate. (ITA)
249) Umschlag einer Studie des Newspaper Advertising Bureau, Inc., über die Nahrungsmittelindustrie in den Vereinigten Staaten. (USA)
250) Grossformatige Einladung an die Vorschau einer Ausstellung von Industrie-Erzeugnissen. Rot und weiss. (USA)
251) 252) Je zwei Felder von zwei monatlichen Veranstaltungskalendern des San Francisco Museum of Art. (USA)

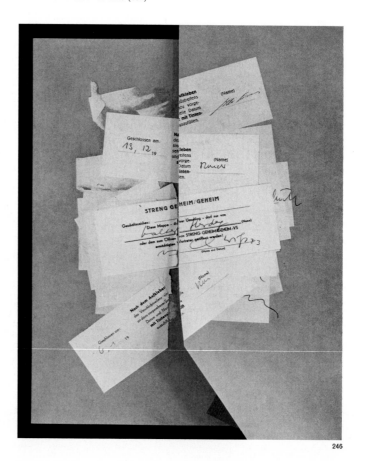

247

Centro Internazionale
degli Scambi

14-25 aprile 1974

FIERA
DI MILANO

248

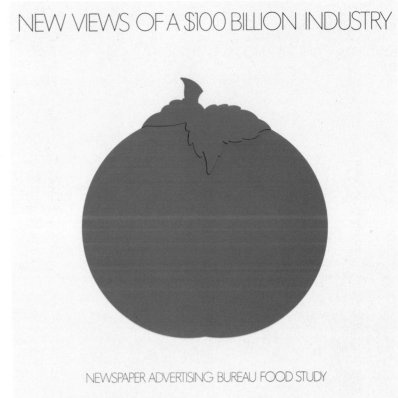

NEWSPAPER ADVERTISING BUREAU FOOD STUDY

249

243) Couverture d'un catalogue de haut-parleurs fabriqués par James B. Lansing Sound, Inc. Noir et blanc, ondes arc-en-ciel. (USA)

244) Invitation à une rétrospective de Calder à la Galerie Maeght de Zurich. Rouge, noir. (SWI)

245) Couverture d'un programme mensuel de la Télévision du Land de Hesse, avec une émission enfantine de la série *Sesame Street*. Noir et blanc. (GER)

246) Page d'une brochure au grand format présentant le cabinet de coalition de la RFA sous forme d'un dossier ultra-secret dont le lecteur doit rompre le sceau. (GER)

247) Invitation couleur de vin pour l'ouverture d'un restaurant turinois. (ITA)

248) Couverture d'un dépliant sur la 52e Foire de Milan. Carrés polychromes. (ITA)

249) Couverture d'une brochure sur l'industrie alimentaire américaine publiée par le Newspaper Advertising Bureau, Inc. (USA)

250) Invitation grand format pour l'avant-première d'une exposition des produits de la société Robert Benjamin, Inc. (USA)

251) 252) Deux fois deux volets de deux calendriers de manifestations publiés mensuellement par le San Francisco Museum of Art. (USA)

250

Booklets / Prospekte
Prospectus

Artist | Künstler | Artiste:

243) DAVE HOLT/DENNIS S. JUETT
244) ALEXANDER CALDER
245) EBERHARD MARHOLD
246) CHARLES WILP
247) ARMANDO TESTA/PAOLO REPETTO
248) VITTORIO CORRADINI
249) ERNIE GARCIA
250) GILBERT LESSER
251) 252) BOB ROSS

Art Director | Directeur artistique:

245) HESSISCHER RUNDFUNK, ABT. PUBLIZISTIK
246) CHARLES WILP
247) ARMANDO TESTA
248) EZIO BONINI
249) TOM CLEMENTE
250) GILBERT LESSER
251) 252) BOB ROSS

Agency | Agentur | Agence – Studio:

243) WELLER & JUETT, INC.
244) ATELIER MAEGHT
247) STUDIO ARMANDO TESTA
248) CBC
249) NEWSPAPER ADVERTISING BUREAU, INC.
251) 252) BOB ROSS DESIGN

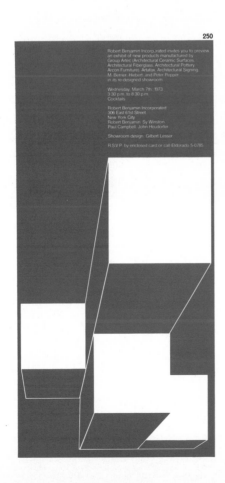

251

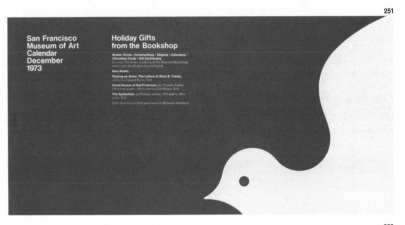

252

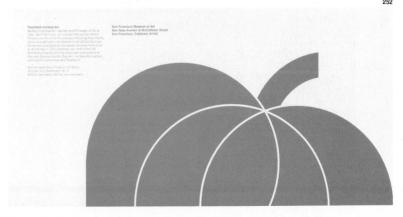

254

The Exhibition The Art Directors Club of Minneapolis and St. Paul Fine Art Exhibit is open to all members in good standing. The scope of this exhibit includes paintings, drawings and prints. Receiving All works must be delivered to the West Lake Gallery, 1612 West Lake Street, Minneapolis, Minnesota 55408 during the hours of 10.30 A.M. to 5:30 P.M. Monday, Tuesday and Wednesday, June 11, 12 and 13. Each work must have an entry label mounted on the back of the work. Judging will be on Friday, June 15, 1973. Conditions of Entry Total number of entries per exhibitor will be limited to two. All works must be suitably framed, ready for hanging. An entry fee of $3.00 must accompany each entry. There will be no hanging fee. All paintings must be for sale. The Gallery commission on all sales is 33⅓%. Please indicate if rental is acceptable. Rentals will be charged at regular Gallery rates and will apply toward purchase. Sold and rented works should remain on exhibit until the end of the show. Returning All works not sold will be held at the Gallery to be called for Monday and Tuesday, July 2 and 3, 1973. Liability The Art Directors Club will insure (against fire, theft, or vandalism) all works submitted at their stated valuation for the period of June 11, 1973 through July 3, 1973. The Gallery takes all possible care of art works left in charge, but assumes no responsibility after this date. Awards Exhibition awards will be presented to the winning artist at the reception to be held at 6 P.M., Tuesday, June 19, 1973, at the West Lake Gallery, 1612 West Lake Street, Minneapolis. The Art Directors Club of Minneapolis and St. Paul Fine Art Show will be on display to the public at the West Lake Gallery from 10 A.M. to 5:30 P.M. on Wednesday, June 20 through Saturday, June 30, 1973. 1973 Minneapolis and St. Paul Art Directors Club Fine Art Exhibit June 19th through June 30th

255

Cultures du soleil
et de la neige

Cultures of the sun
and the snow

L'art des Indiens
et des Esquimaux
du continent américain

Indian and Eskimo art
of the Americas

Exposition
tirée des collections du
Musée des beaux-arts
de Montréal
et présentée
à la *Terre des Hommes*
du 21 juin
au 3 septembre 1973

An exhibition
created from the collections of
The Montreal
Museum of Fine Arts
and presented
at *Man and His World*
from June 21 to
September 3, 1973

Booklets / Prospekte / Prospectus

Artist / Künstler / Artiste:

253) PHIL TRUMBO
254) LUC LE BON
255) FREDY JAGGI
256) DEREK BIRDSALL / ZOË HENDERSON
257) GERHARD PREISS

Art Director / Directeur artistique:

253) RAYMOND GEARY
254) LUC LE BON
255) GOTTSCHALK + ASH LTD.
256) DEREK BIRDSALL
257) GERHARD PREISS

Agency / Agentur / Agence – Studio:

255) GOTTSCHALK + ASH LTD.
256) OMNIFIC LTD.
257) GERHARD PREISS

253) Cover of a magazine published by Virginia Museum. (USA)
254) Call for entries to a fine art show of the Minneapolis and St. Paul Art Directors Club. Corrugated board. (USA)
255) Catalogue for an exhibition of Indian and Eskimo art, Montreal Museum of Fine Arts. Red, green, black. (CAN)
256) Catalogue cover for a German art exhibition. (GER)
257) Catalogue cover for an exhibition in Nuremberg (Franconian artists). Black and white. (GER)

253) Umschlag einer Zeitschrift des Virginia Museums. (USA)
254) Einladung zur Teilnahme an einer Kunstausstellung eines Art Directors Club. Wellkarton. (USA)
255) Katalog für eine Ausstellung über Indianer- und Eskimo-Kunst im Montreal Museum of Fine Arts. Rot, grün und schwarz. (CAN)
256) Katalogumschlag für eine Ausstellung in Hamburg. (GER)
257) Umschlag des Katalogs einer Ausstellung in der Kunsthalle Nürnberg. Schwarzweiss. (GER)

253) Couverture d'un magazine du Virginia Museum. (USA)
254) Appel de participation à une exposition des beaux-arts d'un Art Directors Club. Carton ondulé. (USA)
255) Catalogue pour une exposition d'art indien et esquimau. Museum of Fine Arts, Montréal. Rouge, vert sur noir. (CAN)
256) Couverture de catalogue. Exposition d'art allemand. (GER)
257) Couverture de catalogue pour une exposition à Nuremberg (artistes de Franconie). Noir et blanc. (GER)

Kunst in Deutschland

256

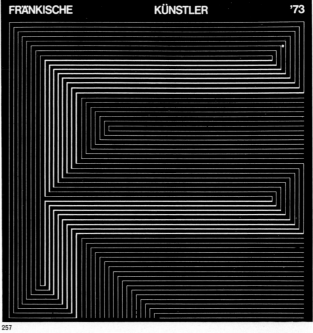

FRÄNKISCHE   KÜNSTLER   '73

257

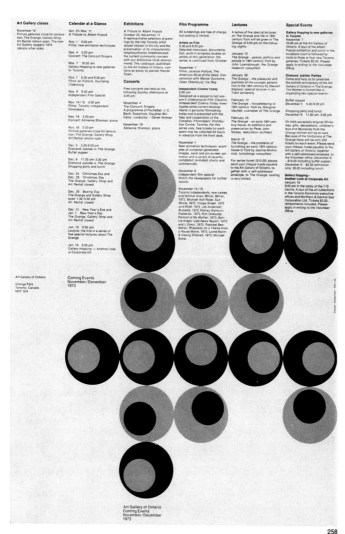

258

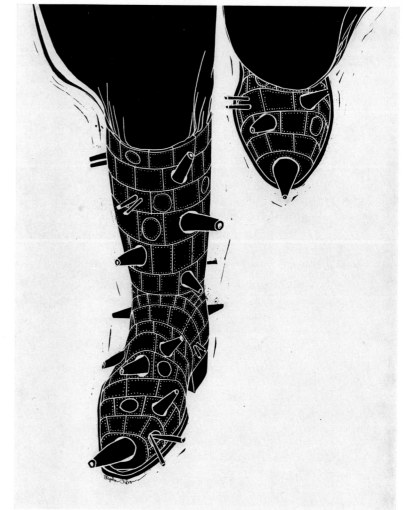

260

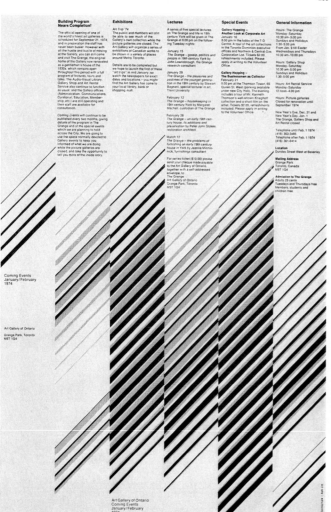

259

258) 259) Two bi-monthly folders, fully opened, announcing coming events in the Art Gallery of Ontario. Fig. 258 in red and deep yellow, fig. 259 in two blues. (CAN)

260) 261) Sheet and drawing from a direct-mail self-promotion portfolio of black-and-white work by the artist. (USA)

262) Small poster announcing a series of lectures on contemporary American art organized by The Art Institute of Chicago. (USA)

263) One side of a mailed invitation to an exhibition on the bicycle in the California Museum of Science and Industry. Lime green and black on pale beige paper. (USA)

264)-266) Cover (in the form of a torn cinema ticket) and two double spreads from the programme of a USA Film Festival in Dallas. (USA)

258) 259) Zweimonatliche Faltprospekte, vollständig geöffnet, als Ankündigung der kommenden Veranstaltungen an der Art Gallery of Ontario. Abb. 258 in Rot und dunklem Gelb, Abb. 259 in Hell- und Dunkelblau. (CAN)

260) 261) Blatt und Zeichnung aus einer Mappe mit schwarzweissen Arbeiten als Eigenwerbung des Künstlers. (USA)

262) Kleinplakat als Ankündigung einer Reihe Vorlesungen über zeitgenössische amerikanische Kunst, die vom Art Institute of Chicago organisiert wurde. (USA)

263) Eine Seite einer Einladung an eine Fahrrad-Ausstellung im California Museum of Science and Industry. Lindengrün und schwarz auf hellbeigem Papier. (USA)

264)-266) Umschlag (in der Form einer zerrissenen Kinoeintrittskarte) und zwei Doppelseiten aus dem Programm eines USA Filmfestivals in Dallas. (USA)

258) 259) Deux dépliants bimestriels, entièrement dépliés, annonçant les expositions de l'Art Gallery de l'Ontario. 258) Rouge, jaune foncé; 259) deux bleus. (CAN)

260) 261) Feuillet et dessin figurant dans un album distribué par un artiste à titre de publicité personnelle. Noir et blanc. (USA)

262) Affichette annonçant une série de conférences sur l'art américain contemporain organisée par l'Art Institute de Chicago. (USA)

263) Un côté d'une invitation pour une exposition sur la bicyclette au Musée californien de la Science et de l'Industrie. Vert citron et noir sur papier beige pâle. (USA)

264)-266) Couverture sous forme d'un ticket de cinéma déchiré et deux doubles pages du programme d'un festival du film américain à Dallas. (USA)

261

262

263

Artist | Künstler | Artiste:

258) 259) MALCOLM WADDELL
260) 261) STEPHEN OSBORN
262) MICHAEL REID
263) DON WELLER
264)–266) JOHN GREEN

Art Director | Directeur artistique:

258) 259) GOTTSCHALK + ASH
260) 261) STEPHEN OSBORN
262) MARGARET BLASALE
263) DON WELLER
264)–266) LARRY SONS

Agency | Agentur | Agence – Studio:

258) 259) GOTTSCHALK + ASH LTD.
260) 261) STEPHEN OSBORN & ASSOC., INC.
263) WELLER & JUETT, INC.
264)–266) THE RICHARDS GROUP

265

264

266

Booklets
Prospekte
Prospectus

267) Cover of a large booklet for *Air France*. Upper horizontal strip in rainbow colours, lower strip black, name in blue. (FRA)
268) Cover illustration for a folder to hold literature on industrial papers made by International Paper Company. (USA)
269) 270) Cover and opening double spread from a theatre programme for a play by Joseph Topol (Two Nights with a Girl). Black and white. (CSR)
271)–273) Illustration (full colour), cover (mauve ground) and spread from a spiral-bound guide to the handling of stars for promotion managers of CBS Television. (USA)
274) Leaflet on a *Solvay* product for packing foodstuffs and beverages. The illustration is chiefly in red shades. (GER)

267) Umschlag einer grossen Broschüre über *Air France*. Obere horizontale Streifen in Regenbogenfarben, untere Streifen in Schwarz, Namenszug in Blau. (FRA)
268) Umschlagsillustration für eine Faltmappe mit Literatur über Industrie-Papiere, die von der International Paper Company hergestellt werden. (USA)
269) 270) Umschlag und erste Doppelseite aus einem Theaterprogramm für ein Stück von Joseph Topol (Zwei Nächte mit einem Mädchen). Schwarzweiss. (CSR)
271)–273) Illustration (violett, braun und Grüntöne), Umschlag (Grund hellviolett) und Doppelseite aus einem spiralgehefteten Ratgeber für Angestellte der CBS Television über den Umgang mit Stars. (USA)
274) Prospekt über einen neuen Kunststoff der Deutschen Solvay-Werke GmbH für die Verpackung von Nahrungsmitteln. Illustration vorwiegend in Rottönen. (GER)

267) Couverture d'une brochure *Air France* au grand format. Bande horizontale supérieure imprimée dans les couleurs de l'arc-en-ciel, bande inférieure noire, nom bleu. (FRA)
268) Illustration de couverture pour un dépliant de l'Industrial Paper Company contenant de la documentation sur les papiers d'industrie. (USA)
269) 270) Couverture et première page initiale d'un programme de théâtre présentant une pièce de Joseph Topol (Deux Nuits avec une fille). Noir et blanc. (CSR)
271)–273) Illustration (mauve, brun et tons verdâtres), couverture au fond mauve et double page d'un guide à reliure spirale enseignant aux publicitaires de la chaîne de télévision CBS le contact avec les vedettes. (USA)
274) Prospectus pour un produit *Solvay* destiné à l'emballage des aliments et boissons. Prédominance de tons rouges dans l'illustration. (GER)

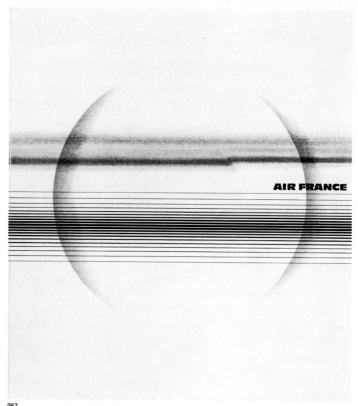

267

268

269

270

271

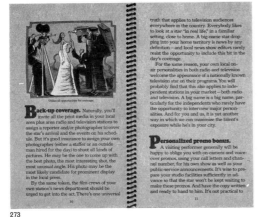

272   273

274

Booklets / Prospekte / Prospectus

Booklets / Prospekte / Prospectus

275

275) Catalogue cover for a Searle exhibition in a Munich gallery. Black and white. (GER)
276) Invitation to a press ball in Hamburg. Lilac paper. (GER)
277) 278) Full-colour illustration and corresponding spread from *Innovations in Paper*, published by the Weyerhaeuser Paper Division. The issue is about nursery rhymes. (USA)
279) Programme cover for the 6th Swiss Juvenile Book Week, held in Basle. The figures are drawn from the Basle carnival tradition. Black and white. (SWI)
280) Cover of a booklet about a national historic park. Black and red. (CAN)
281) Large New Year's card for a furniture transport and removals firm. Orange, magenta, green and black. (SWI)
282) Cover of a booklet on Canada's national historic parks. (CAN)
283) Cover of a catalogue for solidarity days with Cuba, issued by the Istituto Cubano de Amistad con los Pueblos. Blue and red knots. (CUB)

275) Umschlag eines Katalogs für eine Ronald Searle Ausstellung. Schwarzweiss. (GER)
276) Einladung zum Hamburger Presseball 1974. Schwarz auf lila Papier. (GER)
277) 278) Mehrfarbige Illustration und entsprechende Doppelseite aus einer Broschüre eines Papierherstellers mit Gute-Nacht-Versen. (USA)
279) Programmumschlag für die 6. Schweizerische Jugendbuchwoche 1973 in Basel. Die Figuren stammen aus der Basler Fasnachtstradition. Schwarzweiss. (SWI)
280) Umschlag einer Broschüre über einen historischen Park. Schwarz und rot. (CAN).
281) Grosse Neujahrskarte des Transportunternehmens Fritz Kipfer in Bern. Orange, magentarot, grün und schwarz. (SWI)
282) Umschlag einer Broschüre über historische Stätten in Kanada. (CAN)
283) Umschlag eines Katalogs für Solidaritätstage mit Kuba, der vom Istituto Cubano de Amistad con los Pueblos herausgegeben wurde. Knoten in Rot und Blau. (CUB)

275) Couverture de catalogue pour une exposition de Searle à Munich. Noir et blanc. (GER)
276) Invitation à un bal de la presse à Hambourg. Papier lilas. (GER)
277) 278) Illustration polychrome et double page correspondante d'*Innovations in Paper* publié par la Weyerhaeuser Paper Division. Numéro consacré aux rondes enfantines. (USA)
279) Couverture du programme de la 6e Semaine Suisse du Livre d'Enfant à Bâle. Personnages issus de la tradition du carnaval de Bâle. Noir et blanc. (SWI)
280) Couverture d'une brochure sur un parc national historique. Noir et rouge. (CAN)
281) Carte de Nouvel An au grand format pour une entreprise de transports et déménagements Orange, magenta, vert, noir. (SWI)
282) Couverture d'une brochure sur les parcs nationaux historiques du Canada. (CAN)
283) Couverture d'un catalogue en appelant à la solidarité avec le peuple cubain et publié par l'Istituto Cubano de Amistad con los Pueblos. Nœuds bleus et rouges. (CUB)

276

277

Programm

279

278

Ontario **Fort George
Parc historique
national**

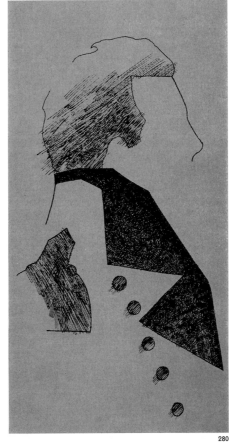

280

281

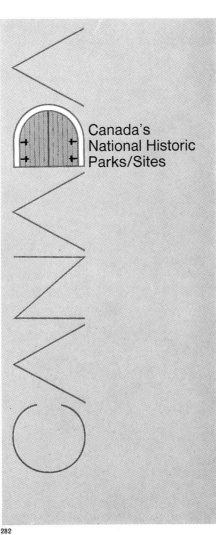

Canada's
National Historic
Parks/Sites

282

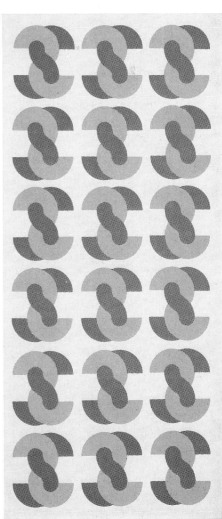

283

284) Mailer from a series demonstrating the quality of papers made by the Scott Paper Company, here showing a make of stoneware. Muted colours. (USA)
285) Cover of a *Ciba-Geigy* corporate identity manual. White on blue. (USA)
286) 287) Two covers of the same booklet of graphic impressions of New York, issued in one case by the Sanders Printing Corp., in the other by the Mead Paper Corp. (USA)
288) Assortment of *Kromekote* papers in the form of a hand. (USA)
289) Cover of a brochure about a CCA heat sealing system for cartons. (USA)
290) Cover for an assortment of new paper qualitites. Black and white. (SWI)

284) Versandkarte aus einer Serie, die die verschiedenen Papierqualitäten und -sorten eines Papier-herstellers präsentiert. In verhaltenen Tönen. (USA)
285) Umschlag eines Handbuches über das Erscheinungsbild von *Ciba-Geigy*. Weiss und Blau. (USA)
286) 287) Zwei verschiedene Umschläge derselben Broschüre mit einer Sammlung graphischer Impressionen von New York, im ersten Fall von einer Druckerei herausgegeben, im zweiten von einem Papierhersteller. (USA)
288) *Kromekote*-Papierkollektion, in der Form einer Hand präsentiert. (SWI)
289) Umschlag einer Broschüre über ein CCA-Verschluss-System für Schachteln. (USA)
290) Umschlag für eine Broschüre mit dem neuen Papiersortiment von Baumgartner Papier AG. Schwarzweiss. (SWI)

284) Elément de publicité directe tiré d'une série destinée à démontrer la qualité du papiers de la Scott Paper Co. Ici, une poterie de grès. Couleurs mates. (USA)
285) Couverture d'un manuel d'identité globale *Ciba-Geigy*. Blanc sur bleu. (USA)
286) 287) Deux couvertures de la même brochure d'impressions graphiques de New York publiée en même temps, mais avec une couverture différente, par la Sanders Printing Corp. et la Mead Paper Corp. (USA)
288) Assortiment de papiers *Kromekote* présenté sous forme d'une main. (SWI)
289) Couverture d'une brochure sur un système CCA de thermoétanchéité de cartons. (USA)
290) Couverture d'un assortiment de qualités nouvelles de papier. Noir et blanc. (SWI)

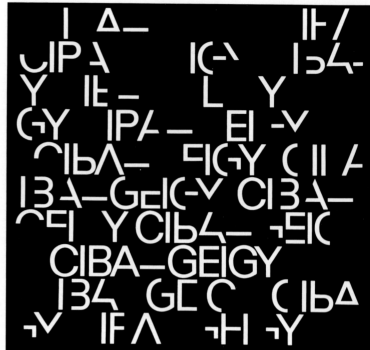

285

284

Lithographed on Scott Vellum Bristol Gray (basis 22½ x 28½—134M)

Bennington Stoneware

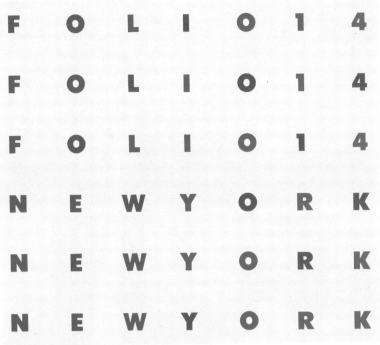

286

287

288

289

Booklets
Prospekte
Prospectus

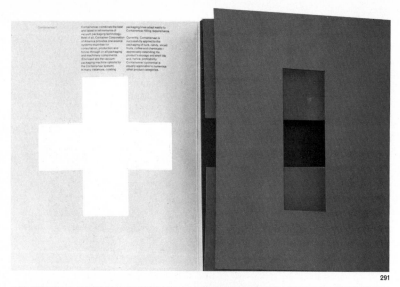

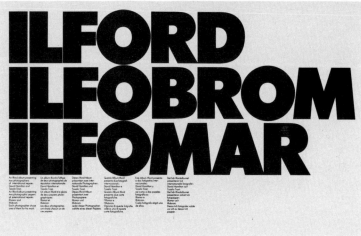

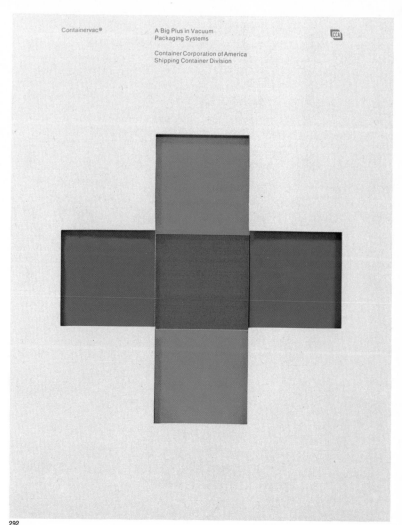

291) 292) Opening and cover of a folder containing loose sheets on vacuum-packing systems and machines offered by the Container Corporation of America. (USA)

293) Cover of an album issued by *Ilford*. It presents two photographic papers through the work of two reputed photographers. Black and white. (GBR)

294) Cover of a folder containing loose sheets on the packaging of soft drinks, for the Container Corporation. A brown board is visible through the die-cut holes. (USA)

295) Double spread from a booklet introducing *Mélange*, a new restaurant, wine shop and club in Houston, Texas. Illustration and initial in full colour. (USA)

296) Direct-mail call for entries for the Art Directors Club of Los Angeles annual show of advertising art. (USA)

297) Paper-sculpture illustration from the New Year's card of a marketing organization. (SWI)

291) 292) Faltmappe – teilweise offen und geschlossen gezeigt – mit losen Blättern über Vakuum-verpackungssysteme und -maschinen der Container Corporation of America. (USA)

293) Umschlag eines von *Ilford* herausgegebenen Albums, in dem zwei Photopapiere durch die Werke von zwei bekannten Photographen vorgestellt werden. Schwarzweiss. (GBR)

294) Umschlag eines Faltprospekts der Container Corporation of America mit losen Blättern über die Verpackung von alkoholfreien Getränken. Durch die ausgestanzten Löcher im Umschlag ist ein brauner Karton sichtbar. (USA)

295) Doppelseite aus einem Prospekt über *Mélange*, ein neues Restaurant mit Weinhandlung und Klub in Houston, Texas. Illustration und Initial mehrfarbig. (USA)

296) Einladung zur Teilnahme an der Ausstellung des Art Directors Club of Los Angeles. (USA)

297) Illustration aus einer Neujahrskarte von Zutter Sommer Marketing in Basel. (SWI)

291) 292) Page initiale et couverture d'un dépliant avec des prospectus décrivant des systèmes et machines d'emballage sous vide de la Container Corporation of America. (USA)

293) Couverture d'un album publié par *Ilford*, qui présente deux papiers photographiques à travers l'œuvre de deux photographes de renom. Noir et blanc. (GBR)

294) Couverture d'un dépliant contenant des prospectus sur l'emballage de boissons sans alcool, pour la Container Corporation. A travers les trous, on aperçoit un carton brun. (USA)

295) Double page d'une brochure présentant un nouveau restaurant, avec cave et club, le *Mélange*, à Houston (Texas). Illustration et lettre initiale en polychromie. (USA)

296) Appel de participation à l'exposition annuelle d'art publicitaire organisée par l'Art Directors Club of Los Angeles. (USA)

297) Illustration sculptée sur papier. Carte de Nouvel An d'une organisation de marketing. (SWI)

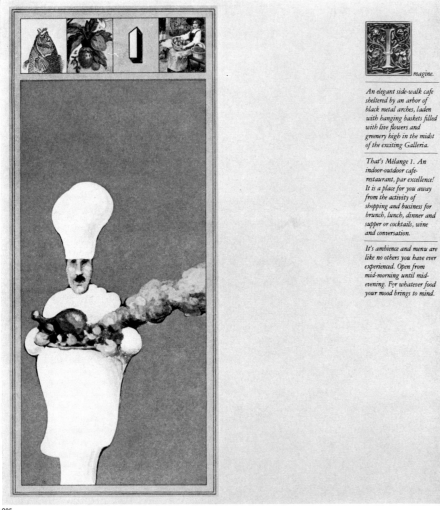

Imagine.

An elegant side-walk cafe sheltered by an arbor of black metal arches, laden with hanging baskets filled with live flowers and greenery high in the midst of the exciting Galleria.

That's Mélange 1. An indoor-outdoor cafe-restaurant, par excellence! It is a place for you away from the activity of shopping and business for brunch, lunch, dinner and supper or cocktails, wine and conversation.

It's ambience and menu are like no others you have ever experienced. Open from mid-morning until mid-evening. For whatever food your mood brings to mind.

295

297

296

Artist | Künstler | Artiste:

291) 292) 294) BILL BONNELL III
293) WILLY FLECKHAUS
295) JERRY JEANMARD / JERRY HERRING
296) IGNACIO GOMEZ
297) ALBERTO SOLBACH

Art Director | Directeur artistique:

291) 292) 294) BILL BONNELL III
293) WILLY FLECKHAUS
295) JERRY HERRING
296) JOHN ANSELMO

Agency | Agentur | Agence – Studio:

291) 292) 294) CONTAINER CORPORATION OF AMERICA
295) KELVIN GROUP
297) ZUTTER SOMMER MARKETING

Booklets / Prospekte / Prospectus

298

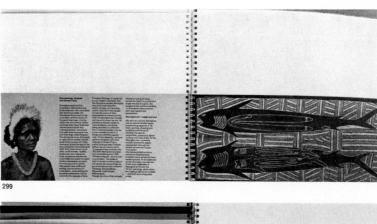

299

300

301

302

303

298)-301) Double spreads from an issue of *Imagination*, a booklet issued at intervals by Champion Papers and using a variety of their paper grades. This issue is devoted to Australia. Fig. 298 shows photographs of the Northern Territory and a seascape by Peter Powditch; fig. 299 has a text on the Australian aborigines and an example of their 'X-ray' art (lower half of pages black on red); fig. 300 deals with the famous Australian outlaw Ned Kelly, who recurs in the paintings of Sidney Nolan (right); and fig. 301 is about sport in Australia, the right-hand page showing a painting on enamel by Bernard Hesling. (AUL)

302) 303) Two double spreads from a booklet about 'symbols of the ancients' to introduce a new dull art paper made by Associated Pulp and Paper Mills Ltd. The right-hand pages are in full colour, with a detail of that in fig. 303 showing through the die-cut circle in fig. 302. (AUL)

304) Panel of a large folder issued as part of a large series by International Typographic Composition Association, Inc. Black and white. (USA)

305) One side of a folder showing a plan of a French 'Disneyland' village. (FRA)

306) Poster announcing an exhibition of American posters in the Mead Library of Ideas, New York. Blue and red. (USA)

307) Cover of an issue of CCA *Today*, brochure of the Container Corporation of America, also conveying season's greetings. Green, red and blue. (USA)

298)-301) Doubles pages d'un numéro d'*Imagination*, brochure périodique de Champion Papers imprimée sur divers papiers de cette entreprise. Numéro consacré à l'Australie : 298) photos du Territoire du Nord et marine de Peter Powditch; 299) texte sur les aborigènes et exemple de leur «art aux rayons X» (partie inférieure de ces pages noir sur rouge); 300) récit sur le célèbre hors-la-loi Ned Kelly, que l'on trouve représenté dans les peintures de Sidney Nolan (à droite); 301) les sports en Australie; la page de droite représente une peinture sur émail due à Bernard Hesling. (AUL)

302) 303) Deux doubles pages d'une brochure sur les «symboles des anciens» présentant un nouveau papier couché mat fabriqué par l'Associated Pulp and Paper Mills Ltd. Les pages de droite sont polychromes; un détail de l'illustration de la fig. 302 apparaît dans le cercle découpé de la fig. 302. (AUL)

304) Volet d'un dépliant grand format figurant dans une série importante publiée par l'International Typographic Composition Association, Inc. Noir et blanc. (USA)

305) Un côté d'un dépliant montrant le projet d'un village «Disneyland» français. (FRA)

306) Affiche annonçant une exposition d'affiches américaines à la Mead Library of Ideas a New York. Bleu et rouge. (USA)

307) Couverture d'un numéro de CCA *Today*, avec des vœux de Nouvel An. Vert/rouge/bleu. (USA)

298)-301) Doppelseiten aus einer Ausgabe von *Imagination*, eine Broschüre, die in unregelmässigen Zeitabständen von Champion Papers unter Verwendung deren verschiedener Papiersorten herausgegeben wird. Diese Nummer ist Australien gewidmet. Abb. 298 zeigt Aufnahmen des Northern Territory und eine Meerlandschaft, Abb. 299 bringt einen Text über die Eingeborenen und deren Kunst (untere Hälfte der Seiten Schwarz auf Rot); Abb. 300 handelt vom bekannten australischen Gesetzlosen Ned Kelly, der in den Gemälden von Sidney Nolan wiederkehrt (rechts), und Abb. 301 ist dem Sport in Australien gewidmet. (AUL)

302) 303) Zwei Doppelseiten aus einer Broschüre über «Symbole der Antike» als Einführung einer neuen matten Kunstpapiersorte von Associated Pulp and Papier Mills Ltd. Die rechten Seiten sind mehrfarbig. Ein Detail derjenigen in Abb. 303 ist durch den ausgestanzten Kreis in Abb. 302 sichtbar. (AUL)

304) Feld eines grossformatigen Faltprospekts, der als Teil einer langen Serie von International Typographic Composition Association Inc. herausgegeben wurde. Schwarzweiss. (USA)

305) Eine Seite eines Prospekts mit dem Plan eines Vergnügungsparks in Frankreich. (FRA)

306) Plakat als Ankündigung einer Ausstellung amerikanischer Plakate in der Mead Library of Ideas in New York. Blau und rot. (USA)

307) Umschlag einer Ausgabe von CCA *Today*, Broschüre der Container Corporation of America, mit Neujahrswünschen. Grün, rot und blau. (USA)

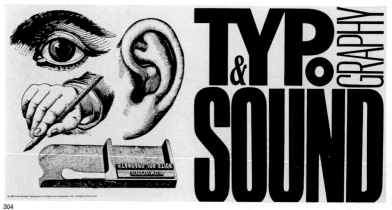

304

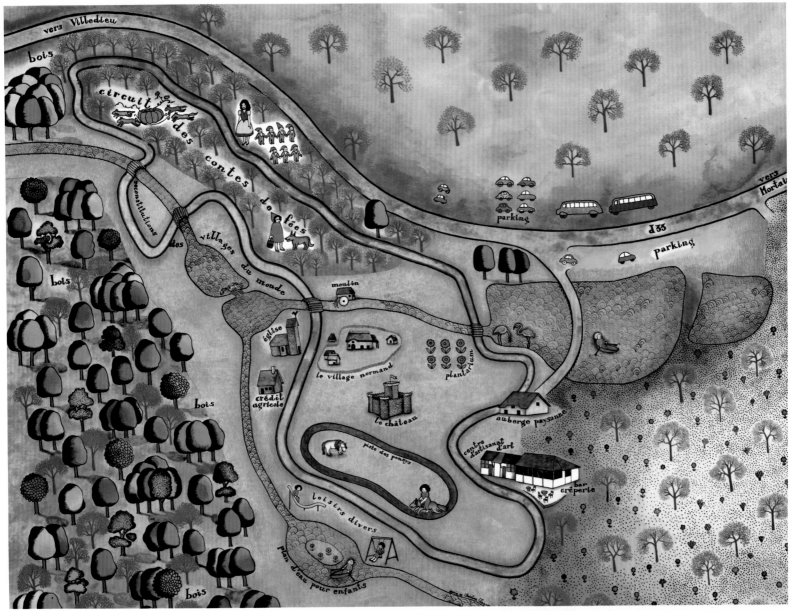

305

Booklets / Prospekte
Prospectus

306

307

308

Bible Readings and Intercessions for Mission

RESPONSE

November December 1973

309

310

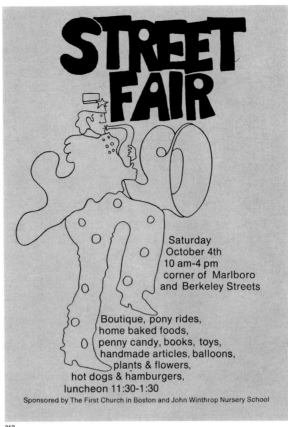

311

312

313

308) Self-promotion card for the design studio of John and Barbara Casado. Black and red. (USA)
309) Cover of a booklet about a religious mission. Black type matter and white stars on red ground. (USA)
310) Invitation to a show of work by students organized by Franklin Typographers Inc. (USA)
311) Poster-size bulletin about the facilities of the California Institute of the Arts. Blue and black on silver-grey. (USA)
312) Card announcing a street fair organized by The First Church in Boston. Printed on orange paper. (USA)
313) Menu for the Hotel Meridien, Guadeloupe. Design in red, white and blue. (FRA)
314) Invitation to a lecture and slide presentation about the discovery of a biblical city, issued by the Hebrew Union College. Dark blue design. (USA)

308) Eigenwerbekarte eines Design-Studios in Los Angeles. Schwarz und rot. (USA)
309) Umschlag einer Broschüre über eine Mission. Schwarze Schrift und weisse Sterne auf rotem Grund. (USA)
310) Einladung an eine Ausstellung der prämierten Werke eines von Franklin Typographers Inc. organisierten Kunstwettbewerbs für Studenten. (USA)
311) Bulletin – in der Grösse eines Plakats – über Studienmöglichkeiten am California Institute of the Arts. Blau und schwarz auf Silber. (USA)
312) Karte als Ankündigung eines Jahrmarktes, der von der First Church in Boston organisiert wurde. Auf orangefarbigem Papier gedruckt. (USA)
313) Menü für das Hotel Meridien, Guadeloupe. Design in Rot, Weiss und Blau. (FRA)
314) Einladung zu einer Vorlesung und Diavorführung des Hebrew Union College über die Entdeckung einer biblischen Stadt. (USA)

308) Carte servant à la publicité personnelle des designers John et Barbara Casado. Noir et rouge. (USA)
309) Couverture d'une brochure consacrée à une mission religieuse. Lettres noires et étoiles blanches sur fond rouge. (USA)
310) Invitation pour une exposition de travaux d'étudiants organisée par la Franklin Typographers Inc. (USA)
311) Bulletin format affiche présentant les installations du California Institute of the Arts. Bleu et noir sur gris argenté. (USA)
312) Carte annonçant une foire organisée dans les rues de Boston par la First Church. Papier orange. (USA)
313) Menu pour l'Hôtel Méridien à la Guadeloupe. Composition bleu/blanc/rouge. (FRA)
314) Invitation pour une conférence avec diapositives sur la découverte d'une cité biblique, organisée par le Hebrew Union College. Bleu foncé. (USA)

314

315

316

Artist / Künstler / Artiste:

315) SIMMS TABACK   318) 319) MABEY TROUSDELL
316) GILBERT STONE   320) AGNÈS GAY-ROSENTIEHL
317) ROY CARRUTHERS   321) MARIA DEFEBO

Agency / Agentur / Agence – Studio:

318) 319) KINCAID ADVERTISING

318

319

317

320

315)–317) Full-page black-and-white illustrations from *The White Elephant Cook Book*, published by *Collins* for a restaurant club. The proceeds from the book go to a children's aid fund. The illustrations shown face the recipes for Gefilte Fish, Chicken Pie and Chicken with Rosemary respectively. (GBR)

318) 319) Direct-mail kit with an invitation to a Western Party at Dallas, sent out by First Union National Bank of Charlotte, N.C. All texts and illustrations have a Western flavour. (USA)

320) Cover of a large portfolio about hair dyeing and tinting handed to women's magazine journalists by *L'Oréal*. (FRA)

321) Programme cover for a gymnastics meeting between the USA and Hungary, issued by Pennsylvania State University. Colours of the Hungarian flag. (USA)

315)–317) Ganzseitige, schwarzweisse Illustrationen aus *The White Elephant Cook Book*, ein von *Collins* für einen Restaurant-Club herausgegebenes Kochbuch. Der Verkaufsertrag geht an einen Kinderfonds. Die gezeigten Bilder illustrieren die Rezepte für ein Fischgericht, Geflügelpastete und Hähnchen mit Rosmarin. (GBR)

318) 319) Direktwerbegarnitur einer Bank, mit einer Einladung zu einer Western Party in Dallas: «Du willst also Cowboy werden?». Sämtliche Texte und Illustrationen haben Western-Charakter. (USA)

320) Umschlag einer grossen Mappe von *L'Oréal*, die an Journalisten von Frauenzeitschriften abgegeben wurde, über das Färben und Tönen der Haare. (FRA)

321) Umschlag eines von der Pennsylvania State University herausgegebenen Programms für ein Treffen zwischen amerikanischen und ungarischen Turnern. Farben der ungarischen Flagge. (USA)

315)–317) Illustrations noir-blanc pleine page pour le *White Elephant Cook Book*, un livre de cuisine publié par *Collins* pour un restaurant-club. La recette de ce livre sera versée à un fonds d'assistance à l'enfance. Les illustrations se rapportent aux recettes suivantes: «gefilte fish», chicken pie et poulet au romarin. (GBR)

318) 319) Eléments de publicité directe comportant une invitation à une fête dans le style du Far-Ouest à Dallas, distribués par la First Union National Bank de Charlotte, N.C. Les textes et illustrations respirent l'atmosphère du Far-Ouest. (USA)

320) Couverture d'un album *L'Oréal* au grand format sur le thème de la teinture et de la coloration des cheveux, distribué aux journalistes des magazines féminins. (FRA)

321) Couverture du programme d'une rencontre de gymnastique USA–Hongrie publié par la Pennsylvania State University. Couleurs du drapeau hongrois. (USA)

Art Director | Directeur artistique :

315)–317) ARNOLD SCHWARTZMAN
318) 319) FRANK RODGERS
320) AGNÈS GAY-ROSENTIEHL
321) MARILYN SHOBAKEN

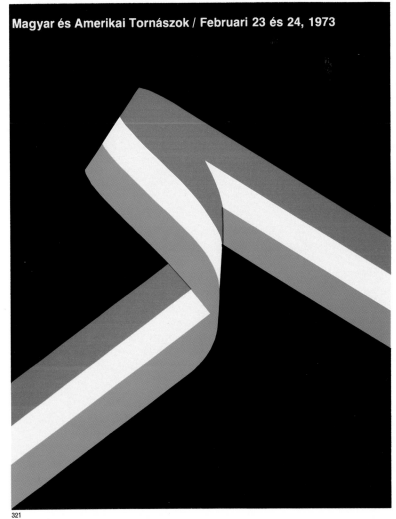

Magyar és Amerikai Tornászok / Februari 23 és 24, 1973

321

322) 323) Illustration in actual size and corresponding double spread from a *Philips* booklet for children about a little girl who liked watching television. (FRA)

324)–326) Three double spreads from an ABC of American football, a 16-page brochure explaining the game, issued by the National Football League. Full-colour illustrations. (USA)

327) Postcard designed, together with a trade mark and menus, for a restaurant in New York called The Russian Tea Room. The copy lists the requirements laid down by Peter the Great when he first invited ladies to dine at his table. (USA)

Philippine est une petite fille de ton âge, qui adore regarder la télévision en couleur. Un jour, alors que son Papa et sa maman étaient sortis, Philippine céda à la tentation. Après avoir usé d'un peu d'ingéniosité pour parvenir jusqu'au bouton, elle escalada l'énorme fauteuil et s'y blottit. ...Soudain, une ambiance irréelle régna dans la pièce.

323

322

322) 323) Illustration in Originalgrösse und entsprechende Doppelseite aus einer *Philips* Broschüre für Kinder über ein kleines Mädchen, das gerne Fernsehen schaute. (FRA)

324)–326) Drei Doppelseiten aus einem ABC des amerikanischen Fussballs, einer von einem Fussballverband herausgegebenen Broschüre mit Erklärungen über das Spiel. Mehrfarbig. (USA)

327) Zusammen mit Emblem und Menükarte gestaltete Postkarte für ein Restaurant in New York (The Russian Tea Room). Auf der Rückseite stehen die Bestimmungen, die Peter der Grosse erliess, als er erstmals Damen einlud, an seiner Tafel zu speisen. (USA)

322) 323) Illustration format original et double page où elle figure. Brochure *Philips* destinée aux enfants. C'est l'histoire d'une fillette qui aimait regarder la télé. (FRA)

324)–326) Trois doubles pages pages d'un ABC du «football américain» (brochure de 16 pages expliquant cette variété originale de football) de la National Football League. (USA)

327) Carte postale réalisée (en même temps que des menus et une marque déposée) pour un restaurant newyorkais, le Russian Tea Room. On y trouve les exigences formulées par Pierre le Grand pour la première invitation de dames à la table impériale. (USA)

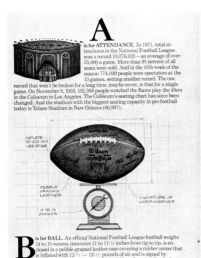

324

325

326

327

Artist | Künstler | Artiste:

322) 323) PATRICK VENTUJOL
324)–326) MABEY TROUSDELL, INC.
327) MILTON GLASER

Art Director | Directeur artistique:

322) 323) PATRICK VENTUJOL
324)–326) DAVE BOSS
327) MILTON GLASER

Agency | Agentur | Agence – Studio:

322) 323) PRESSE REUNIE
327) PUSH PIN STUDIOS, INC.

Booklets / Prospekte / Prospectus

328

332

334

328) Insert in a daily in the form of a red *Levi's* sports shirt. (USA)
329) Educational booklet on anatomy cut to the human figure, for Scott, Foresman & Co. (USA)
330) Cover of a booklet issued by International Typographic Composition Association, Inc. Yellow on taupe grey. (USA)
331) Cover of a folder to hold technical literature on *Saint-Gobain* glass panels. Full colour. (FRA)
332) 333) Cover (leaf and cigarette in colour) and fold-out chart illustrating the manufacture of cigarettes. (SWI)
334)–336) Cover and two spreads from a programme for a bogus Molière play, issued by The Beckett Paper Co. (USA)

328) Prospekt in der Form eines weinroten *Levi's* Sporthemdes als Beilage in einer Fachzeitschrift. (USA)
329) Anatomisches Lehrmittel, herausgegeben vom Papierhersteller Scott, Foresman & Co. (USA)
330) Umschlag einer Broschüre, die von der International Typographic Composition Association Inc. herausgegeben wurde. Mehrfarbig. (USA)
331) Umschlag eines Mäppchens zum Aufbewahren von technischen Notizen über *Saint-Gobain*-Glasplatten. Farbig. (FRA)
332) 333) Umschlag (Blatt und Zigarette farbig) und ausgelegte Darstellung der Herstellung von Zigaretten aus einer von *Rinsoz Ormond* herausgegebenen Broschüre. (SWI)
334)–336) Umschlag und zwei Doppelseiten aus einem von einem Papierhersteller herausgegebenen Theaterprogramm. (USA)

328) Encart de quotidien sous forme d'une chemise de sport rouge *Levi's*. (USA)
329) Brochure éducative sur l'anatomie, en forme de silhouette, pour Scott, Foresman & Co. (USA)
330) Couverture d'une brochure publiée par l'International Typographic Composition Assoc., Inc. Jaune sur gris. (USA)
331) Couverture d'un dépliant renfermant de la documentation sur les panneaux de verre *St-Gobain*. Polychromie. (FRA)
332) 333) Couverture (feuille et cigarette en couleur) et tableau dépliant sur la fabrication des cigarettes. (SWI)
334)–336) Couverture et deux doubles pages d'un programme pour une comédie imaginaire de Molière. Beckett Paper Co. (USA)

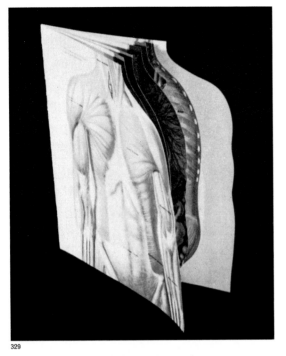

329

Typographic i Vol.3. No 3. Ideas. Information. Inspiration. Type and the tube by Rudi Bass. Aural typography: Transwhichics. The word paintings of Ronald Arnholm. The three families of Century by M.F. McGrew. Morton Goldsholl cries: "Enough!" International Typographic Composition Association, Inc.

330

Panover: panneaux préfabriqués en briques de verre SAINT-GOBAIN

331

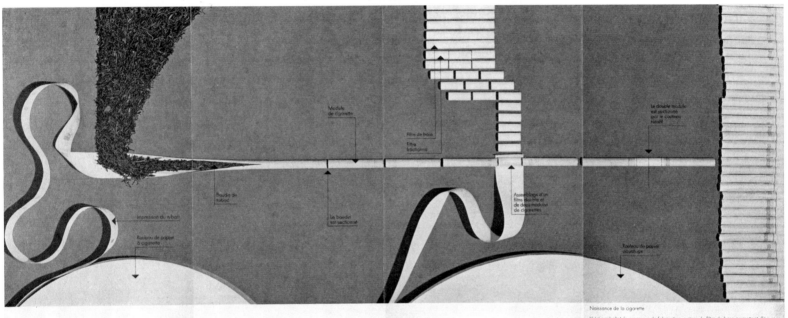

Naissance de la cigarette

Voici symbolisé le processus de fabrication. Le tabac, tressé en un boudin, est enveloppé du ruban de papier. Telle une cigarette géante sans cesse fractionnée, sans cesse renaissante, il défile à une allure vertigineuse dans la confectionneuse. Une imprimante appose au passage la marque sur le papier.
Une seule batterie de machines produit jusqu'à 4000 cigarettes à la minute. Celles qui doivent être dotées d'un filtre sont acheminées directement à l'assembleuse. Les dimensions du filtre de base permettent d'équiper six cigarettes. Il est fractionné en trois parties, chacune d'elles est fixée par un enveloppement de papier aquotuge aux extrémités de deux cigarettes, qui sont séparées ensuite par un couteau rotatif.

333

The Play   Act 1

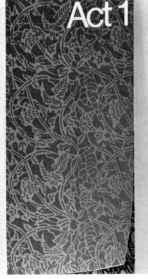

The Cast

Mr. Jourdain	Sir John Morley
Mrs. Jourdain	Arlene Pavan
Elise	Krissa Tyrell
Dorante	Browne Davis
Valere	Bruce Slade
Silvester	Kurt Tremaine
Dr. Filnin	Cameron Michaels
Dr. Meirollin	Eaton Taft
Dr. d'Aguri	Louis Benton
Master Biggs	Hal Polbrock
Cerito	Turhan Fitz
Dame Claude	Marjorie Blazno
La Merouche	Regis Kellerman
Brindavoine	Roberta Shutzner
Music Master	William Baird
Music Master's Pupil	Ralph Richards
Two Lackeys	Charles Hardy, Archer Gardner
The Mufti, Turks, and Dervishes	LeRoy Irvin, Tony Lund, and Homer Ronsen

Note: Our apologies to Molière. This is a totally fictitious drama based on the oeuvre of the Author.

335

336

337

Artist | Künstler | Artiste:

337) 338) YUSAKU KAMEKURA/
  KATSUMI ASABA
339) JOHN MASSEY / RICHARD PREY
340)–343) STEPHAN GEISSBÜHLER

Art Director | Directeur artistique:

337) 338) KATSUMI ASABA
339) JOHN MASSEY / RICHARD PREY
340)–343) STEPHAN GEISSBÜHLER

Agency | Agentur | Agence – Studio:

339) CBT PUBLICATION SERVICES

338

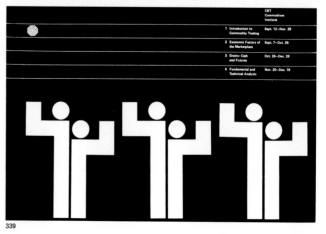

339

337) 338) Detail of the design and complete black-and-white cover for the programme of the 1973 ICSID congress in Kyoto. (JPN)
339) Three panels of a folder about courses in commodity training, issued by the Chicago Board of Trade. Pale blue and white. (USA)
340)–343) Covers of four booklets for the use of children entitled *The Process of Choice*. They are issued by the Group for Environmental Education and published by the MIT Press. The purpose is to persuade children, by an entertaining presentation of the facts, to think about the alternatives of modern society. (USA)

337) 338) Detail der Graphik und vollständiger, schwarzweisser Umschlag für das Programm des ICSID Kongresses 1973 in Kyoto. (JPN)
339) Drei Seiten eines Faltprospekts über Verkaufskurse für Gebrauchsgüter. Der Herausgeber ist die Chicagoer Handelskammer. Hellblau und weiss. (USA)
340)–343) Umschläge von vier für Kinder bestimmte Broschüren mit dem Titel *The Process of Choice*. Sie sind von einer Gruppe für Umgebungserziehung zusammengestellt und von MIT Press herausgegeben. Der Zweck liegt darin, Kinder durch eine unterhaltende Darstellung der Tatsachen dazuzubringen, über Alternativen zur modernen Gesellschaft nachzudenken. (USA)

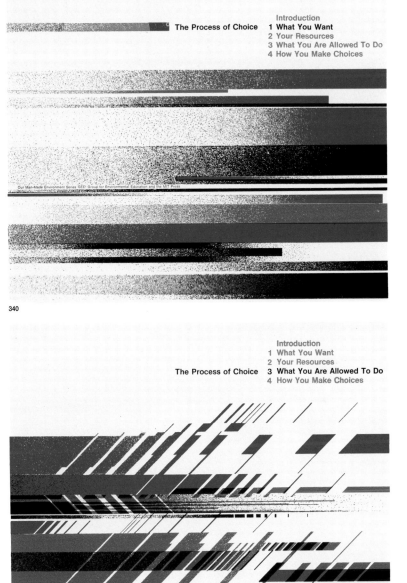

340

341

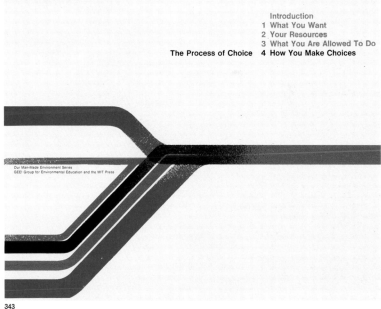

342

343

337) 338) Détail de la composition (JPN) et couverture noir-blanc complète du programme du congrès de l'ICSID à Kyoto en 1973. (JPN)
339) Trois volets d'un dépliant du Chicago Board of Trade annonçant des cours sur le commerce de marchandises spécifiques. Bleu pâle et blanc. (USA)
340)–343) Couverture de quatre brochures publiées par MIT Press et intitulées *The Process of Choice* (La Liberté de choisir). Le Group for Environmental Education entend y convaincre les enfants de l'existence de plusieurs modèles de société à notre époque, en présentant ses idées sous une forme attrayante. (USA)

Booklets / Prospekte / Prospectus

121

the development of leadership among member bands. As an example, member bands, have applied for and received assistance under the Woodlot Improvement Act. Other initiators have been taken by various member bands.

CORAID is an example of how Indian communities can achieve a high level of development more quickly by working in co-operation with each other.

Chippewas of Georgina Island Indian Band

The development of tourist recreation facilities on Snake, Fox and Georgina Islands in Lake Simcoe is providing band members with pride in their own achievements. On Snake Island, there is a cottage sub-division; Fox Island is being preserved as a park and the band community lives on Georgina Island.

A Provincial grant of $24,000 covered the purchase cost of a steel self-propelled non-passenger barge. Band members operate this vehicle to transport equipment to the three islands comprising the reserve and to pump out and remove sewage from resident and cottage holding systems. Local involvement in this project has resulted in the assumption of greater responsibility by community members.

Couchiching Indian Band

To overcome the problem of inadequate transportation facilities on the reserve, the provincial government allocated $5,613.50 to the Couchiching Indian Band to defray the purchase price of a small community bus which, by providing daily access to Fort Frances, allows band members to take part in activities, recreation programmes and special events outside the reserve. A local band member is employed on a part-time basis as the bus driver.

A further grant of $11,500 covered the costs of buying a loader backhoe. The purchase of the equipment is part of a programme of economic and social development initiated by the chief and members of the community.

The loader-backhoe may be utilized in many ways, both on and off reserve. The Federal Department of Indian Affairs and Northern Development has agreed to rent the equipment when available and required by that Department.

These projects improve the physical integration of the community and are examples of a community initiated response to a major local problem.

Constance Lake Indian Band

Members of the Constance Lake Indian Band have felt, for some time, that their economic development interests could best be served if monies now leaving the community could be recirculated within the community.

A special committee was organized to study the problems involved in operating a community store. After examining the size of the local market, the committee made detailed plans outlining the cost breakdown of the construction and operation of the store. The project, in providing a source of employment for band members, is unanimously supported by the entire community of the Constance Lake area. With the assistance of a $12,900 provincial grant, the band proceeded towards the realization of its goal.

Deer Lake Indian Band

In 1969, an experimental project was initiated by Deer Lake Indian Band and involved the training of several native persons of the Sandy Lake area in the use of VTR equipment. Based on the success of this project, in 1970-71, the Indian Community Branch financed the purchase of VTR equipment and covered the operating costs in 1971-72. For 1972-73, a Provincial grant of $13,000 covered operating costs, including salaries and travel expenses, for two persons.

The Sandy Lake VTR Committee, by providing a medium for the exchange of information and views on mutual problems, plays a significant role within the far northern isolated communities in terms of both educational and economic development. The production and showing of tapes serves as an information need which, in turn, enhances local involvement in the decision-making process. This development, by the use of VTR equipment, is an attempt to fill the existing communication gap. Presently the VTR crew are training members from other Reserves.

The Sports and Recreation Branch, Ontario Educational Communication Authority and the Indian Community Branch have been involved in this project from its initiation.

Experimental Housing Programme

In 1970, the Ontario Housing Corporation and the Indian Community Branch, attempting to meet housing needs of low income Indian families, undertook an experimental housing programme. The communities of Armstrong, Dinorwic and Macdiarmid were involved in the local planning, construction and administration of their projects. Advice and guidance from The Ontario Housing Corporation ensured that the houses built were of a high construction standard.

The houses built were occupied before full completion. Further additions were required and in 1972-73, a Provincial grant of $19,600 defrayed costs of the necessary material and labour. An additional grant of $6,000 in the same year was designated to cover the special requirements of Macdiarmid. Monies were made payable to Ontario Housing Corporation to be disbursed by installments on the basis of completed work.

The projects have proved to be a valuable community development learning process in that families have been housed and the homes are being managed by local community councils. This experience has led to operation NOAH under the auspices of Ontario Housing Corporation. In addition, the organizations formed are developing as community councils, which are assessing their situation and seeking further community improvements.

Indian Crafts Foundation of Ontario

The Indian Crafts Foundation of Ontario was recently formed by the merger of Indian Crafts of Ontario and the Craft Foundation of Ontario (First Natale Boutique). Assisted by a provincial grant of $53,650, the new organization consists of two main branches — an education branch which is devoted to improving the quality of Indian crafts, and a retail branch to market crafts.

The educational unit sends craft instructors to various communities to assist Indian craftsmen in up-grading their skills and to teach these skills to younger workers. As part of the retail function, the First Nation Boutique at Ontario Place is considering the establishment of a year-round outlet.

The merger of the two organizations should reduce the administrative overhead, as well as provide a means for rationalized co-ordination of the educational and marketing functions.

Indian Hall of Fame Canadian National Exhibition

For the past six years, the Indian Hall of Fame has presented a display of Indian culture, crafts and history at the Canadian National Exhibition.

The Exhibition and on-site creation of various handicraft objects fostered the development of an Indian identity and cultural pride. It also provided an opportunity for non-Indian visitors to become aware of the valuable contributions which Indians have made to Canadian art, culture and history.

A provincial grant of $10,000 covering administrative costs, salaries, transportation and accommodation supported nine Indian craftsmen in the on-site creation of various handicrafts. Eleven Indian guides explained these display items and discussed matters relating to Indian culture and history with visitors to the exhibit.

Islington Indian Band Whitefish Reserve

In an attempt to attain a degree of self-sufficiency, the Islington Indian Band has been developing a timber and pulp cutting operation. Last winter a woods clean-up operation was begun to prepare the timber for proper harvesting. No profits were realized to date but sufficient monies were generated to pay the salaries of the men involved in the project.

For the past two cutting seasons, the Ministry of Natural Resources has provided the services of a logging supervisor; cutting and harvesting techniques were taught and the project provided jobs for previously unemployed band members.

A provincial grant of $6,500 assisted to defray the summer operating expenses of bush clean-up and covered a portion of the required equipment costs.

Nishnawbe Institute

Nishnawbe Institute, an Indian operated educational, cultural and research centre, has expanded during the past five years into a co-ordinating and administrative agency. In February of 1970, it became incorporated and received grants in the amounts of $40,000 and $32,000 for the two fiscal years, 1970/71 and 1971/72 respectively.

The Nishnawbe Institute, by making resources available to both native and non-native people, has developed specific programmes through which cultural and educational objectives are achieved: for example, the organizing of the annual Indian Ecumenical Conference, Canadian Indian Youth Workshops, and Cross Cultural Workshops.

By supporting and preserving Indian language and culture, the Institute enables native people to enhance their identity and sense of self-worth. It also is a means by which non-Indians can assist native people to pursue their programmes.

A provincial grant of $29,400 in 1972/73 assisted Nishnawbe to defray operating costs, including salaries, administration, travel and consulting fees.

North American Arts and Crafts Association

The North American Indian Arts and Crafts Association is sponsoring a gift show at the Mohawk Institute in Brantford.

A provincial grant of $600 assisted Indian owned and operated firms and Indian craftsmen operated aggressive wholesale and retail outlets. The three day long program included an Indian talent show, film slides, a fashion show and dance performances. An advertising campaign conducted through newspapers, radio and television communications served to familiarize the public with the program. The project was an invaluable learning experience for all involved, both for the native people in planning and carrying out the gift show and non-native people attending the exhibit.

Northeastern Ontario Native Development Association

The bands of the Sudbury-Manitoulin area are seeking to initiate economic and social development programmes. As a result, the Northeastern Ontario Native Development Association has undertaken an organizational process to solve some of the existing problems.

The specific functions of the Association include the co-ordination of the economic planning for member reserves, the researching of various development alternatives, the studying of specific problems within individual reserves and the setting of priorities among programmes initiated by various groups in the area.

A provincial grant of $6,000 covered initial expenditures and enabled the group to continue progressing towards the realization of their goals. The costs of exploratory meetings at the inception of the project were paid to the individuals and groups involved.

344)–347) Spreads from a booklet on Indian affairs with drawings by Indian children. (CAN)
348) Diagram of immunological processes, from Le Nouveau Diascope, a Lepetit magazine. (ITA)
349) From a folder offering The New York Times Index as a record of Supreme Court decisions. (USA)
350) Cover and pages of a booklet about the St. Olaf College student fund. (USA)
351) Double spread from a booklet about Vivitar lenses, for Ponder & Best Inc. (USA)
352) Binding and slip case of a book about postage stamps issued by the Post Office. (GBR)

344)–347) Doppelseiten aus einer Broschüre über indianische Angelegenheiten. (CAN)
348) Diagramm von immunologischen Vorgängen aus Le Nouveau Diascope. (ITA)
349) Aus einem Prospekt für The New York Times Index, der Gerichtsentscheide aufzählt. (USA)
350) Umschlag und Seiten aus einer Broschüre über einen Studentenfonds. (USA)
351) Doppelseite aus einem Prospekt über Vivitar-Objektive von Ponder & Best Inc. (USA)
352) Einband und Schuber eines Buches über Briefmarken, das von der britischen Post herausgegeben wurde. (GBR)

344)–347) Doubles pages d'une brochure sur les affaires indiennes. Dessins d'enfants indiens. (CAN)
348) Graphique (processus immunologiques) du Nouveau Diascope, un magazine Lepetit. (ITA)
349) Dépliant indiquant le New York Times Index comme source de droit (Cours Suprême). (USA)
350) Couverture et pages d'une brochure sur le fonds des étudiants du Collège St-Olaf. (USA)
351) Double page d'une brochure sur les objectifs Vivitar de la Ponder & Best Inc. (USA)
352) Reliure et étui d'un ouvrage de la poste britannique consacré aux timbres-poste. (GBR)

Artist | Künstler | Artiste:

344)–347) STEVE GOLDMAN
348) ELISA PATERGNANI
349) JOHN HAWKINS
350) ROBERT CLARK NELSON
351) KEN PARKHURST
352) ROGER O. DENNING

Art Director | Directeur artistique:

344)–347) STEVE GOLDMAN
348) PUBLICIS CONSEIL
349) ANDREW KNER
350) ROBERT CLARK NELSON
351) KEN PARKHURST
352) ROGER O. DENNING

Agency | Agentur | Agence – Studio:

344)–347) GRAAFIKKO
348) PUBLICIS CONSEIL
351) THE DREYFUS AGENCY

Booklets / Prospekte / Prospectus

3

Magazine Covers
Magazine Illustrations
Newspaper Illustrations
House Organs
Annual Reports
Book Covers

Zeitschriften-Umschläge
Zeitschriften-Illustrationen
Zeitungs-Illustrationen
Hauszeitschriften
Jahresberichte
Buchumschläge

Couvertures de périodiques
Illustrations de périodiques
Illustrations de journaux
Journaux d'entreprises
Rapports annuels
Couvertures de livres

353

354

355

356

Artist | Künstler | Artiste:
353) 357) 358) ANDRÉ FRANÇOIS
354) 356) RONALD SEARLE
355) PIERRE LE-TAN

Art Director | Directeur artistique:
355) LEE LORENZ

Publisher | Verleger | Éditeur:
353)–358) THE NEW YORKER

353)–358) A selection of covers for THE NEW YORKER, with a detail of the artwork for one of them in roughly actual size. Shown are, in order: the morning egg-sun; the man who lives in his shell; the simple (night) life; after closing time; and a Jumbo Father Christmas. (USA)

353)–358) Umschläge für die Zeitschrift THE NEW YORKER, mit Detail einer Illustration in annähernd Originalgrösse. Gezeigt werden: die Morgenei-Sonne; der Mann, der in seiner Schale lebt; das einfache (Nacht-) Leben; nach Polizeistunde; und ein Jumbo-Weihnachtsmann. (USA)

353)–358) Sélection de couvertures du NEW YORKER et détail de la composition pour l'une d'elles, format approx. nature. Sujets, dans l'ordre: soleil ovoïde; l'homme qui vit retiré dans sa coquille; la vie (nocturne) simple; après la fermeture; et un énorme Père Noël. (USA)

Magazine Covers / Zeitschriften-Umschläge
Couvertures de périodiques

357

359

360

361

362

Magazine Covers
Zeitschriften-Umschläge
Couvertures de périodiques

363

364

365

359)–362) Four covers for the illustrated magazine POLAND, which is issued by the Polish Interpress Agency and appears in six languages. Fig. 359 shows a complete cover entitled 'Musicians'. Fig. 360, 'Forest', is in purple, dark blue and three greens; fig. 361, in pale ochres, green and greys, is entitled 'Portraits'; and fig. 362, 'Motorcycle Racing', is in bright colours and anthracite. (POL)

363) Cover for INTELLECTUAL DIGEST; blue ground. (USA)

364) 365) Covers for VISION (South American edition), referring to urban proliferation and the Russo-American struggle for supremacy. (BRA)

366) Cover for LEARNING, a magazine for teachers. (USA)

367) For an annual review of advertising. Blue/red/black. (ITA)

368) For the humorous magazine SZPILKI. Blue/red/black. (POL)

359)–362) Vier Umschläge für die illustrierte Zeitschrift POLAND, die in sechs Sprachen erscheint. Abb. 359 zeigt einen vollständigen Umschlag mit dem Titel «Musiker». Abb. 360, «Wald», ist in Violett, Dunkelblau und drei Grüntönen; Abb. 361, in blassen Ocker-, Grün- und Grautönen, heisst «Portraits»; und Abb. 362, «Motorradrennen», ist in bunten Farben und Anthrazit. (POL)

363) Umschlag für INTELLECTUAL DIGEST. Blauer Grund. (USA)

364) 365) Umschläge für VISION (südamerikanische Ausgabe), die sich auf die Ausdehnung der Städte und den russo-amerikanischen Kampf um Vorherrschaft beziehen. (BRA)

366) Umschlag für LEARNING, Zeitschrift für Pädagogen. (USA)

367) Für ein Jahrbuch der Werbung. Blau/rot/schwarz. (ITA)

368) Umschlag für die humoristische Zeitschrift SZPILKI. (POL)

359)–362) Quatre couvertures pour le magazine POLAND publié en six langues par l'agence polonaise Interpress. La fig. 359 est intitulée «les Musiciens». La «Forêt» de la fig. 360 est en pourpre, bleu foncé et trois verts, la fig. 361, «Portraits», en ocres pâles, vert et divers gris. La «Course de Motos» (362) est en couleurs vives et anthracite. (POL)

363) Couverture d'INTELLECTUAL DIGEST. Fond bleu. (USA)

364) 365) Couvertures pour l'édition sud-américaine de VISION, sur le thème des villes tentaculaires et de la lutte russo-américaine pour la domination de la Terre. (BRA)

366) Couverture de LEARNING, une revue d'enseignants. (USA)

367) Couverture pour une revue publicitaire annuelle. Bleu, rouge, noir. (ITA)

368) Pour le magazine SZPILKI. Bleu, rouge, noir. (POL)

366

367

368

Artist | Künstler | Artiste:

359) 362) ANDRZEJ KRAJEWSKI
360) LESZEK HOLDANOWICZ
361) ANTONI BORATYNSKI
363) ROGER HANE / NORM SCHAEFER
364) 365) ZIRALDO PINTO
366) BRUCE LEVY / RAY DER / MICHEL DATTEL
367) ARMANDO TESTA / ANDREA ARMAGNI
368) JERZY CZERNIAWSKI

Art Director | Directeur artistique:

359)–362) LECH ZAHORSKI
364) 365) MARILYN HOFFNER
366) MICHEL DATTEL
367) ARMANDO TESTA
368) MAREK GOEBEL

Agency | Agentur | Agence – Studio:

366) MICHEL DATTEL & ASSOC.
367) STUDIO ARMANDO TESTA

Publisher | Verleger | Editeur:

359)–362) POLONIA VERLAG
363) INTELLECTUAL DIGEST
364) 365) VISION MAGAZINE
366) HART PRINTING CO.
367) L'UFFICIO MODERNO
368) RSW-PRASA-KSIAZKA-RUCH

369

371

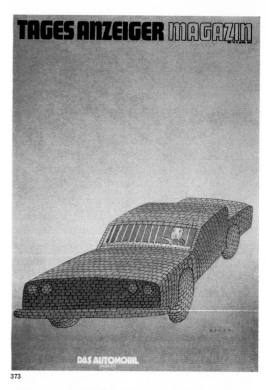

373

370

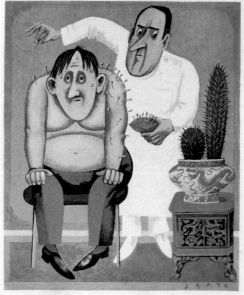

372

374

369)–372) Four covers for the satirical weekly NEBELSPALTER. Fig. 369: a 'bottle' is a German term for a dud; fig. 370: television moves into new fields; fig. 371: new light on parking meters; fig. 372: a skit on acupuncture. (SWI)

373) Cover for the weekly magazine of the daily TAGES-ANZEIGER; the issue contains a feature on the automobile. Blue on red ground. (SWI)

374) Cover, showing an old ornament, for the magazine SICILIA. Red and yellow shades on green. (ITA)

375) Cover for an issue of FORTUNE containing a feature on the US budget. Red and blue with white title. (USA)

376) Cover for the Christmas issue of LONG LINES magazine. In full colour. (USA)

377) Cover for an issue of TIME carrying a feature on Bobby Riggs, an opponent of Women's Lib. (USA)

378) Cover for L'EXPRESS referring to Kissinger's many foreign missions. (FRA)

369)–372) Umschläge der satirischen Wochenschrift NEBELSPAL-TER. Abb. 369 in Brauntönen; Abb. 370: das Fernsehen nimmt grössere Dimensionen an; Abb. 371: Parkingmeter anders gesehen; Abb. 372: eine Satire auf Akupunktur. (SWI)

373) Umschlag für die wöchentliche Beilage TAGES-ANZEIGER MAGAZIN; diese Ausgabe enthält einen Artikel über das Automobil. Blau auf Rot. (SWI)

374) Umschlag, der ein altes Ornament zeigt, für die Zeitschrift SICILIA. Rote und gelbe Schattierungen auf Grün. (ITA)

375) Umschlag einer Nummer von FORTUNE mit einem Beitrag über das Budget der USA. Rot, blau und weiss. (USA)

376) Umschlag der Weihnachtsausgabe von LONG LINES. (USA)

377) Umschlag einer Nummer von TIME mit einem Artikel über Bobby Riggs, einen Gegner der Bewegung für die Gleichberechtigung der Frau. (USA)

378) Umschlag für L'EXPRESS, der sich auf Kissingers viele Auslandmissionen bezieht. (FRA)

369)–372) Quatre couvertures pour l'hebdomadaire satirique NEBELSPALTER. 369: une «bouteille», en allemand, désigne un imbécile, une cloche; 370: la télévision conquiert de nouveaux domaines; 371: pleins feux sur les parcomètres; 372: parodie de l'acupuncture. (SWI)

373) Couverture du supplément hebdomadaire du quotidien TAGES-ANZEIGER. Sujet: l'automobile. Bleu sur rouge. (SWI)

374) Couverture montrant un vieil ornement, pour le magazine SICILIA. Tons rouges et jaunes sur vert. (ITA)

375) Couverture pour un numéro de FORTUNE contenant un article sur le budget des USA. Rouge, bleu, titre blanc. (USA)

376) Couverture du numéro de Noël du magazine LONG LINES. En polychromie. (USA)

377) Couverture d'un numéro de TIME contenant un article sur Bobby Riggs, le fameux anti-féministe. (USA)

378) Couverture de L'EXPRESS sur le thème des nombreuses missions de Kissinger à l'étranger. (FRA)

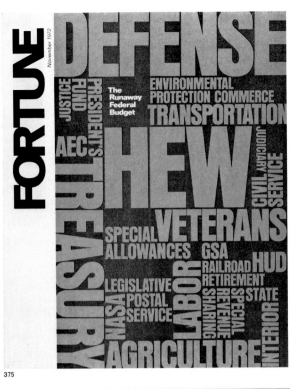

375

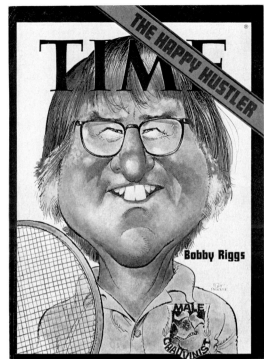

377

376

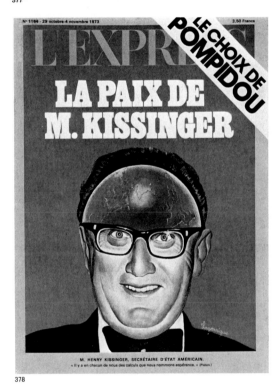

378

Magazine Covers
Zeitschriften-Umschläge
Couvertures de périodiques

379

380

381

382

383

Artist / Künstler / Artiste:

379) 380) H. & U. OSTERWALDER
381) 382) RICHARD HESS /
MILTON GLASER
383) PAUL DAVIS / WALTER BERNARD /
MILTON GLASER
384) DEANNA GLAD

Art Director / Directeur artistique:

379) 380) JOCHEN WIDMANN
381)–383) WALTER BERNARD /
MILTON GLASER
384) ELIN WAITE

Agency / Agentur / Agence – Studio:

384) AUTOMOBILE CLUB OF SOUTHERN
CALIFORNIA

Publisher / Verleger / Editeur:

379) 380) GRUNER & JAHR GMBH & CO.
381)–383) NEW YORK MAGAZINE
384) AUTOMOBILE CLUB OF SOUTHERN
CALIFORNIA

385

386

385)–388) Four covers for the United Nations magazine VISTA. The covers refer respectively to an article entitled 'What now?', to the surveying of earth's resources from space, to hunger and plenty on earth, and to the problems of frontiers. (USA)
389) Cover for the photographic magazine ZOOM using a drawing based on a photograph originally made for ESQUIRE. (FRA)
390) Cover for BUILT ENVIRONMENT referring to the need for health centres. (USA)
391) Cover for the monthly ATLANTIC referring to a feature on speed, sex and heroes. (USA)

385)–388) Umschläge von VISTA, Zeitschrift der Vereinten Nationen. Die Umschläge beziehen sich auf einen Artikel mit dem Titel «Was nun?»; auf das Prüfen von Bodenschätzen aus dem Weltraum; auf Hunger und Überfluss; und auf das Problem der Grenzen. (USA)
389) Umschlag für die photographische Zeitschrift ZOOM. Die Zeichnung basiert auf einer Photographie, die ursprünglich für ESQUIRE aufgenommen wurde. (FRA)
390) Umschlag für eine Nummer der Zeitschrift BUILT ENVIRONMENT mit einem Artikel über die Notwendigkeit von Gesundheitszentren. Mehrfarbig. (USA)
391) Umschlag von ATLANTIC mit einem Artikel über Geschwindigkeit, Sex und Helden. (USA)

385)–388) Couvertures du magazine des Nations Unies, VISTA, consacrées aux sujets suivants: un article intitulé «Et maintenant, quoi faire?»; l'exploration des ressources de la terre par satellite; la faim et l'abondance dans le monde; le problème des frontières. (USA)
389) Couverture du magazine photo ZOOM, avec un dessin d'après une photo réalisé primitivement pour ESQUIRE. (FRA)
390) Couverture de BUILT ENVIRONMENT évoquant le besoin de centres sanitaires. (USA)
391) Couverture de mensuel ATLANTIC. Sujet: la vitesse, le sexe et les héros. (USA)

LE MAGAZINE DE L'IMAGE

ZOOM

389

Artist | Künstler | Artiste:
385) RICHARD HESS
386) PHILIP HAYS/RICHARD HESS
387) SEYMOUR CHWAST/
RICHARD HESS
388) GUY BILLOUT/RICHARD HESS
389) GUY FERY
390) POVEL WEBB
391) SEYMOUR CHWAST

Art Director | Directeur artistique:
385)–388) RICHARD HESS
389) JEAN-PIERRE MONTAGNE/MAURICE CORIAT
390) BOB LAMP
391) DAVID OLIN

Agency | Agentur | Agence – Studio:
385)–388) RICHARD HESS, INC.
390) THE BUILDER GROUP

Publisher | Verleger | Editeur:
385)–388) UNITED NATIONS ASSOCIATION OF THE USA
389) ZOOM
390) BUILDING PUBLISHERS LTD.
391) ATLANTIC MAGAZINE

Magazine Covers

387

388

390

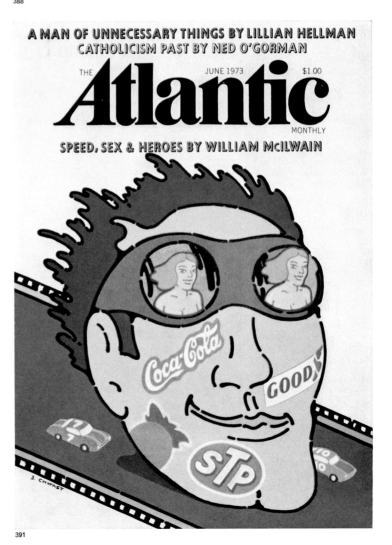

391

392

393

394

395

Magazine Covers

396

397

398

399

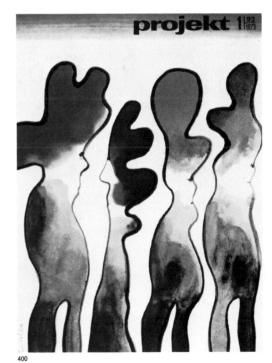

400

392) Superrealistic cover for the design magazine IDEA. (JPN)
393) Cover for a special issue of IDEA magazine on the Push Pin artist Seymour Chwast. (JPN)
394) 395) Two covers of the design magazine PRINT. Fig. 394 with pale colouring chiefly along outlines, fig. 395 with orange reflexes on face. (USA)
396) 397) Complete cover and detail of silkscreen design in actual size for PHP (standing for peace, happiness and prosperity), a critical monthly. (JPN)
398) Air-brushed cover motif for ART DIRECTION. (USA)
399) 400) Two covers for the art and design magazine PROJECT. The cat in fig. 399 and the heads of the figures in fig. 400 are brightly coloured. (POL)

392) Umschlag für die Designzeitschrift IDEA. (JPN)
393) Umschlag einer Spezialausgabe der Zeitschrift IDEA über den Push-Pin-Künstler Seymour Chwast. (JPN)
394) 395) Zwei Umschläge der graphischen Zeitschrift PRINT. Abb. 394 mit Umrandungen in blassen Tönen, Abb. 395 mit orangefarbigen Spiegelungen im Gesicht. (USA)
396) 397) Vollständiger Umschlag und Detail der Graphik in Originalgrösse für PHP (steht für Peace, Happiness and Prosperity), eine kritische Monatsschrift. (JPN)
398) Gespritzter Umschlag für ART DIRECTION. (USA)
399) 400) Zwei Umschläge für die Kunst- und Designzeitschrift PROJECT. Die Katze in Abb. 399 und die Köpfe der Figuren in Abb. 400 sind in bunten Farben gehalten. (POL)

392) Couverture surréaliste pour le magazine IDEA. (JPN)
393) Couverture d'un numéro spécial d'IDEA consacré à Seymour Chwast, des Push Pin Studios. (JPN)
394) 395) Deux couvertures du magazine de design PRINT. 394: couleurs pâles surtout le long des contours; 395: reflets orange sur le visage. (USA)
396) 397) Couverture complète et détail d'une composition séri-graphique pour une revue mensuelle critique, PHP (= paix, happiness = bonheur, prospérité). Format original. (JPN)
398) Couverture peint au pistolet, pour ART DIRECTION. (USA)
399) 400) Deux couvertures pour le magazine d'art et de design PROJECT. Le chat de la fig. 399 et les têtes des personnages de la fig. 400 sont exécutés en couleurs vives. (POL)

401

402

401) 402) Cover and page from RIGHT NOW, a women's newsletter issued by McCALL'S. The subjects are birth control and marriage preparations. (USA)
403) Full-page illustration from the women's magazine NOVA. (GBR)
404) 405) Black-and-white illustrations for a story about drugs in STERN. (GER)
406) Double spread in NOVA preceding a page of anecdotes about the author and actor Noël Coward. Full colour. (GBR)
407) Double spread on bacteria in the home, from NOVA. Full colour. (GBR)

401) 402) Umschlag und Seite aus RIGHT NOW, Bulletin von McCALL'S für Frauen. Die Themen sind Geburtenkontrolle und Heiratsvorbereitungen. (USA)
403) Ganzseitige Illustration aus der Frauenzeitschrift NOVA. (GBR)
404) 405) Schwarzweisse Illustrationen zu einer Drogengeschichte in STERN. (GER)
406) Doppelseite in NOVA zu Anekdoten über Noël Coward. (GBR)
407) Doppelseite aus der Zeitschrift NOVA zu einem Artikel über Bakterien in Haus und Wohnung. Mehrfarbige Zeichnung. (GBR)

401) 402) Couverture et page de RIGHT NOW, un bulletin d'information féminin publié par McCALL'S. Sujets: le planning familial; les fiançailles. (USA)
403) Illustration pleine page pour le magazine féminin NOVA. (GBR)
404) 405) Illustration noir-blanc. Article du STERN sur la drogue. (GER)
406) Double page couleur de NOVA précédant une page d'anecdotes mettant en scène Noël Coward. (GBR)
407) Double page de NOVA sur les microbes dans la maison. Polychromie. (GBR)

Artist | Künstler | Artiste:

401) 402) KIT HINRICHS
403) ALAN CRACKNELL
404) 405) ERHARD GÖTTLICHER
406) ROGER LAW/DAVID HILLMAN
407) JOSSE GOFFIN

Art Director | Directeur artistique:

401) 402) C. KRAMER
403) 406) 407) DAVID HILLMAN
404) 405) WOLFGANG BENKEN

Agency | Agentur | Agence – Studio:

401) 402) HINRICHS DESIGN ASSOC.

Publisher | Verleger | Editeur:

401) 402) MCCALL CORPORATION
403) 406) 407) IPC MAGAZINES LTD.
404) 405) GRUNER & JAHR GMBH & CO.

Magazine Illustrations
Zeitschriften-Illustrationen
Illustrations de périodiques

403

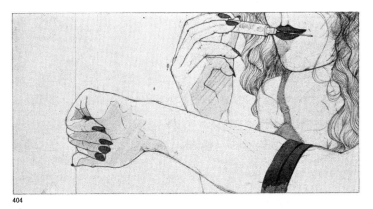

404

405

406

are staphylococci. That is, 6 million *Staphylococcus albus*, the rest *Staphylococcus citreus*. They are resistant to many disinfectants and anti-biotics, and resemble bunches of grapes under a microscope. 50% of people are carriers of potentially dangerous staphylococci – like the food-poisoning types of *Staphylococcus aureus*, the toxin of which can survive an hour's boiling.

After one person has had a bath, a quarter of a teaspoon of the water contains nearly 10 million live organisms. A pinch of hairy dust from the floor contains 29,700; the hairbrush 14,000 – before both kids have had a go of it. The boy's toothbrush contains some 300 million live bugs, and of the 6 million on the handtowel ½ million are *Escherichia coli* – evidence of recent faecal contamination.

The bathroom: Not counting the dead ones, 1440 million organisms live on a face flannel: 8½ million

To put, say, laundry on the draining board creates a short route for live organisms from dirty underwear to the crockery and cutlery.

Parrots and budgerigars can pass on a disease rather like pneumonia called psittacosis.

A bug which is becoming more dangerous is *Pseudomonas aeruginosa*, commonly known as the green pus organism. Most at home in drains and sinks, it is relatively resistant to antibiotics and disinfectant and its pathogenicity has increased in the last 10 years. Causes enteritis, particularly in infants; very dangerous when it contaminates burns.

N.B. All the bacteria counts mentioned here are typical examples from our investigations.

Rubbish-bin lids are a feeding ground, breeding ground and a popular terminus for organisms of all types.

The kitchen: A bacteria count in the kitchen this morning reveals: the washing-up sponge contains 10,000 million, live total; the tea-towel 75 million; the plate-rack 13 million; the water in the kitchen sink U-bend, per millilitre, accommodates 32 million live germs; the

washing-up bowl just over 1 million and the cup with a small crack 5860 live organisms. The washing-up water, incidentally, is 278 times cleaner than the bathwater.

Common kitchen creatures include the Oriental Cockroach which lives at floor level and is shy of light; the German Cockroach or Steam Fly which is brownish in colour (the male is a very good climber) and the Silverfish.

Mouldy bread and the whiskers on the jam may look awful and are best not consumed in great quantities. Nevertheless, neither is pathogenic.

The foods on which germs grow best are cooked meats, gravies, milk and egg dishes, especially when they're moist and warm. Each one of those organisms living in ideal conditions will produce 1 million more between breakfast and supper.

Dogs' droppings, more often puppies', can contain worm eggs which cause dysentery in children – in extreme cases loss of sight. Each gram of cat-litter soil contains 416 million live organisms.

Tortoises and terrapins commonly harbour salmonella, which can give diarrhoea to children and old people. There are over 1000 types of salmonella. They can live in soil and dust for months in temperatures ranging from −70°C. to +45°C, and can also cause severe food poisoning, and typhoid.

407

Artist | Künstler | Artiste:

408) 410) MICHAEL TREVITHICK
409) GUY FERY
411) SIMMS TABACK/CHARLES CURTIS
412) GERVASIO GALLARDO
413) MAGGI BAARING

Art Director | Directeur artistique:

408) RICHARD JORDAN/PAUL DAIZLEY
409) ARTHUR PAUL
411) CHARLES CURTIS
412) HERBERT BLEIWEISS/BRUCE DANBROT
413) LISE NØRGAAD/PAUL MOES

Agency | Agentur | Agence – Studio:

411) CHARLES CURTIS DESIGN

408

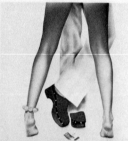

409

410

411

408) Full-colour illustration from a feature on male chauvinist 'pigs' in HIS AND HERS magazine. (GBR)
409) Double spread on shoe fashions, from PLAYBOY. (USA)
410) Opening spread of a story in LUI magazine. Full colour. (FRA)
411) Illustration in full colour from an article in WORLD magazine on the nature of depreciation (sub-title: 'An elephant is not a snake'). (USA)
412) Colour illustration for a poem published in LADIES' HOME JOURNAL. (USA)
413) Colour illustration across a double spread opening a 'dream lexicon' in the magazine HJEMMET. (DEN)

408) Mehrfarbige Illustration zu einer Geschichte über männliche Gegner der Frauenemanzipation. Aus der Zeitschrift HIS AND HERS. (GBR)
409) Doppelseite aus der Zeitschrift PLAYBOY über Schuhmode. (USA)
410) Erste Doppelseite einer Geschichte in der Zeitschrift LUI. Mehrfarbig. (FRA)
411) Mehrfarbige Illustration aus der Zeitschrift WORLD zu einem Artikel über die Natur der Entwertung (Untertitel: «Ein Elephant ist keine Schlange»). (USA)
412) Farbige Illustration zu einem Gedicht im LADIES' HOME JOURNAL. (USA)
413) Farbillustration über eine ganze Doppelseite zu einem «Traumlexikon» in der Zeitschrift HJEMMET. (DEN)

408) Illustration polychrome pour un article consacré aux «cochons» que sont les anti-féministes, dans le magazine HIS AND HERS. (GBR)
409) Double page consacrée à la mode de la chaussure, dans PLAYBOY. (USA)
410) Double page initiale d'un récit publié dans LUI. Polychromie. (FRA)
411) Illustration en polychromie pour un article du magazine WORLD expliquant la technique des amortissements («Un éléphant n'est pas un serpent»). (USA)
412) Illustration couleur pour un poème publié dans LADIES' HOME JOURNAL. (USA)
413) Illustration couleur occupant la double page initiale d'un «lexique des rêves» dans le magazine HJEMMET. (DEN)

WHEN
I WAS NINE
BY ROD
McKUEN

412

413

Publisher | Verleger | Editeur:

408) HIS & HERS MAGAZINE
409) PLAYBOY ENTERPRISES, INC.
410) LUI MAGAZINE
411) WORLD MAGAZINE
412) LADIES' HOME JOURNAL
413) MOGENS FØNSS

Magazine Illustrations
Zeitschriften-Illustrationen
Illustrations de périodiques

414

415

The clumsy ones
by Ted Halbert

Ten-year-old Lisa couldn't cry herself to sleep. Despite the tears in bed at night, she lay awake, hearing the voices — the derisive taunts of her playmates at school.

On the playground every day, they ridiculed or mimicked Lisa's awkward, poorly coordinated, always-failing efforts to take part in games during recess. Lisa grew to despise her own clumsy attempts to join in these physical activities.

Eventually, a teacher asked Lisa's parents if they hadn't noticed the problem — and suggested that they bring her to the University of California at Los Angeles for an evaluation by Dr. Bryant J. Cratty, director of the Perceptual-Motor Learning Laboratory in the Department of Kinesiology.

After the two-hour evaluation and conference with her parents, Dr. Cratty pinpointed the specific kinds of clumsiness troubling Lisa. He suggested that she be enrolled in a special remedial-exercise program that for conducts for clumsy children like her in late afternoon, at an elementary school near UCLA.

But the distance between Lisa's home and the remedial group seemed too great an obstacle. And her parents decided that, eventually, Lisa would grow out of this clumsy stage.

No one knows what became of Lisa. Most likely, by now, she is a very uncomfortable adolescent. Saddled still in the fact that identical stories could be told about any number of other boys and girls.

Researchers like Dr. Cratty agree that as high as 20 percent of all children experience some degree of clumsiness. Unexplainably, boys suffer these coordination troubles more often than girls.

Their inner lives seem infinitely cruel to most clumsy children. Because they lag behind others their age at a time when peer recognition is crucial, the clumsy ones find playgrounds to be torturous

places. Often they anticipate "physical education" classes with a particular dread.

The clumsy boys, as a result of their low physical agility, frequently gravitate toward activities inappropriate to their own sex, but surprisingly, they later may develop greater identification troubles.

When such youngsters are brought to Dr. Cratty for evaluation, inevitably he finds a correlation between their physical awkwardness and emotional self-images. The clumsy children quite carefully see they are the last choices in games, they have trouble making friends, they don't like the way they look, they are sad most of the time.

They may learn to compensate eventually for their deficient agility. One compensation is to achieve academic brilliance. Another attention-getting compensation is anti-social conduct: a study of juvenile arrests reveals the disproportionately high percentage of truancy among children with perceptual-motor problems.

All too often the clumsy child is regarded by teachers as a disruptive element in the classroom. His unreachable tendency to bump into others, or the learning difficulties that may accompany poor coordination, result in "disruptive" rather than sympathetic diagnosis.

Teachers cannot be faulted entirely. Even some family physicians seem convinced that children will "grow out" of these developmental problems. And parents, typically, are reluctant to recognize certain troubles in their own children.

Dr. Cratty finds that failures especially on hesitate to regard their sons as being clumsy.

As age five a child should be able to draw circles and squares with reasonable accuracy; jump feet together over a stick 10 inches above the ground; touch consecutive fingers to the tip of the thumb; hop on one foot two or three times; balance forces on one foot four to six seconds; print first name in letters one or two inches high.

What can sensitive parents do? First, they should learn to detect a clumsiness pattern in the pre-school years, when it's easiest to remedy. In his book Active Learning, Dr. Cratty gives some very conservative guidelines.

At age three a child should be able to walk a two-inch-wide line a distance of about 10 feet; hold a crayon and draw a simple cross; walk with a rhythmic gait, arms relaxed and moving in coordination with feet; jump forward from stairs, feet leaving the ground at the same time; run forward and walk backward short distances without stumbling; and raise body parts.

By age seven a youngster should have a wider range of abilities. He should be able to draw a circle within one foot; throw 1/4-inch-high, skip in a rhythmic manner; throw a playground ball a distance of 15

feet into a four-foot-square target; run expansively and jump upward or forward with proper arm action; touch fingers to thumbs quickly and in sequential order; skip and jump into small narrow one foot in size.

Any child who cannot perform these tasks should be evaluated by a physician and psychologist, and possibly should participate in remedial activities.

Physical education is a perennially-neglected subject in elementary schools, though in some instances enlightened programs are under way.

At the University Elementary School at UCLA, no low-ability youngster is forced into unusual competition with the physically-gifted, since all children in the non-graded school are carefully evaluated and their pinpointed periodically with peers of similar abilities. Applied to every subject area, this concept at UES is providing a model for elementary education elsewhere.

Dr. Cratty estimates that in every elementary school in the nation, one can find at least 30 clumsy children. The need for individual remediation in fine-muscle or gross-muscle control is as real as the more-readily recognized need for remedial reading.

The program can be quickly seen in the model program that Dr. Cratty now conducts near the campus. There is no secret to this success other than persistent, patient repetition of appropriate physical tasks, in a context that includes children of similar abilities.

On one recent afternoon, a group of parents coming to observe confirmed the incredible improvements in their children's physical performance and self-confidence.

The ultimate confirmation, though, came without words from one trouble-haired youngster. He had just succeeded for the first time in a finely-executed trampoline bounce from his seat to his knees and then onto both feet. A broad face betrayed the quiet exultation of his self-confirming success.

18 The Cranbrook Magazine

416

Editors' note: This article is reprinted from the February 1973 issue of the UCLA Monthly because we believe it is of interest, perhaps crucially, not only to parents of Brookside School/Cranbrook children but to parents everywhere.

417

414) Full-page illustration facing an article on aid to the less developed nations in Vista magazine. Old rose background. (USA)
415) Colour illustration in Vista facing an article on a UN assembly. (USA)
416) Double spread opening an article on clumsy children and their problems in The Cranbrook Magazine for Cranbrook school alumni. Black and white. (USA)
417) Black-and-white page facing an article on politics and science in Vista. (USA)
418) Double-spread colour illustration from Redbook magazine. (USA)
419) Colour illustration opening an article in Vista on the oil crisis and the UN's powerlessness to act because of big-power domination. (USA)

414) Ganzseitige Illustration gegenüber einem Artikel in der Zeitschrift Vista über Entwicklungshilfe. Grund in Altrosa. (USA)
415) Farbillustration in Vista zu einem Artikel über eine UNO-Versammlung. (USA)
416) Doppelseite aus einem Artikel über schwerfällige Kinder und deren Probleme. Aus der Zeitschrift The Cranbrook Magazine. Schwarzweiss. (USA)
417) Seite zu einem Beitrag über Politik und Wissenschaft in Vista. (USA)
418) Doppelseitige, mehrfarbige Illustration aus der Zeitschrift Redbook. (USA)
419) Farbillustration zu einem Artikel in Vista über die Ölkrise und die Machtlosigkeit der UNO wegen Beherrschung durch die Grossmächte. (USA)

414) Illustration pleine page en regard d'un article du magazine Vista consacré à l'aide aux pays en voie de développement. Fond vieux rose. (USA)
415) Illustration couleur de Vista en regard d'un article sur l'O.N.U. (USA)
416) Double page initiale d'un article sur les enfants maladroits et leurs problèmes. The Cranbrook Magazine (collège de Cranbrook). Noir, blanc. (USA)
417) Page noir-blanc pour un article de Vista sur la science et la politique. (USA)
418) Illustration polychrome sur double page dans le magazine Redbook. (USA)
419) Illustration couleur au début d'un article de Vista consacré à la crise du pétrole et à l'O.N.U. impuissante face aux grandes puissances. (USA)

418

Magazine Illustrations

419

Artist | Künstler | Artiste:

420) STEVE MYERS/
WALTER BERNARD/
MILTON GLASER
421) DAVID LEVINE/
WALTER BERNARD/
MILTON GLASER
422) SEYMOUR CHWAST
423) ROBERT GROSSMAN/
WALTER BERNARD/
MILTON GLASER
424) EDWARD SOREL/
WALTER BERNARD/
MILTON GLASER
425) MEL FURUKAWA/
WALTER BERNARD/
MILTON GLASER
426) 427) MARVIN MATTELSON/
WALTER BERNARD/
MILTON GLASER

Art Director | Directeur artistique:

420) 421) 423–427) WALTER
BERNARD/MILTON GLASER
422) WALTER BERNARD

Publisher | Verleger | Editeur:

420)–427) NEW YORK MAGAZINE

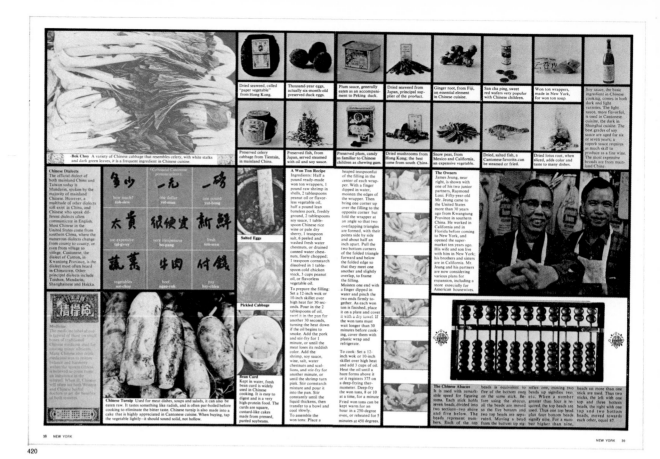

420

420) Double spread in full colour from an article on Chinese groceries and dishes in NEW YORK magazine. (USA)
421) Colour page facing a skit on Nixon in NEW YORK magazine. (USA)
422) Portrait of Ahmet Ertegün in NEW YORK. Black and white, full page. (USA)
423) Illustration of Lindsay from a survey of candidates for the New York mayoralty published in NEW YORK. Full colour. (USA)
424) Double spread of 'imaginary events' from NEW YORK. Full colour. (USA)
425) Illustration for an article on sailing in NEW YORK. Black and white. (USA)
426) 427) Spreads from a guide to New York beaches, from NEW YORK. (USA)

420) Mehrfarbige Doppelseite zu einem Artikel in der Zeitschrift NEW YORK über chinesische Lebensmittelgeschäfte und Gerichte. (USA)
421) Farbseite gegenüber einer Satire über Nixon in NEW YORK. (USA)
422) Portrait von Ahmet Ertegün in NEW YORK. Schwarzweiss, ganzseitig. (USA)
423) Illustration von Lindsay aus einem Bericht über die Kandidaten für das New Yorker Bürgermeisteramt. Aus der Zeitschrift NEW YORK. Mehrfarbig. (USA)
424) Doppelseite aus NEW YORK über «imaginäre Ereignisse». Mehrfarbig. (USA)
425) Illustration zu einem Artikel in NEW YORK über Segeln. Schwarzweiss. (USA)
426) 427) Doppelseiten aus NEW YORK über New Yorks Badestrände. (USA)

420) Double page polychrome d'un article du magazine NEW YORK traitant des produits alimentaires et plats traditionnels chinois. (USA)
421) Page couleur en regard d'une satire anti-nixonienne dans NEW YORK. (USA)
422) Portrait d'Ahmet Ertegün dans NEW YORK. Noir-blanc, pleine page. (USA)
423) Lindsay candidat à la mairie newyorkaise. NEW YORK. En polychromie. (USA)
424) Double page d'«événements imaginaire», dans NEW YORK. Polychromie. (USA)
425) Illustration polychrome d'un article sur les voiliers dans NEW YORK. (USA)
426) 427) Doubles pages d'un guide des plages newyorkaises. NEW YORK. (USA)

425

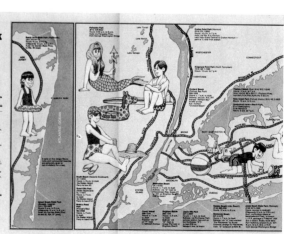

426

421

422

He is tired and everyone else is fresh.

423

Cardinal Cooke takes confession from Andy Warhol.

John Kenneth Galbraith doesn't know the answer.

William F. Buckley leaves Stamford in the middle of the night to get an egg cream on the Lower East Side.

Billy Graham suggests to his wife that they sleep late on Sunday

Thomas Hoving obtains an "important" Claes Oldenburg from Marlborough Gallery in exchange for the east wing of the Metropolitan. (Mr. Hoving explains that "The museum already has a west wing which is far superior.")

424

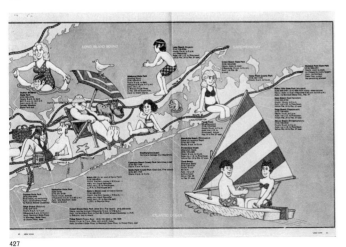

427

Magazine Illustrations
Zeitschriften-Illustrationen
Illustrations de périodiques

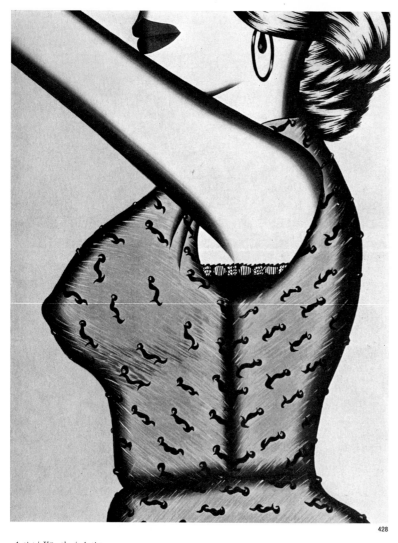

428

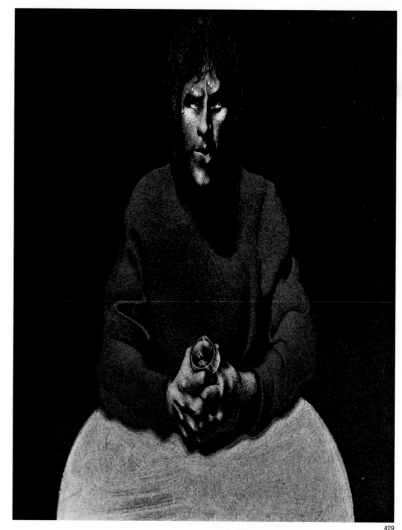

429

Artist | Künstler | Artiste:

428) CHRISTINA RAMBERG
429) 430) GILBERT STONE / LEN WILLIS
431) TOMI UNGERER
432) KATHY CALDERWOOD / BOB POST

Art Director | Directeur artistique:

428)–432) ARTHUR PAUL

Publisher | Verleger | Editeur:

428)–432) PLAYBOY ENTERPRISES, INC.

430

428) Full-page illustration for a story in PLAYBOY. (USA)
429) 430) Full-page illustration in full colour and complete double spread opening a story in PLAYBOY. (USA)
431) Double spread with a car-washing sequence on pink paper, from PLAYBOY magazine. (USA)
432) Full-page illustration for a feature published in PLAYBOY magazine. (USA)

428) Ganzseitige Illustration aus der Zeitschrift PLAYBOY. (USA)
429) 430) Ganzseitige, mehrfarbige Illustration und vollständige Doppelseite aus einer Geschichte in PLAYBOY. (USA)
431) Doppelseite mit Autowasch-Sequenz auf rosa Papier, aus der Zeitschrift PLAYBOY. (USA)
432) Ganzseitige Illustration zu einem Artikel, der in der Zeitschrift PLAYBOY erschienen ist. (USA)

428) Illustration pleine page pour un récit de PLAYBOY. (USA)
429) 430) Illustration pleine page en polychromie et double page complète introduisant un récit dans PLAYBOY. (USA)
431) Double page sur papier rose consacrée au lavage des voitures, dans le magazine PLAYBOY. (USA)
432) Illustration pleine page en polychromie pour un article publié dans le magazine PLAYBOY. (USA)

431

**Magazine Covers
Zeitschriften-Umschläge
Couvertures de périodiques**

Magazine Illustrations
Zeitschriften-Illustrationen
Illustrations de périodiques

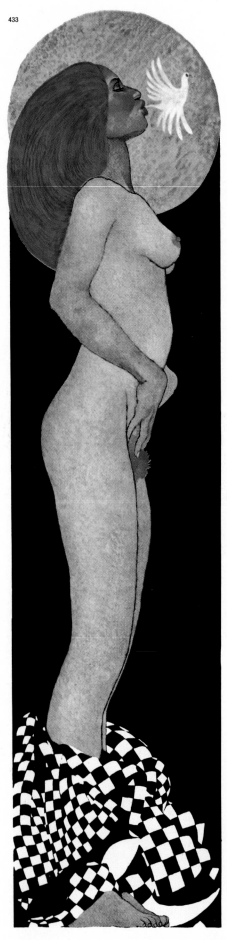

433) Illustration for a Bulgarian folk tale in PLAYBOY. (USA)
434) Double spread from the German PLAYBOY, on the television satellites of the future. (GER)
435) Double spread opening a story in the German PLAYBOY. (GER)
436) Full-colour double spread on fashions, from PLAYBOY. (USA)
437) Illustration from an article on the rescue squad in PLAYBOY. Full colour. (USA)
438) Illustration for PLAYBOY. Full page, full colour. (GER)
439) Illustration of two grandfathers; Italian PLAYBOY. (ITA)

433) Illustration zu einem bulgarischen Märchen. PLAYBOY. (USA)
434) Doppelseite aus dem deutschen PLAYBOY über Fernsehsatelliten der Zukunft. (GER)
435) Doppelseite aus einer Geschichte im deutschen PLAYBOY. (GER)
436) Farbige Doppelseite über Mode. Aus PLAYBOY. (USA)
437) Illustration zu einem Artikel in PLAYBOY über Rettungsmannschaften. Mehrfarbig. (USA)
438) Ganzseitige, mehrfarbige Illustration für PLAYBOY. (GER)
439) Illustration von zwei bekannten Grossvätern. PLAYBOY. (ITA)

433) Illustration d'un conte populaire bulgare. PLAYBOY. (USA)
434) Double page de l'édition allemande de PLAYBOY: les satellites TV de l'avenir. (GER)
435) Double page initiale d'un récit. Ed. all. de PLAYBOY. (GER)
436) Double page polychrome de modes, dans PLAYBOY. (USA)
437) Illustration polychrome d'un article de PLAYBOY. (USA)
438) Illustration pour PLAYBOY. Pleine page, polychrome. (GER)
439) Deux célèbres grands-pères. Illustration pour PLAYBOY. (ITA)

Artist | Künstler | Artiste:

433) BRAD HOLLAND/BOB POST
434) UTE OSTERWALDER
435) GEORGE LACROIX
436) WILSON MCLEAN/ TOM STAEBLER
437) DON IVAN PUNCHATZ
438) JOHN HOLMES
439) TULLIO PERICOLI

Art Director | Directeur artistique:

433) 436) 437) ARTHUR PAUL
434) 435) 438) RAINER WÖRTMANN
439) CARLO RIZZI

Publisher | Verleger | Editeur:

433) 436) 437) PLAYBOY ENTERPRISES, INC.
434) 435) 438) BAUER VERLAG
439) RIZZOLI

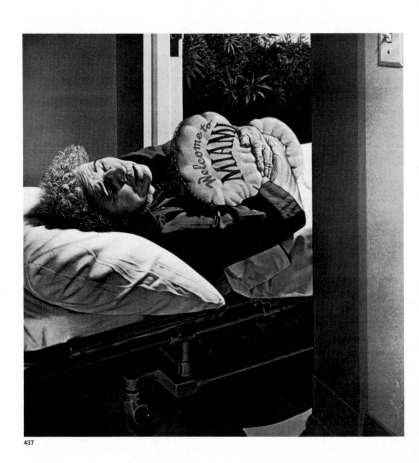

Multicolor polyester/
cotton seersucker
plaid untailored
jacket with notched
lapels and patch
pockets, $25, over an
acetate/nylon knit
shirt with long-
pointed collar, $7,
and cotton-denim
slacks with stitch-
front crease and
wide straight legs,
$12, all by H.I.S.

Front: Cotton/polyester brushed-twill zip-
front jacket, $23, and matching slacks,
$12, both by Landlubbers; plus a
multicolor hibiscus-print short-sleeve
rayon shirt, by Michael Milea/Peter
Sinclair, $12, and kid-leather lace-up
shoes with triple soles and stacked
heels, by Italia Bootwear, about $30.
Rear: Denim zip-front jacket, by
Peters Sportswear, $18; cotton
rib-knit turtleneck, by Puri-
tan Sportswear, $15; and
plaid brushed-cotton slacks,
by Buccaneer, $15.

W.M.

436

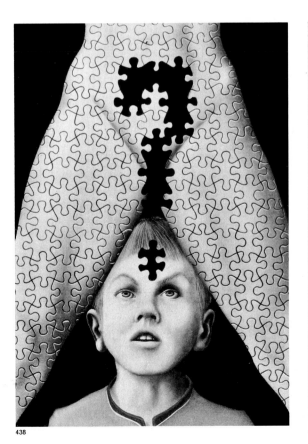

438

439

Magazine Illustrations
Zeitschriften-Illustrationen
Illustrations de périodiques

Artist | Künstler | Artiste:

440) PETER KRUMPELBECK/MIKE GROSS
441) EDWARD GOREY
442) D. BRAUTIGAR/DAVID KAESTLE
443) RICHARD HESS/DAVID KAESTLE

Art Director | Directeur artistique:

440) MIKE GROSS
442) DAVID KAESTLE/MIKE GROSS
443) DAVID KAESTLE

Publisher | Verleger | Editeur:

440)–443) NATIONAL LAMPOON/TWENTY-FIRST
CENTURY COMMUNICATIONS, INC.

440) Full-page illustration for a story about drugs in NATIONAL LAMPOON. Full colour. (USA)
441) Colour illustration for a story by the artist in NATIONAL LAMPOON. (USA)
442) Full-page illustration in full colour for a humorous article on outdoor clothing in NATIONAL LAMPOON. (USA)
443) Full-page illustration for an article in NATIONAL LAMPOON on sexual relations between humans and animals. (USA)

440) Ganzseitige Illustration zu einer Drogengeschichte in NATIONAL LAMPOON. Farbig. (USA)
441) Farbillustration zu einer Geschichte des Illustratoren in NATIONAL LAMPOON. (USA)
442) Ganzseitige, mehrfarbige Illustration zu einem humoristischen Artikel in NATIONAL LAMPOON über Freizeitbekleidung. (USA)
443) Ganzseitige Illustration zu einem Artikel in NATIONAL LAMPOON über sexuelle Beziehungen zwischen Menschen und Tieren. (USA)

440) Illustration couleur pleine page d'un article sur la drogue. NATIONAL LAMPOON. (USA)
441) Illustration couleur pour un texte de l'artiste dans NATIONAL LAMPOON. (USA)
442) Illustration pleine page en polychromie pour un article humoristique sur les vêtements que l'on porte à l'extérieur, dans NATIONAL LAMPOON. (USA)
443) Illustration pleine page pour un article de NATIONAL LAMPOON consacré à la zoophilie. (USA)

441

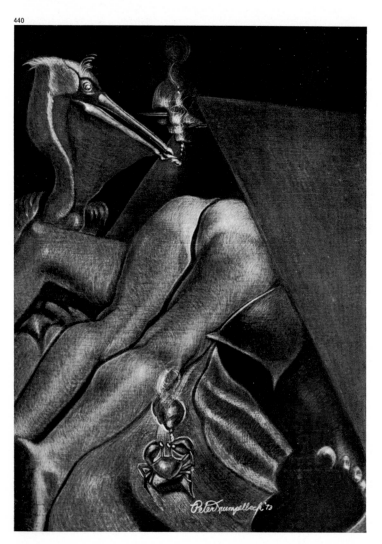

440

442

Richard Hess

444

445

449

450

Artist / Künstler / Artiste:

444) MIRIAM WOSK
445) FRANK OLINSKY
446)–**448)** DON IVAN PUNCHATZ
449) ALAIN LE SAUX/DIETMAR MEYER
450) HANNO RINK/RITA MÜHLBAR/DIETMAR MEYER
451) JOCHEN WIDMANN/DIETMAR MEYER

Art Director / Directeur artistique:

444) 445) BEA FEITLER
446) JEAN-PIERRE HOLLY/DON MENELL
447) 448) JOHN DAVIS/DON MENELL
449)–**451)** DIETMAR MEYER

Publisher / Verleger / Editeur:

444) 445) MS. MAGAZINE
446)–**448)** OUI MAGAZINE
449)–**451)** GRUNER & JAHR GMBH & CO.

446

447

Jasmin-Report: Sekretärin

451

448

444) Illustration for an article on the economics of prostitution in Ms. magazine. (USA)
445) Full-page colour illustration from Ms. magazine. (USA)
446) Full-page colour illustration for an article in Oui on a successful sex magazine. (USA)
447) 448) Illustration in full colour for an article on dolphins in Oui magazine, with the corresponding double spread. (USA)
449) Illustration from JASMIN for an article entitled 'How I love my car'. Flat colours. (GER)
450) Black-and-white illustration for a short story in JASMIN. Full page. (GER)
451) Full-page illustration for a report on secretaries in JASMIN. Black and white. (GER)

444) Illustration zu einem Artikel in der Zeitschrift Ms. über Prostitution. (USA)
445) Ganzseitige, mehrfarbige Illustration aus der Zeitschrift Ms. (USA)
446) Farbillustration in Oui zu einem Artikel über eine erfolgreiche Sex-Zeitschrift. (USA)
447) 448) Mehrfarbige Illustration und entsprechende Doppelseite aus der Zeitschrift Oui zu einem Artikel über Delphine. (USA)
449) Doppelseite aus der Zeitschrift JASMIN. In blassen Tönen. (GER)
450) Schwarzweisse Illustration zu einer Kurzgeschichte in JASMIN. Ganzseitig. (GER)
451) Ganzseitige Illustration in JASMIN zu einem Bericht über Sekretärinnen. (GER)

444) Illustration d'un article sur l'aspect économique de la prostitution, dans Ms. (USA)
445) Illustration couleur pleine page pour le magazine Ms. (USA)
446) Illustration couleur pleine page pour un article de Oui sur un magazine érotique. (USA)
447) 448) Illustration polychrome pour un article du magazine Oui consacré aux dauphins, et double page où elle figure. (USA)
449) Illustration pour un article de JASMIN intitulé «Comment j'aime ma voiture». Couleurs en à-plat. (GER)
450) Illustration noir-blanc pleine page pour une nouvelle publiée dans JASMIN. (GER)
451) Illustration pleine page pour une enquête de JASMIN sur les secrétaires. Noir, blanc. (GER)

452) Double spread in full colour opening a story by Virginia Woolf about a haunted house published in the magazine 20 ANS. (FRA)
453) Double spread from 20 ANS opening an article on the use of make-up by the beat idol Mick Jagger. Black and white in pink frame. (FRA)
454) Drawings by Saul Steinberg (© 1973) from THE NEW YORKER. The lower drawing also appeared in *The Inspector* (Viking Press). See also fig. 455. Black and white. (USA)

452) Mehrfarbige Doppelseite zu einer Geschichte von Virginia Woolf über ein von Gespenstern geplagtes Haus. Aus der Zeitschrift 20 ANS. (FRA)
453) Doppelseite aus der Zeitschrift 20 ANS. Der Artikel beschreibt wie das Beat-Idol Mick Jagger Make-Up gebraucht. Schwarzweiss mit rosa Umrandung. (FRA)
454) Zeichnungen von Saul Steinberg (© 1973). Aus THE NEW YORKER. Die untere Zeichnung erschien auch in *The Inspector* (Viking Press). Siehe auch Abb. 455. Schwarzweiss. (USA)

452) Double page polychrome introduisant un récit de Virginia Woolf sur une maison hantée, publié dans le magazine 20 ANS. (FRA)
453) Double page initiale d'un article de 20 ANS sur l'emploi du maquillage par l'idole beat Mick Jagger. Noir et blanc, cadre rose. (FRA)
454) Dessins de Saul Steinberg (© 1973) pour le NEW YORKER. Le dessin en bas a aussi été publié dans *The Inspector* (Viking Presss). Voir aussi la fig. 455. Noir et blanc. (USA)

Artist | Künstler | Artiste:

452) REMY DUBOIS
453) GUNTER + BERNADETTE BLUM
454) SAUL STEINBERG

Art Director | Directeur artistique:

452) 453) ZAZA VERGEAU
454) LEE LORENZ

Publisher | Verleger | Editeur:

452) 453) PUBLICATION FILIPACCHI
454) THE NEW YORKER

**Magazine Illustrations / Zeitschriften-Illustrationen
Illustrations de périodiques**

455) *The City,* drawing published in THE NEW YORKER and *The Inspector* (Viking Press). (USA)
456) Double spread with colour illustration opening an article on the wine boom in America, published in the Diners Club magazine SIGNATURE. (USA)
457) Three-dimensional construction illustrating an article on traffic in SIGNATURE. (USA)
458) Colour illustration for an article in WEST magazine on a golf-playing comedian. (USA)
459) Colour illustration for an article in SIGNATURE on athletes. (USA)

455) *Die Stadt,* Zeichnung aus THE NEW YORKER und *The Inspector* (Viking Press). (USA)
456) Doppelseite mit Farbillustrationen zu einem Artikel in der Diners-Club-Zeitschrift SIGNATURE über die steigende Popularität des Weines in Amerika. (USA)
457) Illustration (dreidimensional) zu einem Artikel in SIGNATURE über Strassenverkehr. (USA)
458) Farbillustration zu einem Artikel in WEST über einen golfspielenden Komiker. (USA)
459) Farbillustration zu einem Artikel über Athleten. Aus der Zeitschrift SIGNATURE. (USA)

455) *La Ville,* dessin publié dans le NEW YORKER et *The Inspector* (Viking Press). (USA)
456) Double page initiale d'un article sur le boom des vins aux Etats-Unis, avec illustration couleur, publié dans le magazine SIGNATURE du Diners Club. (USA)
457) Construction à trois dimensions illustrant un article de SIGNATURE sur la circulation. (USA)
458) Illustration couleur pour un article de WEST sur un comédien joueur de golf. (USA)
459) Illustration couleur pour un article de SIGNATURE consacré aux athlètes. (USA)

Artist / Künstler / Artiste:
455) SAUL STEINBERG
456) JOHN TRULL
457) VIN GIULIANI / DAVID OLIN
458) 459) SEYMOUR CHWAST

Art Director / Directeur artistique:
455) LEE LORENZ
456) 457) 459) DAVID OLIN
458) MIKE SALISBURY

Publisher / Verleger / Editeur:
455) THE NEW YORKER
456) 457) 459) DINER'S CLUB
458) LOS ANGELES TIMES

Magazine Illustrations
Zeitschriften-Illustrationen
Illustrations de périodiques

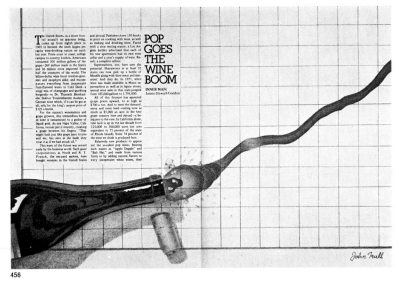

456

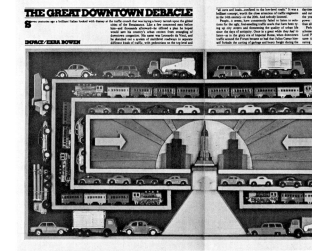

457

458

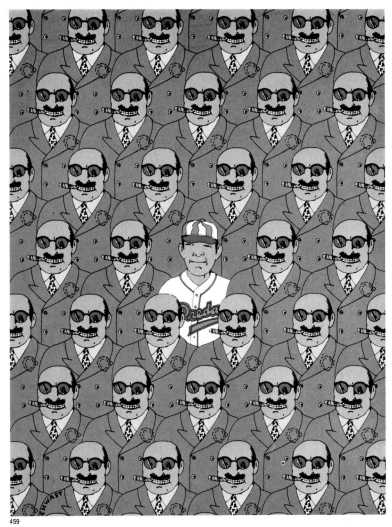

459

460

460)–462) Three double spreads in black and white from a feature entitled *Abilene Reporter* about a 'brazen railroad robbery' in a magazine published by Mladá Fronta. (CSR)
463) Full-page illustration from ESQUIRE magazine. (USA)
464) Black-and-white illustration for an article entitled 'Railroads off the rails' published in the business magazine MANAGEMENT TODAY. (GBR)

460)–462) Drei Doppelseiten mit schwarzweissen Illustrationen zu einem Beitrag über einen «frechen Raub» im Wilden Westen, aus einer von Mladá Fronta herausgegebenen Zeitschrift. (CSR)
463) Ganzseitige Illustration aus der Zeitschrift ESQUIRE. (USA)
464) Schwarzweisse Illustration in der Handels- und Finanzzeitschrift MANAGEMENT TODAY zu einem Artikel mit dem Titel «Entgleiste Eisenbahnen». (GBR)

460)–462) Trois doubles pages noir et blanc d'un article intitulé *Abilene Reporter* et rapportant le pillage crapuleux d'un train. Magazine publié par Mladá Fronta. (CSR)
463) Illustration pleine page pour le magazine ESQUIRE. (USA)
464) Illustration noir et blanc pour un article intitulé «Chemins de fer déraillés» et publié dans le magazine d'affaires MANAGEMENT TODAY. (GBR)

463

Artist | Künstler | Artiste:

460)–462) JIRI SALAMOUN / MILAN KOPRIVA
463) JEAN LAGARRIGUE
464) MICHAEL TREVITHICK / ROLAND SHENK

Art Director | Directeur artistique:

460)–462) MLADÁ FRONTA
463) RICHARD WEIGAND
464) ROLAND SHENK

Publisher | Verleger | Editeur:

460)–462) MLADÁ FRONTA
463) ESQUIRE, INC.
464) MANAGEMENT TODAY

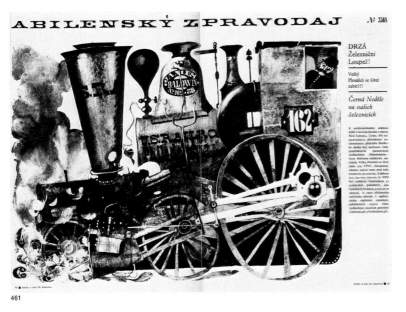

461

462

Magazine Illustrations

464

465

466

467

468

469

470

471

472

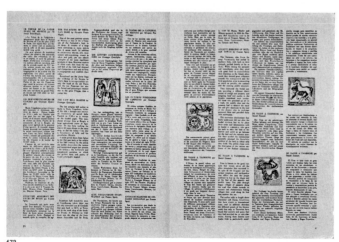
473

**Magazine Illustrations / Zeitschriften-Illustrationen
Illustrations de périodiques**

Artist | Künstler | Artiste:

465)–473) SANTUZZA CALI
474) DON WELLER
475) SEYMOUR CHWAST

Art Director | Directeur artistique:

474) JOE IWANAGA
475) NEIL SHAKERY

Agency | Agentur | Agence – Studio:

474) HOUSE OF DESIGN

Publisher | Verleger | Editeur:

465)–473) S. F. FLACCOVIO
474) FISH LIFE MAGAZINE
475) SATURDAY REVIEW, INC.

465)–473) Selected vignettes and typical double spread from a summary of contents and short notes contained in the tourist magazine SICILIA. Black and white. (ITA)
474) Full-page illustration from the magazine FISH LIFE. Full colour. (USA)
475) Illustration in actual size from THE SATURDAY REVIEW. (USA)

465)–473) Einzelne Vignetten und typische Doppelseite aus einer Inhaltsübersicht mit Kurznotizen in der touristischen Zeitschrift SICILIA. Schwarzweiss. (ITA)
474) Ganzseitige Illustration aus der Zeitschrift FISH LIFE. Mehrfarbig. (USA)
475) Illustration in Originalgrösse aus der Zeitschrift THE SATURDAY REVIEW. (USA)

465)–473) Quelques vignettes et double page type extraites d'une table des matières et de nouvelles brèves contenues dans un numéro du magazine de tourisme SICILIA. Noir, blanc. (ITA)
474) Illustration pleine page pour le magazine FISH LIFE. En polychromie. (USA)
475) Illustration grandeur nature pour THE SATURDAY REVIEW. (USA)

474

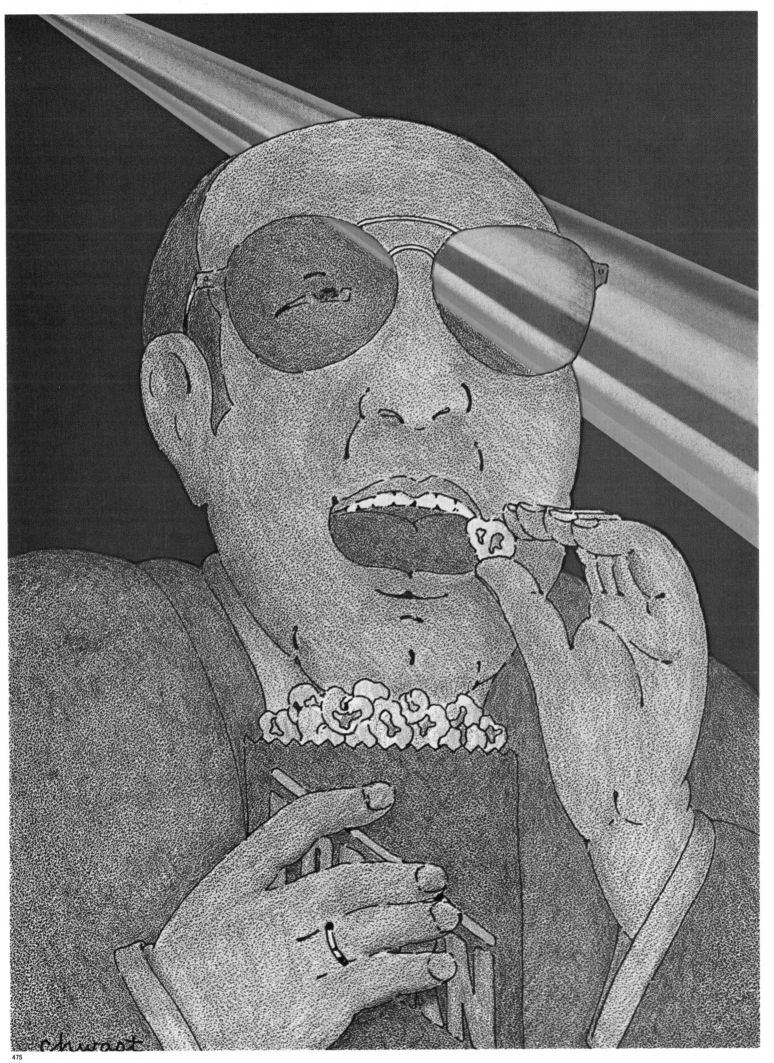

476

476) Drawing from ESQUIRE of Malcolm McDowell as a cricketer, accompanying an article on the British actor. Full page. (USA)
477)–479) Illustrations from an article on caricature in ESQUIRE magazine. (USA)
480) Full-page drawing in flat colours from the satirical weekly NEBELSPALTER. (SWI)
481) Illustration in pastel shades from the magazine EMERGENCY MEDICINE. (USA)
482) Illustration from the magazine PRACTICAL RADIOLOGY. Full page, full colour. (USA)

476) Zeichnung aus der Zeitschrift ESQUIRE von Malcolm McDowell als Cricketspieler, zu einem Artikel über den britischen Schauspieler. Ganzseitig. (USA)
477)–479) Illustrationen zu einem Artikel in der Zeitschrift ESQUIRE über Karikaturen. (USA)
480) Ganzseitige Zeichnung aus der satirischen Wochenschrift NEBELSPALTER. In blassen Tönen. (SWI)
481) Illustration in Pastellfarben aus der Zeitschrift EMERGENCY MEDICINE. (USA)
482) Illustration aus der Zeitschrift PRACTICAL RADIOLOGY. Ganzseitig, mehrfarbig. (USA)

476) Dessin d'ESQUIRE présentant Malcolm McDowell comme joueur de cricket, pour un article sur le célèbre acteur britannique. Pleine page. (USA)
477)–479) Illustrations d'un article consacré à la caricature. Magazine ESQUIRE. (USA)
480) Dessin pleine page de l'hebdomadaire satirique NEBELSPALTER. Couleurs en à-plat. (SWI)
481) Illustration aux tons pastels pour le magazine EMERGENCY MEDICINE. (USA)
482) Illustration du magazine PRACTICAL RADIOLOGY. Pleine page, polychromie. (USA)

Artist / Künstler / Artiste:

476) DAVID LEVINE
477) JEAN MULATIER
478) 479) PATRICE RICORD/RICHARD WEIGAND
480) HEINZ STIEGER
481) FRANK BOZZO/TOM LENNON
482) SIMMS TABACK

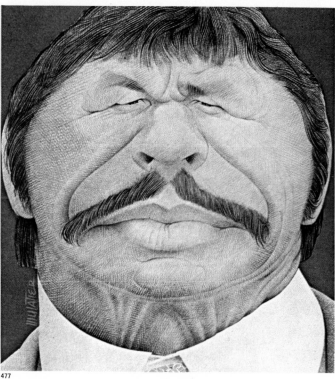

477

478

Art Director / Directeur artistique:

476)–479) RICHARD WEIGAND
481) IRA SILBERLICHT
482) DAVID BARBA

Agency / Agentur / Agence – Studio:

482) NAIMARK & BARBA, INC.

Publisher / Verleger / Editeur:

476)–479) ESQUIRE, INC.
480) NEBELSPALTER-VERLAG
481) FISCHER-MURRAY, INC.
482) PRACTICAL RADIOLOGY

Magazine Illustrations
Zeitschriften-Illustrationen
Illustrations de périodiques

480

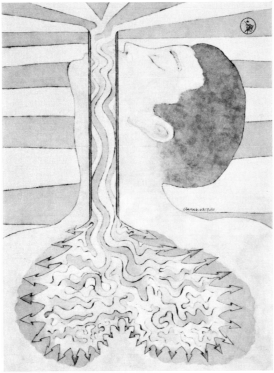

481

482

479

Artist / Künstler / Artiste:

483) ALEX GNIDZIEJKO / PAUL HARDY
484) GUY BILLOUT / PAUL HARDY
485) BARBARA BASCOVE / RAYMOND WAITES
486) EDWARD SOREL / MARTIN BERTHOMMIER
487)–489) RALPH STEADMAN

483

484

485

486

Art Director / Directeur artistique:

483) 484) PAUL HARDY
485) RAYMOND WAITES
486) ETIENNE DELESSERT
487)–489) BOB KINGSBURY

Agency / Agentur / Agence – Studio:

483) 484) HINRICHS DESIGN ASSOC.

Publisher / Verleger / Editeur:

483) 484) SUPER-8 FILMAKER
485) A.D. MAGAZINE
486) BAYARD PRESSE
487)–489) STRAIGHT ARROW PUBLISHERS, INC.

Magazine Illustrations
Zeitschriften-Illustrationen
Illustrations de périodiques

487

488

489

165

490) 491) Double spread in full colour and two-colour illustration from BERUFSBILDER 73, an annual booklet on career possibilities, here referring to trades connected with wood and to office professions. (SWI)
492) 493) Full-colour covers of a magazine for children published by Zenon Music Co. (JPN)
494) Illustration for a short story published in the daily LA NACION. Black and white. (ARG)
495) Black-and-white illustration from THE TIMES. (GBR)
496) Double spread from McGRAPHIC, a newspaper published by 'graphic artists and writers for McGovern/Shriver' before the American elections of 1972. Black and white. (USA)

490) 491) Double page polychrome et illustration en deux couleurs tirées de BERUFSBILDER 73, une brochure d'orientation professionnelle distribuée chaque année. Ici, on discute les métiers du bois et les professions du bureau. (SWI)
492) 493) Couvertures polychromes d'un magazine d'enfants publié par la Zenon Music Co. (JPN)
494) Illustration d'une nouvelle publiée dans le quotidien LA NACION. Noir et blanc. (ARG)
495) Illustration noir-blanc pour le journal THE TIMES. (GBR)
496) Double page de McGRAPHIC, un journal préélectoral publié par «les artistes graphiques et écrivains supporters de McGovern et Shriver» en 1972. Noir et blanc. (USA)

490

491

490) 491) Mehrfarbige Doppelseite und zweifarbige Illustration aus BERUFSBILDER 73, einer Jahresbroschüre über Karrieremöglichkeiten, hier mit bezug auf Berufe im Zusammenhang mit Holz und auf Büroberufe. (SWI)
492) 493) Umschläge einer von Zenon Music Co. herausgegebenen Kinderzeitschrift. (JPN)
494) Illustration für eine Kurzgeschichte in der Tageszeitung LA NACION. Schwarzweiss. (ARG)
495) Schwarzweisse Illustration aus THE TIMES. (GBR)
496) Doppelseite aus McGRAPHIC, einer Zeitung, die von einer Gruppe von Graphikern und Schriftstellern für McGovern/Shriver vor den amerikanischen Wahlen von 1972 herausgegeben wurde. (USA)

492

493

494

495

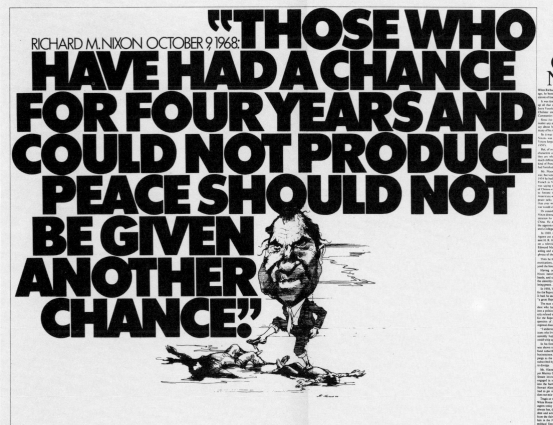

496

Artist | Künstler | Artiste:

490) 491) URS FURRER
492) 493) MAKOTO OBO
494) ROBERTO PÁEZ
495) FRANKLIN WILSON /
JEANETTE COLLINS
496) DAVID LEVINE / HERB
LUBALIN / SEYMOUR CHWAST /
ELLEN SHAPIRO

Art Director | Directeur artistique:

490) 491) URS FURRER
492) 493) MAKOTO OBO
495) JEANETTE COLLINS
496) HERB LUBALIN / SEYMOUR
CHWAST

Agency | Agentur | Agence – Studio:

496) LUBALIN, SMITH, CARNASE /
PUSH PIN STUDIOS

Publisher | Verleger | Editeur:

490) 491) ABC VERLAG
492) 493) ZENON MUSIC CO. LTD.
494) DIARIO LA NACION
495) TIMES NEWSPAPERS LTD.
496) GRAPHIC ARTISTS & WRITERS
FOR MCGOVERN

497)–499) Cover page, double spread and cartoon strip from REVUE SMARAGD. Fig. 497 opens a story by Knut Hamsun (The Gravedigger Is Late), and figs. 498 and 499 are illustrated stories with captions by the artists. Black and white. (CSR)

497)–499) Umschlagseite, Doppelseite und Comic-Strip aus REVUE SMARAGD. Abb. 497 eröffnet eine Geschichte von Knut Hamsun (Der Totengräber ist verspätet), Abb. 498 und 499 sind illustrierte Geschichten mit Legenden der Künstler. Schwarzweiss. (CSR)

497)–499) Première page de couverture, double page et bande dessinée tirées de la REVUE SMARAGD. La fig. 497 introduit un récit de Knut Hamsun (Le Fossoyeur est en retard). Les fig. 498 et 499 sont des récits en images, avec des légendes fournies par les dessinateurs. Noir et blanc. (CSR)

497

498

Artist | Künstler | Artiste:

497) 499) JIRI SALAMOUN / MILAN KOPRIVA
498) ZDENEK MEZEL

Art Director | Directeur artistique:

497)–499) MLADÁ FRONTA

Publisher | Verleger | Editeur:

497)–499) MLADÁ FRONTA

Newspaper Illustrations
Zeitungs-Illustrationen
Illustrations de journaux

Hle! Pyšná tvář ukrutné zbohatlice, zrůzněná vášní! Kamenné srdce pod brokátem a zlatohlavem!

Hle! Ruka obtížená klenoty vrhá ve zvrácené pýše do líných vln Vltavy prsten, klenot nesmírné ceny, aby pokořila nuzáka, jenž ji ťal do živého ...

Ale běda! Tiché kletby nuzných rtů klenby nebeské dosáh Styď, zpanělá ženo, hrůzanou ozvěnu!

499

4.

A nastojte! Žádný strom neroste do nebe
a kolo Štěstěny se obrací!
Chmurné hlubiny vltavské vracejí prokletý kov!

5.

Z útrob nenasytného lupiče zelenavých tůní vrací se
zházonosný šperk zlé ženě, ovoce pýchy
– zlověstné znamení nadcházejících strastí!

6.

A skutečně!
Nastaly zlé časy.
Co nedokázal věrolomný správce, rozkacené živly . . .

7.

. . . a chamtivá čeládka,
co nestrávily trestající plameny,
dokonala zhoubná choroba . . .

8.

Ano, tot ona!
Se sinalou tváří a okem vyhaslým
v divném rámci šedin zoufalství . . .

500

501

500)–505) A selection of illustrations, all in black and white, from the Op-Ed page of THE NEW YORK TIMES, with one example of a complete page (fig. 503). The articles to which the illustrations relate deal with the Watergate scandal (fig. 500), with a divorce story (fig. 501), cross-examination (fig. 502), an excerpt (about apples) from a forthcoming book (fig. 503), the beginnings of flight (fig. 504) and brain surgery (fig. 505). (USA)

Art Director | Directeur artistique:
500)–505) J.C. SUARES

Publisher | Verleger | Editeur:
500)–505) THE NEW YORK TIMES

500)–505) Sélection d'illustrations de la page de tribunes libres – «op-ed» – du NEW YORK TIMES, avec un exemple de page complète (fig. 503). Les articles auxquels se rapportent ces illustrations traitent de Watergate (500), d'une histoire de divorce (501), de l'interrogatoire contradictoire (502), de l'extrait d'un livre à paraître (503; il s'agit de pommes), des débuts de l'aviation (504) et de la chirurgie du cerveau (505). (USA)

500)–505) Eine Auswahl Illustrationen, alle schwarzweiss, aus der Op-Ed-Seite (gegenüber dem Leitartikel) in der NEW YORK TIMES mit einem Beispiel einer vollständigen Seite (Abb. 503). Die Illustrationen begleiten Artikel über den Watergate-Skandal (Abb. 500), eine Scheidungsgeschichte (Abb. 501), das Kreuzverhör (Abb. 502), einen Auszug (über Äpfel) aus einem Buch, das demnächst erscheint (Abb. 503), die Anfänge der Fliegerei (Abb. 504) und Neurochirurgie (Abb. 505). (USA)

502

504

Newspaper Illustrations
Zeitungs-Illustrationen
Illustrations de journaux

503

505

506) Large illustration for an article about living on the Los Angeles freeways, published in THE NEW YORK TIMES MAGAZINE. Black and white. (USA)
507) 508) Collage illustration and complete page with an article on the return of war veterans from Vietnam in THE NEW YORK TIMES BOOK REVIEW. (USA)

506) Grosse Illustration zu einem Artikel über Wohnmöglichkeiten auf den Autobahnen von Los Angeles. Aus dem NEW YORK TIMES MAGAZINE. Schwarzweiss. (USA)
507) 508) Collage-Illustration und vollständige Seite mit einem Artikel über die Rückkehr von Kriegsveteranen aus Vietnam. Aus der Zeitschrift THE NEW YORK TIMES BOOK REVIEW. (USA)

506) Illustration grand format pour un article sur les possibilités d'habitation sur les autoroutes de Los Angeles publié dans le NEW YORK TIMES MAGAZINE. Noir et blanc. (USA)
507) 508) Collage et page complète où figure cette illustration d'un article sur le retour des soldats américains du Viêt-nam publié dans le NEW YORK TIMES BOOK REVIEW. (USA)

507

Newspaper Illustrations
Zeitungs-Illustrationen
Illustrations de journaux

Artist | Künstler | Artiste:
506) BILL BASSO
507) 508) ANITA SIEGEL / J.C. SUARES

Art Director | Directeur artistique:
506) STAN MACK
507) 508) J.C. SUARES

Publisher | Verleger | Editeur:
506)–508) THE NEW YORK TIMES

508

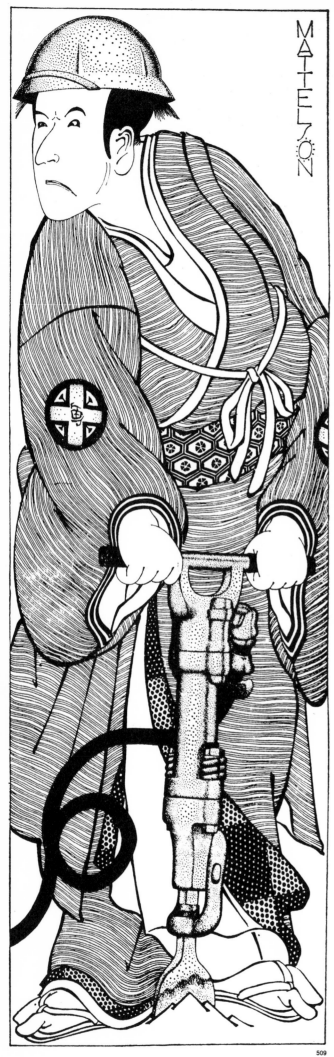

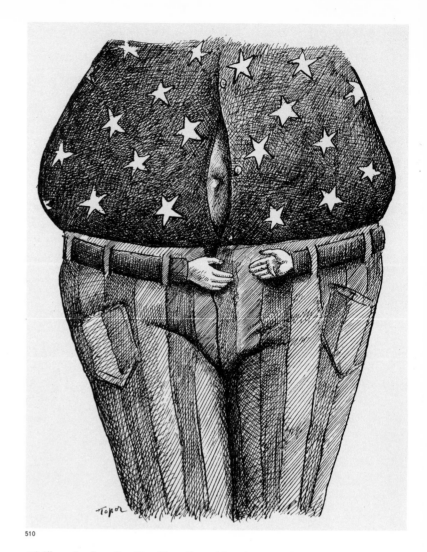

510

509) Illustration from THE NEW YORK TIMES. The subject is building construction in Tokyo. Black and white. (USA)
510) Illustration for an article on 'the idea of fraternity in America' from THE NEW YORK TIMES BOOK REVIEW. (USA)
511) From the Op-Ed page of THE NEW YORK TIMES. Subject: American political leadership. (USA)
512) Illustration from THE NEW YORK TIMES, on the responsibilities of a landlord. (USA)
513) Illustration from THE NEW YORK TIMES BOOK REVIEW. (USA)
514) Illustration of the cogwheels of industry, from THE NEW YORK TIMES. (USA)

509

511

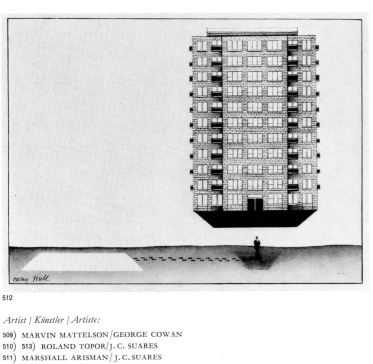

512

Artist | Künstler | Artiste:

509) MARVIN MATTELSON/GEORGE COWAN
510) 513) ROLAND TOPOR/J.C. SUARES
511) MARSHALL ARISMAN/J.C. SUARES
512) CATHY HULL/GEORGE COWAN
514) MEL FURUKAWA/GEORGE COWAN

Art Director | Directeur artistique:

503) 512) 514) GEORGE COWAN
510) 511) 513) J.C. SUARES

Publisher | Verleger | Editeur:

509)–514) THE NEW YORK TIMES

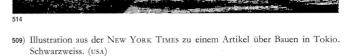

514

509) Illustration aus der NEW YORK TIMES zu einem Artikel über Bauen in Tokio. Schwarzweiss. (USA)
510) Illustration zu einem Artikel über «die Idee der Brüderlichkeit in Amerika» aus der NEW YORK TIMES BOOK REVIEW. (USA)
511) Op-Ed Seite der NEW YORK TIMES, über politische Führung in den USA. (USA)
512) Aus der NEW YORK TIMES, über die Verantwortung eines Hausbesitzers. (USA)
513) Illustration aus der NEW YORK TIMES BOOK REVIEW. (USA)
514) Illustration über die Räder der Industrie, aus der NEW YORK TIMES. (USA)

509) Illustration du NEW YORK TIMES. Le sujet traité est la construction à Tokyo. Noir et blanc. (USA)
510) Illustration pour un article sur «l'idée de fraternité en Amérique», dans le NEW YORK TIMES BOOK REVIEW. (USA)
511) Une page op-ed du NEW YORK TIMES. Thème: les dirigeants politiques US. (USA)
512) Illustration du NEW YORK TIMES, sur les responsabilités d'un propriétaire. (USA)
513) Illustration du NEW YORK TIMES BOOK REVIEW. (USA)
514) Illustration des rouages de l'industrie. THE NEW YORK TIMES. (USA)

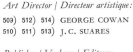
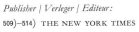

513

Newspaper Illustrations
Zeitungs-Illustrationen
Illustrations de journaux

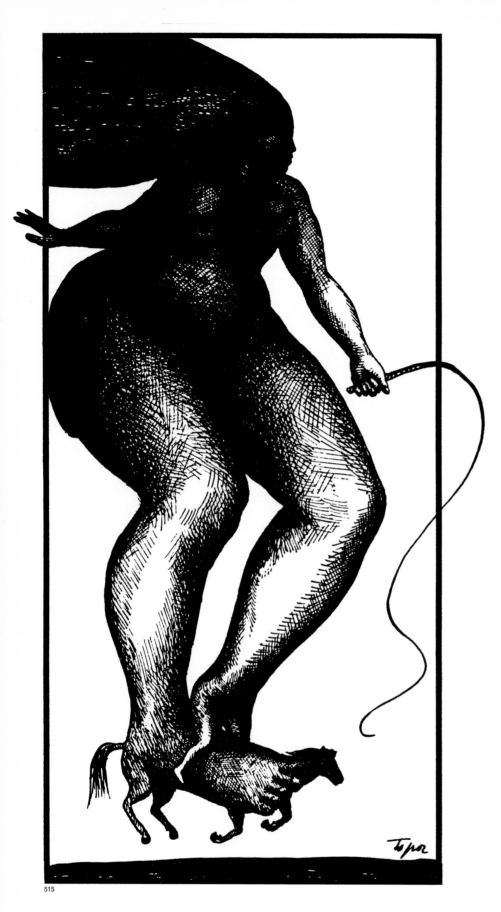

515

516

517

518

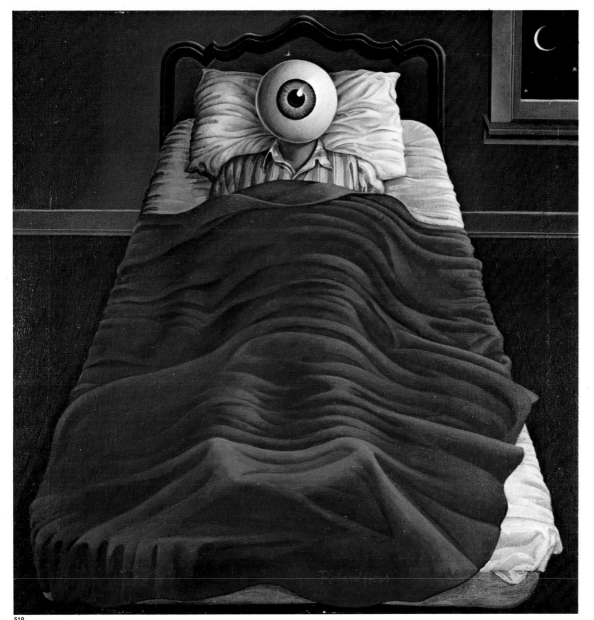

519

520

The New York Times Magazine

The Insomniac / CONTENTS PAGE 24

Artist | Künstler | Artiste:

515) ROLAND TOPOR / J.C. SUARES
516) ANITA SIEGEL / J.C. SUARES
517) 518) CAROL ANTHONY / J.C. SUARES
519) 520) RICHARD HESS / STAN MACK
521) R.O. BLECHMAN / J.C. SUARES
522) PHILIP HAYS / STAN MACK

Art Director | Directeur artistique:

515)–518) 521) J.C. SUARES
519) 520) 522) STAN MACK

Publisher | Verleger | Editeur:

515)–522) THE NEW YORK TIMES

515) Illustration from the Op-Ed page of THE NEW YORK TIMES. (USA)
516) Illustration for a review of a psychological novel published in THE NEW YORK TIMES BOOK REVIEW. (USA)
517) 518) Spread and detail of illustration from THE NEW YORK TIMES BOOK REVIEW. (USA)
519) 520) Illustration in full colour and complete cover of an issue of THE NEW YORK TIMES MAGAZINE. Subject: sleeplessness. (USA)
521) Illustration from THE NEW YORK TIMES BOOK REVIEW alluding to the Black Panthers. (USA)
522) Cover illustration of THE NEW YORK TIMES MAGAZINE. Full colour. (USA)

515) Illustration aus der Op-Ed-Seite der NEW YORK TIMES. (USA)
516) Illustration zu einer Besprechung eines Bildungsromans in der Zeitschrift THE NEW YORK TIMES BOOK REVIEW. (USA)
517) 518) Doppelseite und Detail der Illustration aus THE NEW YORK TIMES BOOK REVIEW. (USA)
519) 520) Mehrfarbige Illustration und ganzer Umschlag einer Nummer des NEW YORK TIMES MAGAZINE. Thema: Schlaflosigkeit. (USA)
521) Illustration aus THE NEW YORK TIMES BOOK REVIEW. Thema: die Black Panthers. (USA)
522) Umschlagillustration für das NEW YORK TIMES MAGAZINE. Mehrfarbig. (USA)

515) Illustration pour la page de tribunes libres («op-ed») du NEW YORK TIMES. (USA)
516) Illustration du compte rendu d'un roman psychologique, dans le NEW YORK TIMES BOOK REVIEW. (USA)
517) 518) Double page et détail de l'illustration. THE NEW YORK TIMES BOOK REVIEW. (USA)
519) 520) Illustration polychrome et couverture complète d'un numéro du NEW YORK TIMES MAGAZINE. Thème: l'insomnie. (USA)
521) Illustration du NEW YORK TIMES BOOK REVIEW. Thème: les Panthères Noires. (USA)
522) Illustration de couverture polychrome pour le NEW YORK TIMES MAGAZINE. (USA)

The New York Times Book Review

AUGUST 26, 1973   SECTION 7

The Black Panthers: large threats, small guilt

The Briar Patch

The People of the State of New York v. Lumumba Shakur, et al.
By Murray Kempton
282 pp. New York: E. P. Dutton Co. $7.95.

By GARRY WILLS

521

The New York Times Magazine

JUNE 17 1973/SECTION 6

Here comes Mr. Brezhnev / CONTENTS: PAGE 4

522

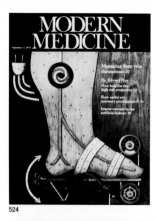

Artist | Künstler | Artiste:

523) ALAIN LE FOLL / MARTIN BERTHOMMIER
524) 525) VIN GIULIANI / PHILIP DYKSTRA
526) ROLAND TOPOR / MARTIN BERTHOMMIER
527) MORDILLO / MARTIN BERTHOMMIER

Art Director | Directeur artistique:

523) 526) 527) ETIENNE DELESSERT
524) 525) PHILIP DYKSTRA

Publisher | Verleger | Editeur:

523) 526) 527) BAYARD PRESSE
524) 525) MODERN MEDICINE

524

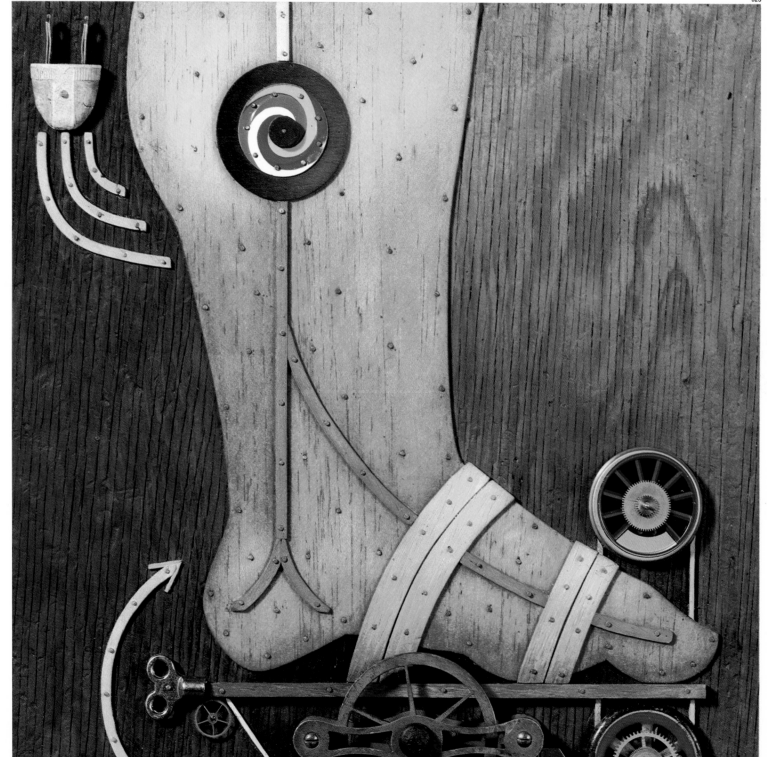

525

526

527

523) 526) 527) Illustrations from RECORD, a new magazine for
children and young people. Fig. 523 is a double-spread
poster illustrating a quotation from Ikhnaton's hymn to the
sun, fig. 526 is a large colour drawing referring to a dream
and its interpretation, and fig. 527 is an uncaptioned full-
colour double-spread poster. (FRA)

524) 525) Complete cover of the monthly MODERN MEDICINE
and detail of the artwork – using a three-dimensional wooden
construction – in actual size. The reference is to an article on
thrombosis. (USA)

523) 526) 527) Illustrationen aus RECORD, einer neuen Zeitschrift
für Kinder und junge Leute. Abb. 523 ist ein Poster (Doppelseite), der ein Zitat aus Echnatons Hymne auf die Sonne
illustriert; Abb. 526 ist eine Farbzeichnung, die sich auf
einen Traum und dessen Auslegung bezieht, und Abb. 527
ist ein unbeschrifteter, mehrfarbiger Poster. (FRA)

524) 525) Vollständiger Umschlag der Monatsschrift MODERN
MEDICINE und Detail der Illustration – es wurde eine drei-
dimensionale Holzkonstruktion verwendet – in Originalgrösse, mit Bezug auf einen Artikel über Thrombose. (USA)

523) 526) 527) Illustrations de RECORD, un nouveau magazine
pour enfants et jeunes gens. La fig. 523 est un poster double
page illustrant une citation de l'hymne au soleil d'Améno-
phis IV-Akhenaton; 526: dessin couleur grand format sur
le thème de l'interprétation des rêves; 527: poster polychrome, double page, sans légende. (FRA)

524) 525) Couverture complète de la revue mensuelle MODERN
MEDICINE et détail grandeur nature de la composition basée
sur une maquette tridimensionnelle en bois. Le thème traité
est celui de la thrombose. (USA)

528

529

530

528)–530) Vignette-like illustrations for a story in the children's magazine SLUNICKO. Full colour. (CSR)

531) Double spread in the magazine SCHULE opening an account by a teacher of how she handles sexual instruction. White heads on grey. (GER)

532) Page from the teacher's magazine SCHULE. The title of the article is: 'Is my child going to be a giant?' Black and white. (GER)

533)–535) Illustrations from SESAME STREET, a magazine for children of pre-school age which encourages participation in games and puzzles. On the right in fig. 535, for instance, a suitcase which can be cut out and taped together. All in full colour. (USA)

528)–530) Vignettenhafte Illustrationen zu einer Geschichte in der Kinderzeitschrift SLUNICKO. Mehrfarbig. (CSR)

531) Doppelseite aus der Zeitschrift SCHULE. Eine junge Lehrerin berichtet, wie sie Sexualkunde unterrichtet. Weisse Köpfe auf grauem Grund. (GER)

532) Seite aus der Lehrerzeitschrift SCHULE mit einem Artikel über Riesenkinder. Schwarzweiss. (GER)

533)–535) Illustrationen aus SESAME STREET, einer Zeitschrift für Kinder von 5 bis 8 Jahren, die zehnmal im Jahr erscheint und zur Teilnahme an Spielen und Puzzles ermutigt. Der Koffer rechts in Abb. 535 zum Beispiel kann ausgeschnitten und zusammengeklebt werden. Alle Illustrationen sind mehrfarbig. (USA)

528)–530) Illustrations-vignettes d'une histoire publiée dans le magazine pour enfants SLUNICKO. En polychromie. (CSR)

531) Double page initiale du rapport d'une maîtresse sur son expérience de l'éducation sexuelle, dans le magazine SCHULE. Têtes blanches sur fond gris. (GER)

532) Page du magazine SCHULE destiné aux enseignants. L'article est intitulé: «Mon enfant sera-t-il un géant?» Noir et blanc. (GER)

533)–535) Illustrations pour SESAME STREET, un magazine pour les petits les invitant à participer à des jeux et devinettes de toutes sortes. La partie droite de la fig. 535, par exemple, montre comment découper une valise et l'assembler à l'aide de ruban adhésif. Polychromie. (USA)

531

532

Artist | Künstler | Artiste:

528)–530) KVETA PACOVSKÁ
531) HEINZ EDELMANN
532) EDDA KÖCHL
533) JAMES MC MULLAN
534) PAUL DAVIS
535) ISADORE SELTZER / DOUG TAYLOR / GARY SCHENK

Magazine Illustrations
Zeitschriften-Illustrationen
Illustrations de périodiques

533

534

A Night Away from Home

535

Art Director | Directeur artistique:

528)–530) KVETA PACOVSKÁ
531) 532) GÜNTER HALDEN
533)–535) HENRY WOLF

Agency | Agentur | Agence – Studio:

533)–535) HENRY WOLF PRODUCTIONS

Publisher | Verleger | Editeur:

528)–530) MLADÁ FRONTA
531) 532) GRUNER & JAHR GMBH & CO.
533)–535) CHILDREN'S TELEVISION WORKSHOP

536

The Epicurean is the official
magazine of the Wine and Food Society
of Australia
Number Forty-three, June-July 1973
A J Holdsworth, Editor
H N McCarty, Sydney Manager
Les Mason, Art Director
South Australian Representative:
A J Ludbrook
The Epicurean is published by
Lawrence Publishing Co. Pty. Ltd.
Melbourne: 13-31 Barrett Street
Kensington, Vic. 33 0571
Sydney: 437 Kent Street
29 4817, 29 5432
Telegrams: Corks, Melbourne
and Sydney
Yearly subscription: $3.60
(6 issues postpaid)
Next issue: August-September 1973
Reproduction in whole
or part without permission
is prohibited.
Distributed by Gordon and Gotch
(A/asia) Limited

537

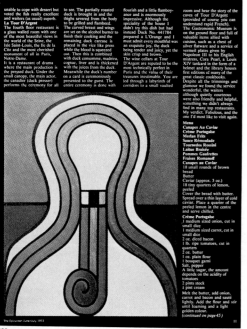

538

540

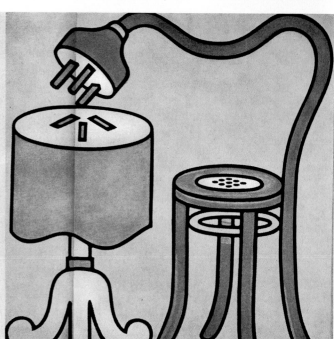

OENOLOGISTS VIEW
By Ian Hickinbotham

This time of nationalistic fervour about those French, has caused me to think again about their permissiveness in winemaking. I refer of course to their long standing practice of adding sugar to wines in some years, and under official approval.

I have long pondered why our industry has been so silent about this practice. Perhaps we are just gentlemen or were! Now, may be the time to grind our teeth and launch a campaign to prevent entry of wines to which sugar has been added and which are therefore not natural wines by our standards.

It is a fact that our standards are specific in this field. No Australian winemaker is permitted by law to add sugar to wine and more important, no winemaker would want to do so because they appreciate that quality would suffer.

539

541

536) Cover of the wine and food magazine EPICUREAN. Artwork in pastel shades against a background of sausages. (AUL)

537)–539) Contents spread, page and double spread from issues of EPICUREAN magazine. The illustrations are in shades of grey. (AUL)

540) Page opening a special section, printed on coloured paper, of TRANSAMERICA, house magazine of the Transamerica Corporation. (USA)

541) 542) Complete cover and artwork in roughly actual size from a winter issue of the quarterly house magazine GUINNESS TIME. (GBR)

536) Umschlag für die kulinarische Zeitschrift EPICUREAN. Komposition in Pastellfarben auf einem Hintergrund von Würsten. (AUL)

537)–539) Indexseite, Seite und Doppelseite aus der Zeitschrift EPICUREAN. Die Illustrationen sind in Grautönen. (AUL)

540) Seite als Anfang eines Sonderteils – auf farbigem Papier gedruckt – von TRANS-AMERICA, Hauszeitschrift der Transamerican Corporation. (USA)

541) 542) Vollständiger Umschlag und Illustration in ungefähr Originalgrösse aus einer Winterausgabe der vierteljährlichen Hauszeitschrift GUINNESS TIME. (GBR)

536) Couverture du magazine de vins et de cuisine EPICUREAN. Composition aux tons pastels sur un fond de saucisses. (AUL)

537)–539) Double page avec le sommaire, page et double page de divers numéros du magazine EPICUREAN. Les illustrations sont exécutées en divers gris. (AUL)

540) Page initiale d'une section spéciale sur papier couleur de TRANSAMERICA, revue d'entreprise de la Transamerica Corporation. (USA)

541) 542) Couverture complète et composition grandeur approx. nature d'un numéro d'hiver de la revue d'entreprise trimestrielle GUINNESS TIME. (GBR)

Artist | Künstler | Artiste:

536)–539) LES MASON
540) MIKE VANDERBYLE /
   MICHEL DATTEL
541) 542) ANDRÉ AMSTUTZ

Art Director | Directeur artistique:

540) MIKE VANDERBYLE
541) 542) GUY CHALLIS

542

Agency | Agentur | Agence – Studio:

540) SOYSTER & OHRENSCHALL, INC.

Publisher | Verleger | Editeur:

536)–539) LAWRENCE PUBLISHING CO. PTY. LTD.
540) JEFFRIES BANKNOTE CO.
541) 542) ARTHUR GUINNESS & SON CO.

House Organs
Hauszeitschriften
Journaux d'entreprises

543

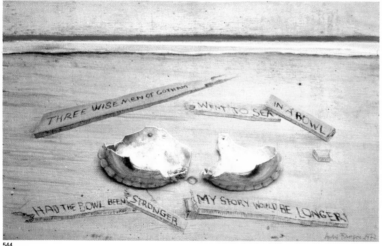

544

545

Artist | Künstler | Artiste:

543) 544) 546) ANDRÉ FRANÇOIS
545) VIN GIULIANI / HARRY O. DIAMOND

Art Director | Directeur artistique:

543)–546) HARRY O. DIAMOND

Publisher | Verleger | Editeur:

543)–546) EXXON CORPORATION

House Organs / Hauszeitschriften
Journaux d'entreprises

543) 544) 546) Three illustrations in actual size from an article entitled 'André François Meets the Sea' in a special issue of the *Exxon* house organ THE LAMP devoted to the oceans. Fig. 543 shows Noah's ark, the other two figures contain their own rhyming captions. (USA)

545) Cover of an issue of THE LAMP containing an article on the debate about the limits to growth, which is illustrated with photographs of three-dimensional wooden constructions of this kind incorporating printed circuits. (USA)

543) 544) 546) Illustrationen in Originalgrösse zu einem Artikel «André François begegnet dem Meer» in einer dem Ozean gewidmeten Ausgabe der *Exxon*-Zeitschrift THE LAMP. Abb. 543 stellt die Arche Noahs dar, die beiden anderen enthalten ihre eigenen Legenden. (USA)

545) Umschlag einer Nummer von THE LAMP mit einem Artikel über die Debatte zum Thema der Grenzen des Wachstums, das mit Photographien von dreidimensionalen Holzkonstruktionen illustriert wird. (USA)

543) 544) 546) Illustrations grandeur nature pour l'article «André François à la rencontre de la mer». Numéro spécial de la revue *Exxon*, THE LAMP, consacré aux océans. Fig. 543 montre l'arche de Noé. Les deux autres figures contiennent leurs légendes en vers. (USA)

545) Couverture d'un numéro de THE LAMP contenant un article sur le problème de la limitation de la croissance industrielle. Les illustrations sont des photos de maquettes tridimensionnelles avec circuits imprimés incorporés, du genre de celle présentée ici. (USA)

546

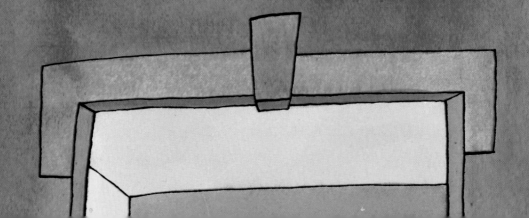

Artist | Künstler | Artiste:

547)–549) JEAN MICHEL FOLON
550) LEE O. WARFIELD III / PHIL JORDAN
551) JEAN ALESSANDRINI

Art Director | Directeur artistique:

547)–549) GIORGIO SOAVI
550) PHIL JORDAN
551) ANDRÉ CHANTE

Agency | Agentur | Agence – Studio:

550) BEVERIDGE & ASSOC.
551) HOLLENSTEIN CRÉATION

Publisher | Verleger | Editeur:

547)–549) ING. C. OLIVETTI & C., S.P.A.
550) NATIONAL SOCIETY OF PROFESSIONAL ENGINEERS
551) IBM FRANCE

547)–549) Page, corresponding double spread and a further illustration from an edition of Kafka's *Metamorphosis* published as a gift by *Olivetti*. (ITA)
550) Cover of the magazine PROFESSIONAL ENGINEER. Black and white. (USA)
551) One of a 'gallery of ancestors' of information, published in IBM-INFORMATIQUE. Polyphile is the man who never finishes his many tasks. (FRA)

547)–549) Seite, entsprechende Doppelseite und eine weitere Illustration aus einer Ausgabe von Kafkas *Die Verwandlung,* die als Geschenk der Firma *Olivetti* an ihre Kunden herausgegeben wurde. (ITA)
550) Umschlag der Zeitschrift PROFESSIONAL ENGINEER. Schwarzweiss. (USA)
551) Illustration aus einer «Ahnengalerie» der Information. Aus IBM-INFORMATIQUE. Polyphil ist jemand, der seine vielen Aufgaben nie beendet. (FRA)

547)–549) Page, double page correspondante et une autre illustration d'une édition de *La Métamorphose,* de Kafka, un livre-cadeau *Olivetti.* (ITA)
550) Couverture du magazine PROFESSIONAL ENGINEER. Noir et blanc. (USA)
551) L'un des personnages figurant dans la «galerie des ancêtres» de l'information: Polyphile, l'homme qui ne vient jamais à bout des nombreux travaux qui lui sont commandés. IBM-INFORMATIQUE. (FRA)

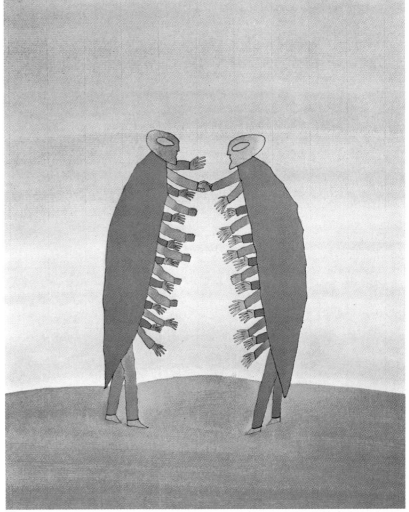

548

549

550

551

552) Cover of Forces, house organ of *Hydro-Québec*. The issue contains an article on stress, the cover composition is entitled 'Stress and the City'. Full colour. (CAN)

553) 554) Illustrations (three-quarter spread and page) from The Texaco Star. Fig. 553 presents the Greek legends behind some constellations (Texaco Inc. has named some of its products after stars). Fig. 554 illustrates an article on automotive emissions and clean air legislation. Both in full colour. (USA)

555) Cover of Ex Libris, magazine of a book and record club. Black and white. (SWI)

556) 557) Cover of Petrole Progres, house organ of the French *Esso*, with an oil map of the North Sea, and colour illustration entitled 'The Moebius motorway' from an article on road signs in the same issue. (FRA)

558) Black-and-white drawing used on a cover of the magazine Serigrafia. The cover is printed in silk-screen. (ITA)

552) Umschlag von Forces, Hauszeitschrift der *Hydro-Québec*. Die Ausgabe enthält einen Artikel über Stress (Titel der Umschlagkomposition: «Stress und die Stadt»). Farbig. (CAN)

553) 554) Illustrationen aus The Texaco Star. Abb. 553 zeigt die griechischen Sagen, die den Konstellationen ihre Namen gegeben haben (Texaco, Inc. hat einige ihrer Produkte nach Sternen benannt). Abb. 554 illustriert einen Artikel über Auspuffgase und die Gesetzgebung zur Reinhaltung der Luft. Beide mehrfarbig. (USA)

555) Umschlag von Ex Libris, Zeitschrift eines Buch- und Schallplattenklubs. (SWI)

556) 557) Umschlag von Petrole Progres, Hauszeitschrift von *Esso* in Frankreich, mit einer Ölkarte der Nordsee, und Farbillustration mit dem Titel «Die Autobahn von Moebius» zu einem Artikel in der gleichen Nummer über Verkehrssignale. (FRA)

558) Schwarzweisse Zeichnung als Umschlag der Zeitschrift Serigrafia. Der Umschlag ist im Siebdruckverfahren hergestellt. (ITA)

552) Couverture polychrome de Forces, la revue d'entreprise d'*Hydro-Québec*. Le numéro contient un article sur le stress, illustré sur la couverture («Le stress et la ville»). (CAN)

553) 554) Illustrations polychromes (trois quarts d'une double page et page) du Texaco Star. La fig. 553 présente les légendes grecques des constellations (Texaco a donné à certains de ses produits des noms d'étoiles). La fig. 554 illustre un article sur les gaz d'échappement des voitures et la législation en la matière. (USA)

555) Couverture d'Ex Libris, revue d'une guilde du livre et du disque. Noir et blanc. (SWI)

556) 557) Couverture de Petrole Progres, revue d'entreprise d'*Esso*-France, avec une carte des gisements pétroliers en mer du Nord et une illustration couleur intitulée «l'autoroute Moebius» (référence à un article sur la signalisation routière). (FRA)

558) Dessin noir et blanc utilisé pour la couverture du magazine Serigrafia. Couverture exécutée en sérigraphie. (ITA)

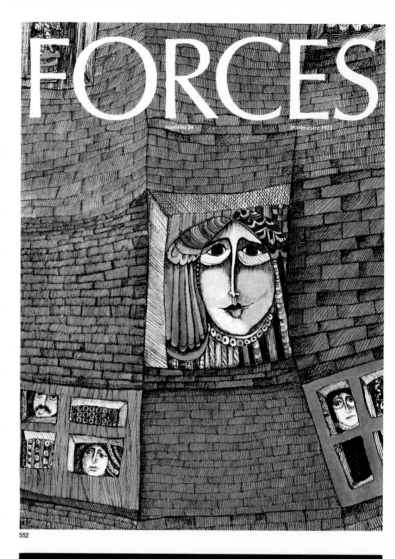

552

555

556

Artist | Künstler | Artiste.

552) MICHÈLE THÉORÊT
553) JEROME SNYDER
554) ISADORE SELTZER
555) HEINZ STIEGER
556) PHILIPPE KAILHENN
557) PIERRE-PAUL DARIGO
558) GIANCARLO ILIPRANDI

Art Director | Directeur artistique:

553) LESLIE A. SEGAL
555) OSWALD DUBACHER
556) 557) JACQUES TRIBONDEAU
558) GIANCARLO ILIPRANDI

House Organs / Hauszeitschriften
Journaux d'entreprises

553

554

557

558

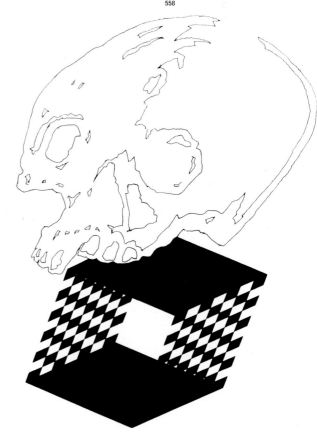

Agency | Agentur | Agence – Studio:

556) 557) DÉPT. INFORMATION ESSO S.A.F.
558) GIANCARLO ILIPRANDI

Publisher | Verleger | Editeur:

552) HYDRO-QUÉBEC
553) 554) TEXACO, INC.
555) EX LIBRIS VERLAG AG
556) 557) MCCANN-ERICKSON
558) EDITORIALE A.Z.

559) Illustration for an article on the treatment of mucoviscidosis published in Essentiala, house organ of UCB. Orange target. (BEL)

560) Colour page from an issue of Kaiser News devoted to the American Dream. (USA)

561)–564) Cover design, illustrations and spread from a *Xerox* recruitment brochure. (USA)

565) Double spread with one of a series of drawings forming a commentary on an Africa Long-Distance Run organized in 1973 by *Citroën, Total* and RTL. From the *Citroën* house organ Le Double Chevron. (FRA)

566) 567) Covers of Esso Rivista, house magazine of the Italian *Esso*. They show compositions by a Japanese artist (yellow, orange, blue and pink) and by an Italian artist (black, grey and red on silver). (ITA)

559) Illustration zu einem Artikel über die Behandlung von Schleimhauterkrankungen. Aus Essentiala, Hauszeitschrift von UCB. Zielscheibe in Orange. (BEL)

560) Seite aus Kaiser News, dem Amerikanischen Traum gewidmete Ausgabe. (USA)

561)–564) Umschlagbild, Illustrationen und Doppelseite aus einer *Xerox*-Broschüre. (USA)

565) Doppelseite mit einer Zeichnung als Teil eines Berichts über eine Dauerfahrt in Afrika, die in 1973 von *Citroën, Total* und RTL organisiert worden war. Aus der *Citroën*-Hauszeitschrift Le Double Chevron. (FRA)

566) 567) Umschläge von Esso Rivista, Hauszeitschrift von *Esso* in Italien. Sie zeigen Kompositionen eines japanischen Künstlers (gelb, orange, blau und rosa) und eines italienischen Künstlers (schwarz, grau und rot auf Silber). (ITA)

559) Illustration d'un article sur le traitement de la mucoviscidose publié dans Essentiala, revue d'entreprise d'UCB. Cible orange. (BEL)

560) Page couleur d'un numéro de Kaiser News sur le Rêve Américain. (USA)

561)–564) Design de couverture, illustrations et double page d'une brochure *Xerox* destinée au recrutement de personnel. (USA)

565) Double page avec l'un des dessins commentant une traversée d'Afrique organisée en 1973 par *Citroën, Total* et RTL. Le Double Chevron, revue d'entreprise de Citroën. (FRA)

566) 567) Couvertures d'Esso Rivista, la revue d'entreprise d'*Esso*-Italie, avec les compositions d'un artiste japonais (jaune, orange, bleu, rose) et d'un artiste italien (noir, gris, rouge sur argent). (ITA)

House Organs
Hauszeitschriften
Journaux d'entreprises

559

560

561

562

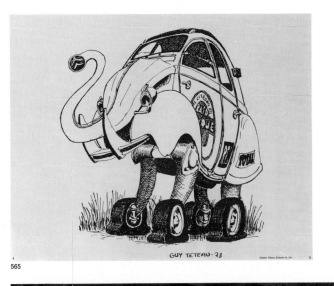

GUY TÉTEAU-73

ESSO RIVISTA

Shu Takahashi

566

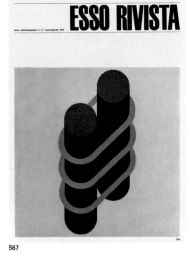

ESSO RIVISTA

Zen

567

564

563

House Organs / Hauszeitschriften
Journaux d'entreprises

568) Full-page illustration for an article on fire hazards published in DIALOGUE 3, house organ of the Insurance Company of North America. (USA)

569)–571) Detail of drawing and corresponding double spread on workmen's compensation, and cover (portrait of a worker) of the same issue of DIALOGUE 3. All in black and white. (USA)

572) 573) Two further colour pages from issues of DIALOGUE 3 (see figs. 568–571). (USA)

568) Ganzseitige Illustration zu einem Artikel über Feuergefahren. Aus DIALOGUE 3, Hauszeitschrift der Insurance Company of North America. (USA)

569)–571) Detail der Illustration und entsprechende Doppelseite über Arbeiter-Entschädigung sowie Umschlag (Porträt eines Arbeiters) der gleichen Nummer von DIALOGUE 3. Alle schwarzweiss. (USA)

572) 573) Zwei weitere Farbseiten aus DIALOGUE 3 (siehe Abb. 568–571). (USA)

568) Illustration pleine page pour un article sur les risques d'incendie publié dans DIALOGUE 3, la revue d'entreprise de l'Insurance Company of North America. (USA)

569)–571) Détail d'un dessin, double page où il figure et couverture (portrait d'un ouvrier) du même numéro de DIALOGUE 3. Noir et blanc. (USA)

572) 573) Deux pages couleurs tirées d'autres numéros de DIALOGUE 3 (cf. les fig. 568–571). (USA)

Artist | Künstler | Artiste:

568) JOHN O'LEARY / BOB WARKULWIZ
569) 570) CHR. PIPER / PUSH PIN STUDIOS
571) STEVE TARANTAL
572) BOB WARKULWIZ
573) LEN BRUNO / BILL DAVIDSON

Art Director | Directeur artistique:

568)–573) KEITH MEASE / LEN BRUNO / BOB WARKULWIZ

Agency | Agentur | Agence – Studio:

568)–573) BRUNO / MEASE, INC.

Publisher | Verleger | Editeur:

568)–573) INSURANCE COMPANY OF NORTH AMERICA

570

Workmen's Compensation Reform—
The Case for Federal Action Now

571

572

Monthly reports: EIS becomes MIS for producers

Many large companies today design their computer systems for the prime purpose of providing a Management Information System for themselves. The EIS system is unusual in that it starts by redesigning and improving the existing system; places emphasis on the availability and accuracy of information in the field; and then plans eventually to build an effectual MIS for itself.

Up to now, most companies have wanted MIS because it would fill a gap —an absence of information. These attempts at building a management information system without any basic information as a base is an exercise in futility . . . resulting in failure. The EIS system, on the other hand, will grow from a substantial base of basic information.

Plus the structure of EIS, in effect, does provide every producer with his own Management Information System —basic information to build on. Monthly reports to agents under EIS will reflect all business actually transacted in a month. Current time lags leave these monthly reports not

reflecting up to 15 days' worth of business for the month. The EIS system will only be off 24 hours . . . the time it takes for any input to the system to be recorded.

Agents will be able to use the new accurate monthly reports as an effective gauge to their business, as a means of evaluating policyholders, and an accurate means of forecasting future business.

Receivables: you're in the money

Because EIS calculates what's due agents and the company faster, payments are faster. Instead of many locations being involved in the payment process, EIS adds and subtracts via the service office terminals. You're in the money . . . sooner.

Growth: for you and for us

Many of the factors of the EIS system that will encourage both agency and company growth have already been discussed. What hasn't been discussed is the fact that without EIS and its speed and accuracy, the peripheral elements of doing business in insurance today would eventually eat up all the time in a business day . . . leaving no time for the actual selling and servicing of accounts.

EIS is obviously a necessity for growth . . . for both of us.

One of today's agency force's biggest complaints about all insurance companies is that they can't handle the new business volume and underwriting capacity. Lines are arbitrarily declined. Decisions are based on old, incorrect information.

With EIS, service offices will be able to respond immediately to unique underwriting situations . . . giving agencies more time to write and handle new business.

With personal lines business, the agent wants to be able to assure his customer that he's covered immediately, what the policy will cost him exactly . . . and EIS will help him here.

With commercial lines, the agent wants to know if the company can provide coverage, the capacity and cost, and the flexibility to change these as the customer's business grows . . . and EIS will help him here.

Studies indicate that as more insurance companies initiate more sophisticated computer systems, agents will turn to those companies which eliminate paperwork, respond with service and facility, give him what he needs for growth and success. The agent will deal with fewer companies than he does now, but these fewer companies must be able to provide capacity, and facilities—all lines facilities, and service. Here, EIS is designed to grow, help and serve both INA and its agency force.

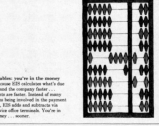
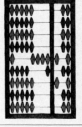

569

573

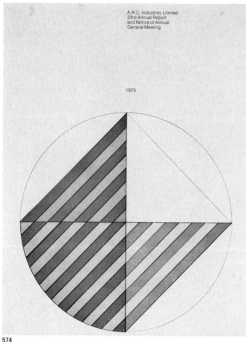

574

1973

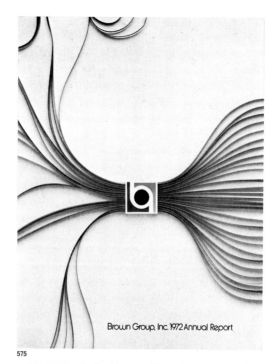

Brown Group, Inc. 1972 Annual Report

575

La Société canadienne des Télécommunications transmarines

23ᵉ Rapport annuel pour l'année se terminant le 31 mars 1973

576

Flagstaff Corporation

Annual Report 1973

577

Federal National Mortgage Association

Annual Report 1971

578

574) Cover of the 1973 annual report of A.R.C. Industries Ltd., suppliers of steel and wire reinforcements for concrete. Design in green, red, blue and yellow. (AUL)
575) Cover of an annual report for the Brown Group, Inc., a diversified shoe company. Brown shades. (USA)
576) Cover, in shades of blue, for an annual report of Canadian Overseas Telecommunication Corporation. (CAN)
577) Cover of the 1973 annual report of Flagstaff Corporation, a company operating in the food services field. (USA)
578) Cover of an annual report of Federal National Mortgage Association. White plaster ground. (USA)
579) Cover of an annual report of Union Commerce Corporation, a financial institution. Ochre and blue on beige. (USA)
580) Annual report cover for the A.B. Dick Co., makers of duplicating machines. Brown, yellow, white on black. (USA)
581) Double-spread colour illustration from an annual report of the Questor Corporation. (USA)
582) Double-spread graph in an annual report of The Flying Tiger Corp., an airline and leasing enterprise. (USA)

574) Umschlag des Jahresberichts für 1973 von A.R.C. Industries Ltd., Hersteller von Stahl- und Drahtverstärkungen für Beton. Graphik grün, rot, blau und gelb. (AUL)
575) Umschlag eines Jahresberichts der Brown Group, Inc., ein Schuhherstellungskonzern. Brauntöne. (USA)
576) Umschlag, in Blautönen, eines Jahresberichts der Canadian Overseas Telecommunication Corporation. (CAN)
577) Umschlag des Jahresberichts für 1973 einer Gesellschaft der Nahrungsmittelbranche. (USA)
578) Umschlag eines Jahresberichts der Federal National Mortgage Association. Weisse Gipsunterlage. (USA)
579) Umschlag eines Geschäftsberichts eines Finanzinstituts. Ocker und blau auf Beige. (USA)
580) Umschlag des Jahresberichts eines Herstellers von Vervielfältigungsapparaten. Braun, gelb, weiss auf Schwarz. (USA)
581) Doppelseitige Farbillustration aus einem Jahresbericht der Questor Corporation. (USA)
582) Doppelseitiges Diagramm aus einem Jahresbericht einer Flug- und Vermietungsgesellschaft. (USA)

574) Couverture du rapport annuel d'A.R.C. Industries Ltd. (armatures d'acier en barres et treillis pour béton) pour 1973. Composition verte, rouge, bleue, jaune. (AUL)
575) Couverture d'un rapport annuel pour le Brown Group, Inc., une compagnie de chaussures diversifiée. Tons bruns. (USA)
576) Couverture aux tons bleus pour un rapport annuel de la Canadian Overseas Telecommunication Corporation. (CAN)
577) Couverture du rapport annuel 1973 de la Flagstaff Corp., société spécialisée dans les services alimentaires. (USA)
578) Couverture d'un rapport annuel de la Federal National Mortgage Association. Fond de plâtre blanc. (USA)
579) Couverture d'un rapport annuel de l'Union Commerce Corp., une société financière. Ocre et bleu sur beige. (USA)
580) Couverture de rapport annuel pour l'A.B. Dick Co. (duplicateurs). Brun, jaune, blanc sur noir. (USA)
581) Illustration couleur double page pour un rapport annuel de la Questor Corporation. (USA)
582) Graphique occupant deux pages d'un rapport annuel de la Flying Tiger Corp., compagnie aérienne et de leasing. (USA)

Union Commerce Corporation Annual Report 1972

579

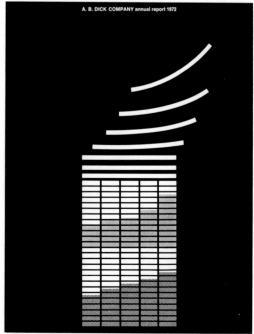

A. B. DICK COMPANY annual report 1972

580

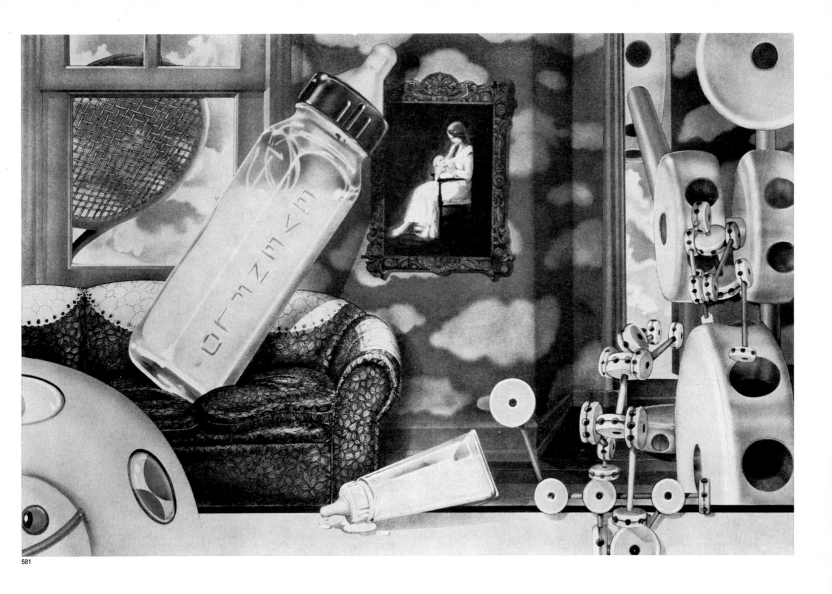

581

Artist | Künstler | Artiste:

574) SANDIE CLARK / LES MASON
575) MORTON GOLDSHOLL / JOHN WEBER / TOM MILLER
576) HERBIE BOSSARDT / JACQUES LATREILLE
577) FRED TROLLER
578) PHIL JORDAN / TED ZEIGLER
579) WILLIAM R. TOBIAS
580) LARRY CRETER
581) CHARLES E. WHITE III / CAROL BOUMAN / FLUID DRIVE STUDIO
582) RUSTY KAY

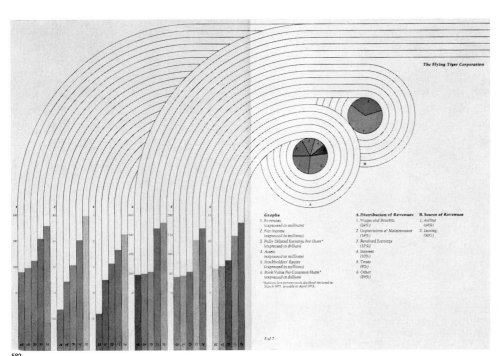

582

Art Director | Directeur artistique:

574) LES MASON
575) MORTON GOLDSHOLL
576) JACQUES LATREILLE
577) FRED TROLLER
578) PHIL JORDAN
579) WILLIAM R. TOBIAS
580) BRUCE BECK
581) ROLLIN BINZER
582) ROBERT MILES RUNYAN

Agency | Agentur | Agence – Studio:

574) HAYES ADVERTISING
575) GOLDSHOLL ASSOC.
576) TRIPLUS
577) ROSE WILLETT ASSOC.
578) BEVERIDGE & ASSOC., INC.
580) THE DESIGN PARTNERSHIP, INC.
581) BILL TAILFORD ASSOC.
582) ROBERT MILES RUNYAN & ASSOC.

Annual Reports
Jahresberichte
Rapports annuels

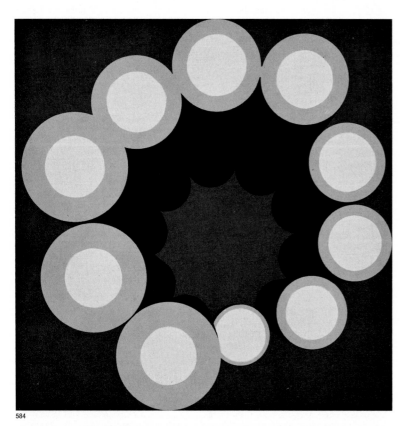

584

585

586

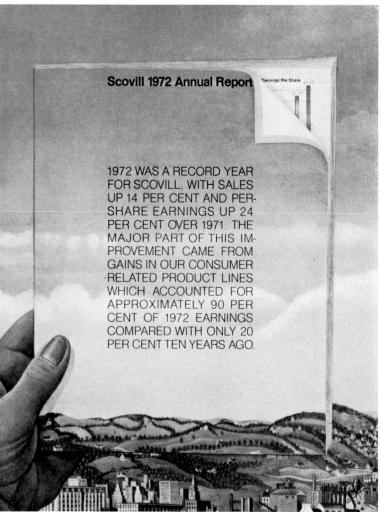

Scovill 1972 Annual Report Earnings Per Share

1972 WAS A RECORD YEAR
FOR SCOVILL, WITH SALES
UP 14 PER CENT AND PER-
SHARE EARNINGS UP 24
PER CENT OVER 1971. THE
MAJOR PART OF THIS IM-
PROVEMENT CAME FROM
GAINS IN OUR CONSUMER
RELATED PRODUCT LINES
WHICH ACCOUNTED FOR
APPROXIMATELY 90 PER
CENT OF 1972 EARNINGS
COMPARED WITH ONLY 20
PER CENT TEN YEARS AGO.

587

Artist | Künstler | Artiste:

583)–585) CLAUS ROSTRUP
586)–589) RICHARD HESS / LESLIE A. SEGAL

583)–585) Cover design (actually a profits diagram), double spread and corresponding colour page (diagram showing European alcohol production figures, with transparent overlay) from an annual report of A/S De Danske Spritfabrikker. (DEN)

586)–589) From the 1972 annual report of the Scovill Manufacturing Company, a diversified enterprise. Fig. 586 is a colour illustration of detailed planning, fig. 587 is the cover-within-a-cover, fig. 588 is a colour graph of product group earnings, and fig. 589 is a colour illustration of a household appliance division (actual size). (USA)

583)–585) Umschlaggraphik (eigentlich ein Gewinndiagramm), Doppelseite und entsprechende Farbseite (Diagramm der europäischen Alkoholherstellungsziffern, mit durchsichtigem Zwischenblatt) aus dem Jahresbericht der A/S De Danske Spritfabrikker. (DEN)

586)–589) Aus dem Jahresbericht für 1972 der Scovill Manufacturing Company, ein Konglomerat. Abb. 586 ist eine Farbillustration der ausführlichen Planung, Abb. 587 ist der Umschlag, Abb. 588 ist ein Farbdiagramm der Produktegruppen-Erträge, und Abb. 589 ist eine Farbillustration der Haushaltgeräteabteilung (in Originalgrösse). (USA)

583)–585) Design de couverture (graphique montrant l'évolution des bénéfices), double page et page couleur correspondante (graphique montrant la production européenne d'alcool, avec cache transparente). Rapport annuel, De Danske Spritfabrikker. (DEN)

586)–589) Rapport annuel 1972 de la Scovill Manufacturing Company, une société diversifiée. 586: Illustration couleur d'un planning détaillé; 587: une couverture dans la couverture; 588: graphique en couleur présentant les bénéfices par groupes de produits; 589: illustration couleur, grandeur nature, d'une division d'équipements ménagers. (USA)

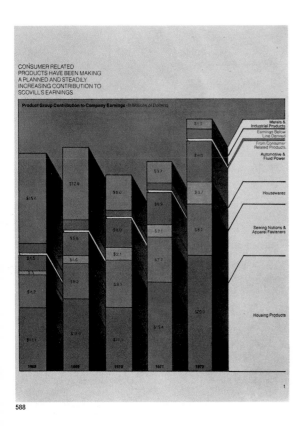

588

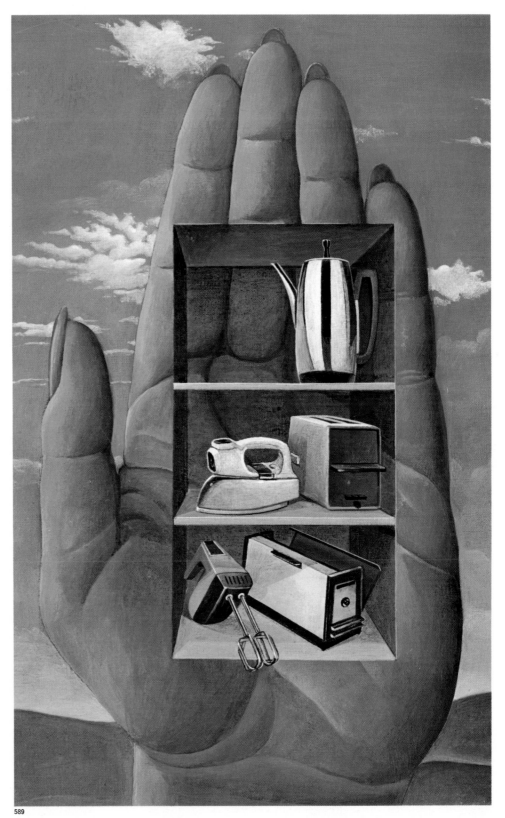

589

Art Director | Directeur artistique:

583)–585) PETER WEYRICH
586)–589) LESLIE A. SEGAL

Agency | Agentur | Agence – Studio:

583)–585) WA & BATES A/S
586)–589) CORPORATE ANNUAL REPORTS, INC.

Annual Reports / Jahresberichte / Rapports Annuels

Artist | Künstler | Artiste:

590) THE WORKSHOP / JOHN CHEPELSKY
591) DANIEL WILL
592) S.D.E.
593) ISADORE SELTZER
594) TOM CARNASE / HERB LUBALIN / ELLEN SHAPIRO
595) PETER J. BLANK / DON MENELL
596) ARNOLD SAKS / INGO SCHARRENBROICH
597) 598) SHELDON SEIDLER

Art Director | Directeur artistique:

590) JOHN CHEPELSKY / KENT PUCKETT
591) CHRISTIAN SCHMUTZ
593) LESLIE A. SEGAL
594) HERB LUBALIN
596) ARNOLD SAKS
597) 598) SHELDON SEIDLER

590

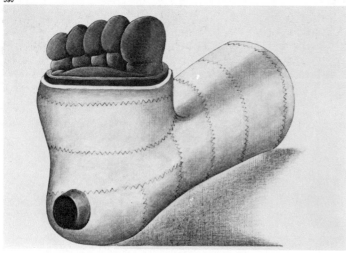

591

592

International Foodservice Systems, Inc. 1973 Annual Report

593

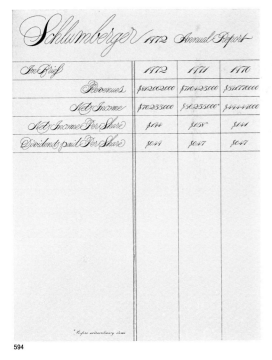

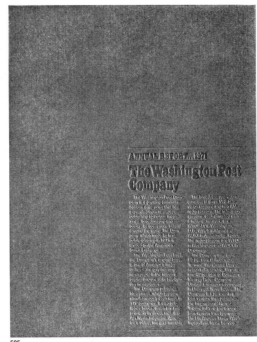

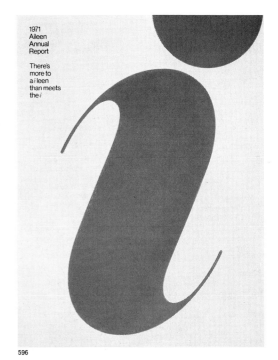

594   595   596

590) Colour illustration of a plaster cast from an annual report of Roanoke Memorial Hospitals. (USA)
591) Cover illustration for the annual report of a bank. (SWI)
592) Annual report cover for *Nicolas,* wine merchants. (FRA)
593) Cover of an annual report of International Foodservice Systems, Inc. (USA)
594) Cover of a *Schlumberger* annual report. (USA)
595) Cover of an annual report in the form of a matrix for The Washington Post Company. (USA)
596) Cover of an annual report of Aileen, Inc., a fashion company. Red 'i'. (USA)
597) 598) Cover (black with embossed printed circuit) and page with a diagram from an annual report of Redactron Corporation, office equipment manufacturers. (USA)

590) Farbillustration eines Gipsverbandes aus einem Jahresbericht eines Krankenhauses. (USA)
591) Umschlagillustration für den Jahresbericht der Bank für Anlagen und Beteiligungen AG. (SWI)
592) Umschlag eines Jahresberichts für einen Weinhändler. (FRA)
593) Umschlag eines Jahresberichts von International Foodservice Systems, Inc. (USA)
594) Umschlag eines *Schlumberger*-Jahresberichts. (USA)
595) Umschlag eines Jahresberichts in der Form einer Mater für die Washington Post Company. (USA)
596) Umschlag eines Jahresberichts für eine Modefirma. (USA)
597) 598) Umschlag (schwarz mit blindgeprägter Druckschaltung) und Seite mit Diagramm aus einem Bericht der Redactron Corporation, Hersteller von Büroausstattungen. (USA)

590) Illustration couleur d'un plâtre, pour un rapport annuel des Roanoke Memorial Hospitals. (USA)
591) Illustration de couverture. Rapport annuel bancaire. (SWI)
592) Rapport annuel du négociant en vins *Nicolas.* (FRA)
593) Couverture d'un rapport annuel d'International Foodservice Systems, Inc. (USA)
594) Couverture d'un rapport annuel *Schlumberger.* (USA)
595) Couverture d'un rapport annuel sous forme d'un flan d'imprimerie pour la Washington Post Company. (USA)
596) Couverture d'un rapport annuel d'Aileen, Inc., un spécialiste des modes. Le «i» est rouge. (USA)
597) 598) Couverture (noire, avec circuit imprimé en relief) et page avec un graphique. Rapport annuel de la Redactron Corp. (équipements de bureaux). (USA)

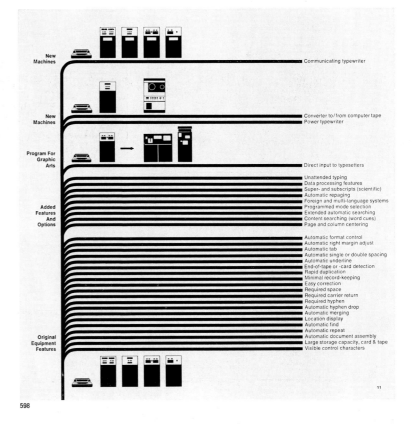

597   598

Agency | Agentur | Agence – Studio:

590) BRAND-EDMONDS & PUCKETT
591) CREATION 3 S.A.
592) S.D.E.
593) CORPORATE ANNUAL REPORTS, INC.
594) LUBALIN, SMITH, CARNASE
595) WKA CORPORATE GRAPHICS
596) ARNOLD SAKS, INC.
597) 598) SHELDON SEIDLER, INC.

599

600

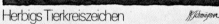

601

602

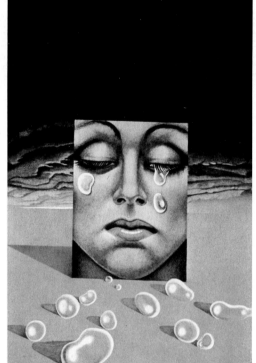

603

604

599)–601) Colour covers for small books for those born in the various Signs of the Zodiac. (AUS)

602)–604) Colour covers from a mystery and horror series. (GER)

605) Cover of a crime story. Lock and key in black and yellow, red blood. (USA)

606) Colour cover for a small book containing tales of imaginary villages in Masuria. (GER)

607) 608) Cover, with detail, of a book about the film world (The Crimes of Hollywood). (ITA)

599)–601) Farbumschläge für Tierkreiszeichenbüchlein. (AUS)

602)–604) Farbumschläge für eine Buchreihe mit Grusel- und Horrorgeschichten. (GER)

605) Umschlag für eine Kriminalgeschichte. Schloss und Schlüssel in Schwarz und Gelb, rotes Blut. (USA)

606) Farbumschlag für ein kleines Buch mit masurischen Geschichten von Siegfried Lenz. (GER)

607) 608) Umschlag, mit Detail der Illustration, für ein Buch über die Welt des Films (Die Verbrechen von Hollywood). (ITA)

599)–601) Couvertures couleurs de petits livres astrologiques pour les natifs des différents signes du zodiaque. (AUS)

602)–604) Couvertures couleurs. Série de mystère. (GER)

605) Couverture d'un roman policier. Serrure et clé noires et jaunes, sang rouge. (USA)

606) Couverture couleur d'un petit livre de nouvelles sur des villages imaginaires en Mazurie. (GER)

607) 608) Couverture, avec détail de celle-ci. Ouvrage consacré au monde du cinéma (Les Crimes d'Hollywood). (ITA)

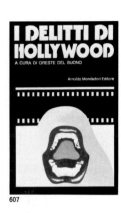

605

606

607

Artist | Künstler | Artiste:

599)–601) WALTER SCHMÖGNER
602)–604) HANS-ULRICH + UTE OSTERWALDER
605) STANISLAW ZAGORSKI
606) EDUARD PRÜSSEN
607) 608) FERENC PINTÉR

Art Director | Directeur artistique:

605) RALLOU HARSHAW
607) 608) BRUNO BINOSI

Publisher | Verleger | Editeur:

599)–601) F. A. HERBIG, VERLAGSBUCHHANDLUNG
602)–604) INSEL VERLAG
605) DOUBLEDAY & CO., INC.
606) EUROPÄISCHE BILDUNGSGEMEINSCHAFT VERLAGS GMBH
607) 608) ARNOLDO MONDADORI

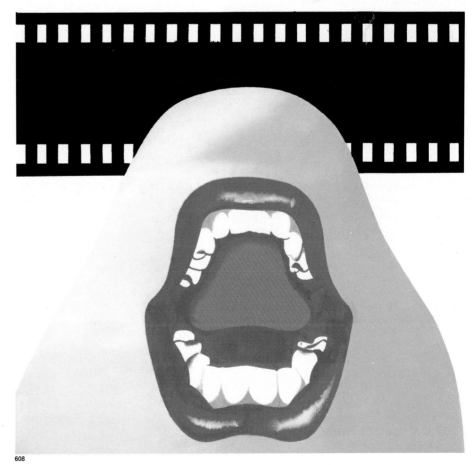

Book Covers
Buchumschläge
Couvertures de livres

608

609) 616) Artwork and complete cover for a spy story. (USA)
610) Cover for a book about an aspect of university life. (USA)
611) Cover for a novel about growing up on a farm. (USA)
612) Cover for a collection of short stories by Nabokov. Butterfly in red and yellow shades. (USA)
613) Cover of a book issued on the occasion of an Arts Council exhibition about mechanisms contributing to the destruction of the environment. (GBR)
614) Cover for a collection of satirical pieces by a well-known Israeli writer. (NLD)
615) Cover for an illustrated collection of poems. Black and red-brown, embossed title. (SPA)
617) 618) Complete cover, with detail of artwork, for a thriller about brain-washing. (USA)

609) 616) Illustration und vollständiger Umschlag für eine Spionagegeschichte (Enger Ausgang). (USA)
610) Umschlag eines Buches über einen Aspekt des Lebens in Hochschulen. (USA)
611) Umschlag eines Romans (Jugend auf dem Lande). (USA)
612) Umschlag für Kurzgeschichten von Nabokov. Farbig. (USA)
613) Umschlag eines Buches, das anlässlich einer Kunstausstellung über Mechanismen der Umweltzerstörung herausgegeben wurde. (GBR)
614) Buchumschlag für eine Sammlung satirischer Stücke des israelischen Schriftstellers Ephraim Kishon. (NLD)
615) Umschlag für einen illustrierten Gedichtband. Schwarz und rötlich-braun mit geprägtem Titel. (SPA)
617) 618) Vollständiger Umschlag, mit Detail der Illustration, für einen Schauerroman über Gehirnwäsche. (USA)

609) 616) Couverture d'un roman d'espionnage. (USA)
610) Couverture d'un livre traitant des universités. (USA)
611) Couverture de roman (une enfance au Vermont). (USA)
612) Couverture d'un recueil de nouvelles de Nabokov. Papillon aux tons rouges et jaunes. (USA)
613) Couverture d'un livre publié à l'occasion d'une exposition de l'Arts Council sur les mécanismes responsables de la destruction de notre environnement. (GBR)
614) Couverture d'un recueil de textes satiriques par un écrivain israélien connu. (NLD)
615) Couverture d'un recueil poétique. Noir, brun rouge. (SPA)
617) 618) Couverture complète et détail de la composition. Roman à suspense sur un lavage de cerveau. (USA)

609

610

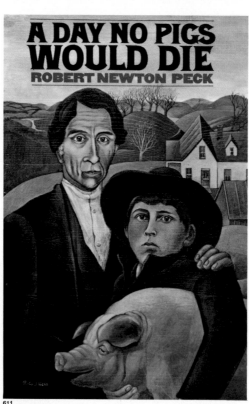

611

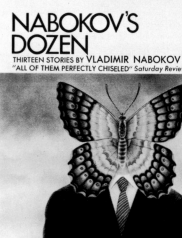

612

Artist | Künstler | Artiste:

609) 616) ROGER HANE
610) WILLI BAUM
611) RICHARD HESS / ROBERT SCUDELLARI
612) GERVASIO GALLARDO
613) ALAN FLETCHER / COLIN FORBES
614) FRISO HENSTRA
615) ANTONI TÀPIES
617) 618) DON IVAN PUNCHATZ

Art Director | Directeur artistique:

609) 616) FRANK METZ
610) WILLI BAUM
611) ROBERT SCUDELLARI
612) 617) 618) BARBARA BERTOLI
613) ALAN FLETCHER
614) WIM MOL
615) R. GIRALT MIRACLE

**Book Covers / Buchumschläge
Couvertures de livres**

Agency | Agentur | Agence – Studio:

613) PENTAGRAM DESIGN PARTNERSHIP

Publisher | Verleger | Editeur:

609) 616) SIMON & SCHUSTER, INC.
610) JOSSEY-BASS, INC.
611) ALFRED KNOPF, INC.
612) 617) 618) AVON BOOKS
613) THE ARTS COUNCIL OF GREAT BRITAIN
614) DE ARBEIDERSPERS
615) FILOGRAF-R.G.M.

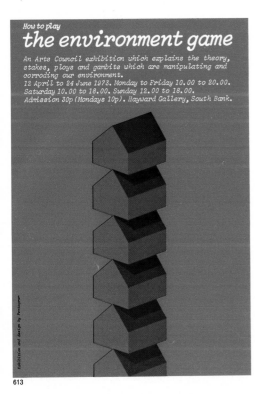

613

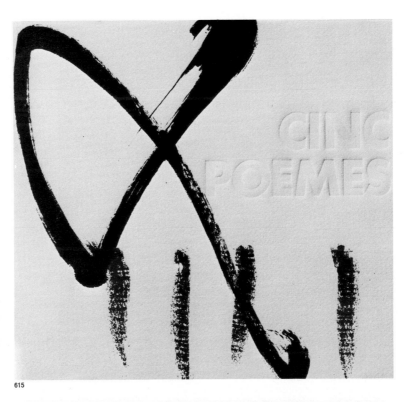

615

616

617

614

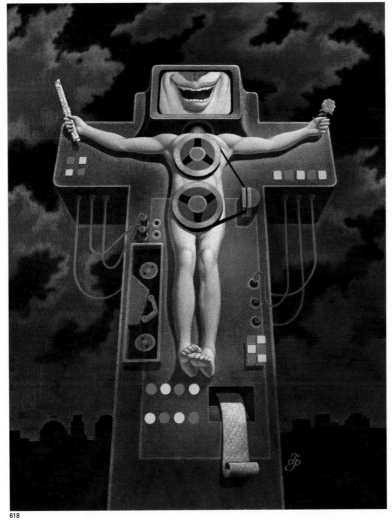

618

619

620

621

623

624

625

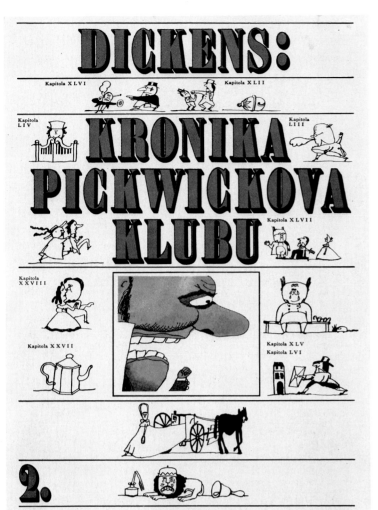

622

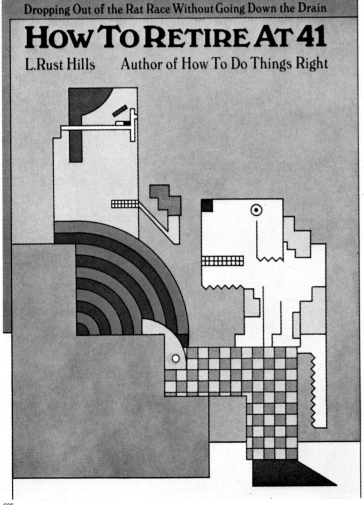

626

627

A Midsummer Night's Dream

628

The Rape of Lucrece

629

The Merry Wives of Windsor

630

Artist | Künstler | Artiste:

628)–630) DAVID GENTLEMAN
631) TURGAY BETIL
632) JAROSLAV SURA
633) WILLI BAUM
634) JEAN ALESSANDRINI
635) 636) ANDRÉ FRANÇOIS
637) FRISO HENSTRA
638) MARLENKA STUPICA

Art Director | Directeur artistique:

631) TURGAY BETIL
633) WILLI BAUM
634)–636) MASSIM
637) MILDRED KANTROWITZ

Publisher | Verleger | Editeur:

628)–630) PENGUIN BOOKS LTD.
631) HÜR YAYINEVI
632) MELANTRICH
633) JOSSEY-BASS, INC.
634)–636) GALLIMARD
637) PARENTS' MAGAZINE
PRESS

628)–630) Three covers for the new *Penguin* series of the works of Shakespeare. (GBR)
631) Cover for a paperback novel. Artwork yellow, purple, green and black, green title. (TUR)
632) Cover for a Czech version of a work by an Italian novelist. Red and purple on black. (CSR)
633) Cover for a psychological work. Yellow drawing on black, white lettering. (USA)
634) Colour cover for a paperback novel. (FRA)
635) 636) Covers in muted colours for paperback translations of famous American novels. (FRA)
637) Cover for an illustrated children's book about a princess who rescued a prince. (USA)
638) Cover for a book of short stories for children. Full colour on blue ground. (CSR)

628)–630) Drei Umschläge für eine neue *Penguin*-Serie mit den Werken von Shakespeare. (GBR)
631) Umschlag der Taschenbuchausgabe eines Romans. Illustration gelb, violett, grün und schwarz. Titel in Grün. (TUR)
632) Umschlag für die tschechische Version eines Werkes von Alberto Moravia. Rot und violett auf Schwarz. Weisse Schrift. (CSR)
633) Umschlag eines psychologischen Werkes. Gelbe Zeichnung auf schwarzem Grund mit weisser Schrift. (USA)
634) Umschlag für einen Roman in Taschenbuchausgabe. Mehrfarbig. (FRA)
635) 636) Umschläge für Taschenbuchausgaben von zwei bekannten amerikanischen Romanen. In dumpfen Tönen. (FRA)
637) Umschlag für ein illustriertes Kinderbuch. Mehrfarbig. (USA)
638) Buchumschlag für Kurzgeschichten für Kinder. Mehrfarbig auf blauem Grund. (CSR)

628)–630) Trois couvertures pour la nouvelle série *Penguin* des œuvres de Shakespeare. (GBR)
631) Couverture d'un roman de poche. Composition jaune, pourpre, verte et noire, titre vert. (TUR)
632) Couverture de l'édition tchèque d'un roman italien. Rouge et pourpre sur noir. (CSR)
633) Couverture d'un ouvrage de psychologie. Dessin jaune sur noir, lettres blanches. (USA)
634) Couverture d'un roman de poche. (FRA)
635) 636) Couverture aux tons mats pour des traductions de poche de deux grands romans américains. (FRA)
637) Couverture d'un livre d'enfants illustré (une princesse y vient au secours d'un prince). En polychromie. (USA)
638) Couverture d'un recueil de nouvelles pour enfants. Polychromie, fond bleu. (CSR)

631

632

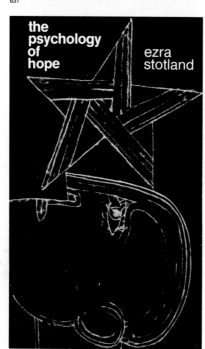

633

634

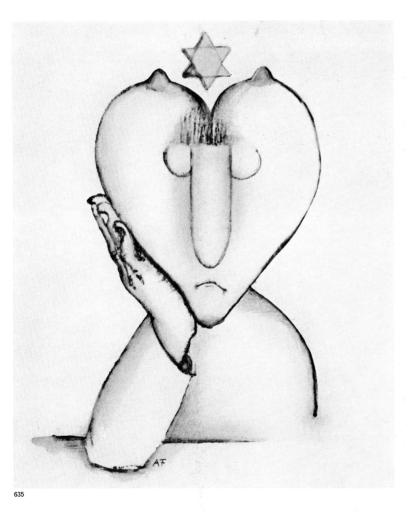

635

636

Petronella

by JAY WILLIAMS

with pictures by FRISO HENSTRA

637

KROJAČEK HLAČEK

638

Book Covers / Buchumschläge / Couvertures de livres

4

Calendars

Trade Marks and Symbols

Letterheads

Packaging

Gramophone Record Covers

Kalender

Schutzmarken

Briefköpfe

Packungen

Schallplatten-Umschläge

Calendriers

Marques et emblèmes

En-têtes

Emballages

Pochettes de disques

639

640

639)–643) Illustrations and one complete sheet from an issue of *Push Pin Graphic,* a publication of the Push Pin Studios, in the form of a calendar for 1974, with illustrations done in the style of the twenties. (USA)

644) Artwork, showing the ruins of Baalbek, from a sheet of a large calendar for the Brazilian airline *Varig.* Full colour. (BRA)

645) 'Good printing is our beer!' Sheet of a calendar for the printer Alfred Pfaff KG. Bright colours. (GER)

646) 647) Calendar for the Container Corporation of America, shown flat and in three-dimensional form (with lid flaps tucked in). White print on dark red. (USA)

639)–643) Illustrationen und ein vollständiges Blatt aus einer Nummer von *Push Pin Graphic,* einer Publikation der Push Pin Studios, in der Form eines Kalenders für das Jahr 1974, der an den Stil der zwanziger Jahre erinnert. (USA)

644) Darstellung der Ruinen von Baalbek auf einem Blatt des grossformatigen Kalenders der brasilianischen Fluggesellschaft *Varig.* Mehrfarbig. (BRA)

645) Blatt aus einem Kalender der Druckerei Al'Press Alfred Pfaff KG, Offset- und Buchdruck. In bunten Farben. (GER)

646) 647) Kalender für die Container Corporation of America, hier flach und in dreidimensionaler Form gezeigt (mit eingesteckten Deckelklappen). Weiss auf Dunkelrot. (USA)

644

Gut drucken   ist unser Bier!

645

641

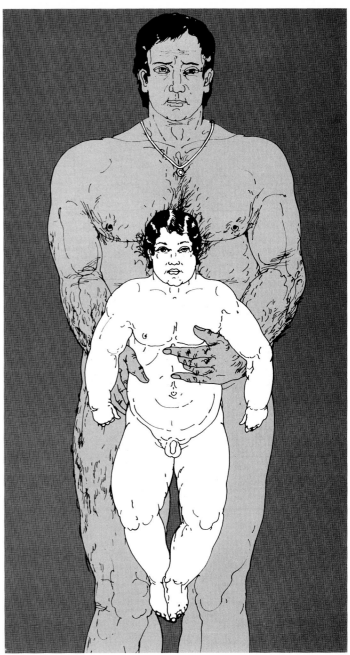

642

639)–643) Illustrations et un feuillet complet d'un numéro de *Push Pin Graphic,* publication des Push Pin Studios, présenté sous forme d'un calendrier style rétro pour 1974. (USA)
644) Composition montrant les ruines de Balbek. Illustration d'un feuillet pour un calendrier au grand format de la compagnie aérienne brésilienne *Varig.* En polychromie. (BRA)
645) «L'impression de qualité est notre affaire» – ou notre bière, comme disent les Allemands. Feuillet de calendrier pour l'imprimerie Alfred Pfaff KG. Couleurs vives. (GER)
646) 647) Calendrier pour la Container Corporation of America, montré à plat et sous forme tridimensionnelle, avec les languettes du couvercle insérées et rabattues. Impression blanche sur fond rouge foncé. (USA)

Artist | Künstler | Artiste:

639) SEYMOUR CHWAST
640) 641) HARUO MIYAUCHI
642) 643) CHRISTIAN PIPER
644) NELSON JUNGBLUTH
645) ADRIAN LACOUR
646) 647) BILL BONNELL III

Art Director | Directeur artistique:

639)–643) SEYMOUR CHWAST
644) NELSON JUNGBLUTH
645) ADRIAN LACOUR
646) 647) BILL BONNELL III

Agency | Agentur | Agence – Studio:

639)–643) PUSH PIN STUDIOS
644) VARIG PROPAGANDA
645) LEONHARDT & KERN
646) 647) CONTAINER CORP. OF AMERICA

646

647

643

Calendars / Kalender
Calendriers

648

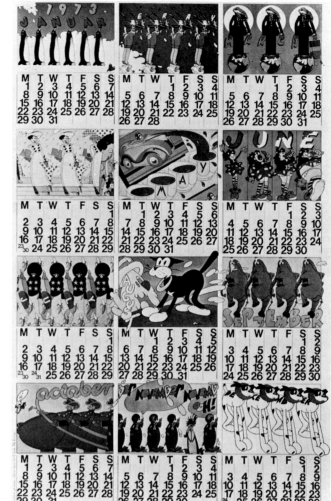

650

649

651

Artist / Künstler / Artiste:

648) PAUL WILLIAMS
649) KEN DALLISON /
     E. YOCHUM
650) CHRIS MCEWAN
651) WALTER GRIEDER
652) GERD GRIMM
653) STEPHAN ZAVREL
654) COLMAN COHEN

Art Director / Directeur artistique:

649) E. YOCHUM
651) WALTER GRIEDER
652) GERD GRIMM
653) 654) PINO USICCO

Agency / Agentur / Agence – Studio:

649) KETCHUM, MACLEOD
     & GROVE, INC.
650) CONRAN ASSOC. LTD.
653) 654) QUADRAGONO

Calendars
Kalender
Calendriers

652

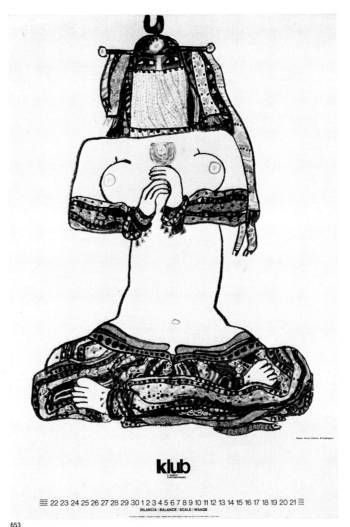

653

648) Sheet of a large calendar entitled 'Americana' for the Scott Paper Co. The 1973 issue was dedicated to the legendary folk hero. The full-colour illustration shows Captain Kidd with some of his booty. (USA)
649) Sheet of the Scott Paper Co.'s calendar for 1974, devoted to the conquest of the skies. This month illustrates the work of Sikorsky. (USA)
650) Complete *habitat* calendar in comic-strip style with the names of the months incorporated in the full-colour drawings. (GBR)
651) Sheet of a calendar issued by a publisher of children's picture books. Full colour. (SWI)
652) Sheet of a large calendar for a printer, August Faller KG. (GER)
653) 654) Sheets of a large calendar for *klub*, a furniture supplier, with interpretations of the Signs of the Zodiac by twelve different artists. The Scales (Libra) and the Fishes (Pisces) are shown here. (ITA)

648) Blatt aus einem grossformatigen Kalender mit dem Titel «Americana» für die Papierfabrik Scott Paper Co. Die Ausgabe für das Jahr 1973 war dem legendären Volkshelden gewidmet. Die Illustration zeigt Captain Kidd mit seiner Raubbeute. In bunten Farben. (USA)
649) Blatt aus dem Kalender für 1974 der Scott Paper Company, der der Eroberung der Luft gewidmet ist. Dieser Monat zeigt die Leistungen Sikorskys (die Helikopter). (USA)
650) Vollständiger *habitat*-Kalender im Comic-Strip-Stil. Die Namen der Monate sind in den mehrfarbigen Zeichnungen integriert. (GBR)
651) Blatt aus einem Kalender der Bilderbücher der Sechs, Herausgeber von farbigen Bilderbüchern. Mehrfarbig. (SWI)
652) Blatt aus dem Kalender der Offsetdruckerei August Faller KG. (GER)
653) 654) Blätter aus einem grossformatigen Kalender für *klub*, einen Möbellieferanten, mit Interpretationen der Tierkreiszeichen durch zwölf verschiedene Künstler – hier Waage und Fische. (ITA)

648) Feuillet d'un calendrier au grand format, intitulé «Americana», de la Scott Paper Co. Celui de 1973 était consacré au héros légendaire; ici le capitaine Kidd avec une partie de son butin de pirate. (USA)
649) Feuillet du calendrier de la Scott Paper Co. pour 1974, consacré à la conquête du ciel: ici, l'œuvre de Sikorsky (les hélicoptères). (USA)
650) Calendrier *habitat* complet, style bandes dessinées, avec les noms des mois incorporés dans les dessins polychromes. (GBR)
651) Feuillet d'un calendrier publié par un éditeur de livres d'enfants. En polychromie. (SWI)
652) Feuillet du calendrier grand format de l'imprimerie August Faller KG. En polychromie. (GER)
653) 654) Feuillets d'un calendrier grand format pour la maison d'ameublement *klub*. Interprétation des signes du zodiaque par douze artistes différents: ici, la Balance (Libra) et les Poissons (Pisces). (ITA)

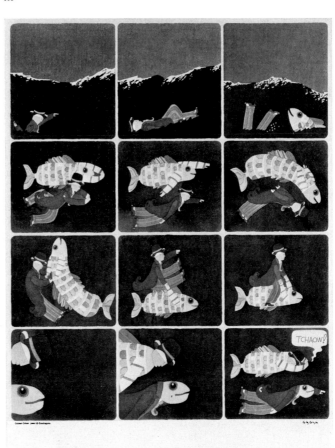

654

Artist | Künstler | Artiste:
655)–659) F.-K. WAECHTER / H. HARALD SCHMITZ
660) KURT HALBRITTER / H. HARALD SCHMITZ

Art Director | Directeur artistique:
655)–660) HANNGEORG VOTTELER

Agency | Agentur | Agence – Studio:
655)–660) VOKO WERBEABTEILUNG

655

656

655)–660) Complete sheet and a selection of the colour illustrations from a large calendar issued by *Voko,* office furniture manufacturers, and taking as its theme the relation of the human being to the office. The drawings reproduced here illustrate: fig. 656, the supervisory duties of the boss; fig. 657, satisfaction in one's work; fig. 658, 'Who is the greatest?'; fig. 659, the cult of authority; fig. 660, sexual equality (black-and-white drawing). (GER)

655)–660) Vollständiges Blatt und eine Auswahl der Farbillustrationen aus einem grossformatigen Kalender der *Voko*-Büromöbelfabriken in Giessen. Der Kalender behandelt verschiedene Aspekte der Beziehungen des Menschen zum Büro. Die hier reproduzierten Zeichnungen illustrieren: Abb. 656, die Aufsichtspflichten des Chefs; Abb. 657, Befriedigung in der Arbeit; Abb. 658, «Wer ist der Grösste?»; Abb. 659, den Autoritätskult; Abb. 660, sexuelle Gleichberechtigung (schwarzweisse Zeichnung). (GER)

655)–660) Feuillet complet et choix d'illustrations couleurs tirés d'un calendrier grand format de *Voko,* un fabricant d'équipements de bureaux, sur le thème de l'homme et du bureau. Les dessins reproduits ici illustrent la fonction de contrôle du patron (656), la satisfaction au travail (657), la lutte pour le pouvoir (658), le culte de l'autorité (659) et l'égalité des sexes (660, dessin noir et blanc). (GER)

657

658

659

660

217

661

661) 662) Covers of calendars for the Viennese printers Brüder Rosenbaum. Fig. 661 green, brown, black and silver on orange, fig. 662 black and silver on yellow. (AUS)

663) Calendar printed on linen board for the bookbinding materials of the *Zanders* paper company. The available colours are shown on the elephant's legs. (GER)

664)–666) Two double spreads in colour and a typical calendar page from the 1974 *Olivetti* agenda. The paintings of American scenes have the cracked effect of old canvases. (ITA)

667) 668) Colour pages from a Reserve Officers' Training Corps appointments schedule, illustrating a quotation from Carl Sandburg and the meeting of the Trans-American railroad. (USA)

669) 670) Examples of the trees shown in the 1974 calendar of Matsushita Electric Co. Ltd. Black and white on blue (fig. 669) and on yellow (fig. 670). (JPN)

661) 662) Umschläge der Kalender für die Wiener Druckerei Brüder Rosenbaum. Abb. 661 Grün, Braun, Schwarz und Silber auf Orange, Abb. 662 Schwarz und Silber auf Gelb. (AUS)

663) Auf Leinwand gedruckter Kalender für die Einbandstoffe der *Zanders* Feinpapiere GmbH. Die erhältlichen Farben sind auf den Beinen des Elefanten ersichtlich. (GER)

664)–666) Mehrfarbige Doppelseiten und typische Kalenderseite aus der *Olivetti*-Agenda für 1974. Die Gemälde von Szenen aus dem amerikanischen Leben haben die rissige Wirkung von alter Leinwand. (USA)

667) 668) Farbseiten aus einem Terminkalender für ein Armeekorps. Sie illustrieren ein Zitat von Carl Sandburg und die Fertigstellung der amerikanischen Eisenbahn. (USA)

669) 670) Beispiele der Bäume aus dem Kalender für 1974 der Matsushita Electric Co. Ltd. Schwarzweiss auf Blau (Abb. 669) und auf Gelb (Abb. 670). (JPN)

661) 662) Couvertures de calendriers pour l'imprimerie viennoise Brüder Rosenbaum: (661) vert, brun, noir, argent sur orange; (662) noir, argent sur jaune. (AUS)

663) Calendrier imprimé sur carton toilé, pour les matériaux de reliure de la papeterie *Zanders*. Les couleurs disponibles sont indiquées sur les pattes de l'éléphant. (GER)

664)–666) Deux doubles pages couleur et page type de calendrier tirées de l'agenda *Olivetti* pour 1974. Les peintures de genre américaines ont l'aspect craquelé de vieux tableaux. (ITA)

667) 668) Pages couleur d'un carnet de rendez-vous du Reserve Officers' Training Corps. Thème: citation de Carl Sandburg; la rencontre des tronçons ouest et est du chemin de fer transaméricain. (USA)

669) 670) Exemples des arbres du calendrier 1974 de Matsushita Electric Co. Ltd. Noir-blanc sur bleu (669) et sur jaune (670). (JPN)

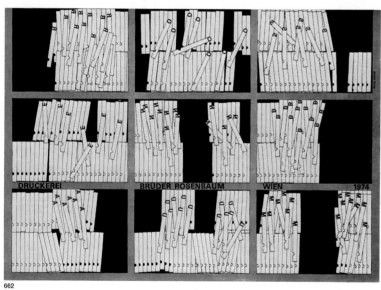
662

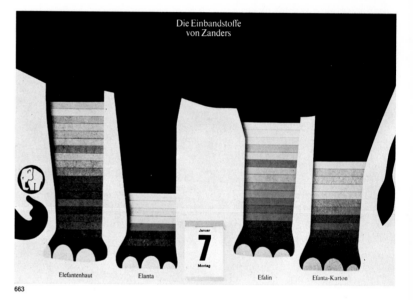
663

664

665

667

668

669

670

666

	19 AUGUST SONNTAG	20 AUGUST MONTAG	21 AUGUST DIENSTAG	22 AUGUST MITTWOCH	23 AUGUST DONNERSTAG	24 AUGUST FREITAG	25 AUGUST SAMSTAG

Artist | Künstler | Artiste:

661) 662) GEORG SCHMID
663) KLAUS WINTERHAGER
664) 665) PAUL DAVIS
666) ENZO MARI
667) 668) MABEY TROUSDELL, INC.
669) 670) HENRY TOMURA / MASAO
SUZUKI / MASAYA FUJIMOTO

Art Director | Directeur artistique:

664)—666) GEORGIO SOAVI
667) 668) MABEY TROUSDELL, INC.
669) 670) HIDEHIKO BAMBA

Agency | Agentur | Agence – Studio:

664)—666) OLIVETTI, UFFICIO PUBBLICITÀ
667) 668) MABEY TROUSDELL, INC.

**Calendars
Kalender
Calendriers**

671) Symbol for a new shopping centre called *Rotunda*. (USA)
672) Symbol for Happy Hotels, Inc. (FIN)
673) Quality symbol for national use. (YUG)
674) Symbol for *Serena,* an international chain of hotels and lodges. (USA)
675) Symbol for Denver Symphony Orchestra. (USA)
676) Symbol for the Sonja Henie-Niels Onstad Foundations in Oslo. (NOR)
677) Symbol for a computer game for students. (USA)
678) A new KOOR emblem based on the Hebrew letter K. (ISR)
679) Emblem for the XXI Olympic Games in Montreal. The sign combines a track (centre), the winners' podium (top, also a stylized M for Montreal) and the five Olympic rings. Standard colour: red. (CAN)
680) Trade mark for Shapell Industries, Inc., Beverly Hills. (USA)
681) Logotype for a menu cover of the Hotel Meridien, Dakar. (SEN)
682) Symbol for Evanston Hospital, Chicago. (USA)
683) Symbol for the All-India Federation of Master Printers. (IND)
684) Symbol for Mountain Lake Sanctuary, Florida, which has a carillon tower. (USA)
685) Logotype for a brand of razor blades. (IND)

671) Zeichen für das neue Einkaufszentrum *Rotunda.* (USA)
672) Schutzmarke für Happy Hotels, Inc. (FIN)
673) Symbol, das im nationalen Gebrauch für Qualität steht. (YUG)
674) Emblem für *Serena,* eine internationale Kette von Hotels und Herbergen. (USA)
675) Symbol für das Denver Symphony Orchestra. (USA)
676) Symbol für die Sonja Henie-Niels Onstad-Stiftung in Oslo. (NOR)
677) Emblem für ein Computer-Spiel für Studenten. (USA)
678) Ein neues KOOR-Emblem, das auf dem hebräischen Buchstaben K basiert. (ISR)
679) Emblem für die XXI. Olympischen Spiele in Montreal. Das Zeichen vereinigt eine Aschenbahn (Mitte), das Siegerpodest (oben, auch ein stilisiertes M für Montreal) und die fünf olympischen Ringe. Standardfarbe: Rot. (CAN)
680) Schutzmarke für Shapell Industries, Inc., Beverly Hills. (USA)
681) Schriftzug für einen Menü-Umschlag des Hotels Meridien, Dakar. (SEN)
682) Symbol für das Evanston-Krankenhaus, Chicago. (USA)
683) Emblem für die All-India Federation of Master Printers. (IND)
684) Symbol für Mountain Lake Sanctuary in Florida. (USA)
685) Schriftzug für eine Marke Rasierklingen. (IND)

671) Emblème d'un nouveau centre commercial du nom de *Rotunda.* (USA)
672) Emblème de la chaîne d'hôtels Happy Hotels, Inc. (FIN)
673) Label de qualité national. (YUG)
674) Emblème de la chaîne internationale d'hôtels et de résidences *Serena.* (USA)
675) Emblème de l'Orchestre Symphonique de Denver. (USA)
676) Emblème des Fondations Sonja Henie-Niels Onstad à Oslo. (NOR)
677) Emblème d'un jeux-ordinateur pour étudiants. (USA)
678) Nouvel emblème KOOR basé sur la lettre hébreue K. (ISR)
679) Emblème des XXIes Jeux Olympiques de Montréal, combinant une piste cendrée (au centre), le podium des vainqueurs (en haut; aussi un M stylisé pour Montréal) et les cinq anneaux olympiques. Couleur standard: le rouge. (CAN)
680) Marque déposée pour Shapell Industries, Inc., à Beverly Hills. (USA)
681) Logotype pour une fourre à menu de l'Hôtel Méridien à Dakar. (SEN)
682) Emblème de l'Evanston Hospital de Chicago. (USA)
683) Emblème de la fédération nationale des maîtres-imprimeurs de l'Inde. (IND)
684) Emblème du Mountain Lake Sanctuary (Floride). (USA)
685) Logotype pour une marque de lames de rasoir. (IND)

672

675

678

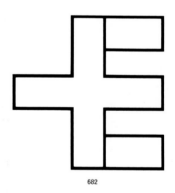

682

671

Art Director | Directeur artistique:

671) 677) I. MURRY GELBERG
672) PENTTI VARTIAINEN
674) JOHN LEES / MASON MORFIT
675) JOHN R. RIEBEN
678) DAN GELBART
679) GEORGES HUEL
680) JAMES CROSS
681) ANNEGRET BEIER
682) EDWARD HUGHES
683) PANNA JAIN
684) PETER BRADFORD
685) YESHWANT CHAUDHARY

673

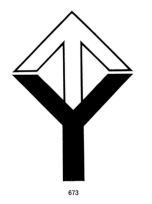

674

Artist | Künstler | Artiste:
671) 677) I. MURRY GELBERG
672) PENTTI VARTIAINEN
673) IVAN DVORSAK
674) JOHN LEES / MASON MORFIT
675) JOHN R. RIEBEN
676) ROSMARIE TISSI
678) GIDI KEICH
679) GEORGES HUEL
680) ROSALIE HANSEN
681) ANNEGRET BEIER
682) EDWARD HUGHES
683) SURESH CHINCHANKAR / PANNA JAIN
684) PETER BRADFORD
685) YESHWANT CHAUDHARY

676

677

679

680

681

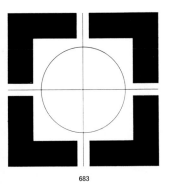

683

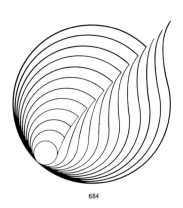

684

685

Agency | Agentur | Agence – Studio:
671) 677) DAVID M. PESANELLI, INC.
672) ADAX ADVERTISING AGENCY LTD.
674) HERMAN & LEES ASSOC.
675) RIEBEN & CRAIG
676) ODERMATT & TISSI
679) GEORGES HUEL & ASSOC., INC.
680) JAMES CROSS DESIGN OFFICE, INC.
681) DELPIRE ADVICO S.A.
682) EDWARD HUGHES DESIGN
683) MASS COMMUNICATION & MARKETING LTD.
684) PETER BRADFORD & ASSOC.
685) COMMUNICA / CORPORATE COMMUNICATIONS

Advertiser | Auftraggeber | Client:
671) MANNEKIN BROTHERS
672) HAPPY HOTELS, INC.
673) JUSK
674) SERENA HOTELS & LODGES
675) DENVER SYMPHONY ORCHESTRA
676) SONJA HENIE-NIELS ONSTAD FOUNDATIONS
677) ENVIROMETRICS
678) KOOR INDUSTRIES
679) COMITÉ ORGANISATEUR DES JEUX DE LA XXIᵉ OLYMPIADE
680) SHAPELL INDUSTRIES, INC.
681) HOTEL MERIDIEN
682) EVANSTON HOSPITAL
683) ALL INDIA FEDERATION OF MASTER PRINTERS
684) THE AMERICAN FOUNDATION
685) CENTRON INDUSTRIAL ALLIANCE LTD.

686) Symbol for *Irihama* sea-side restaurants. (JPN)
687) Trade mark for the *Bredanardi* helicopter factory. (ITA)
688) Trade mark for *Delta,* a pharmaceutical company. (GER)
689) Trade mark for *Asilin* patent plastic tubes. (SWI)
690) Symbol based on water and sun for a University of Minnesota summer arts school. (USA)
691) Trade mark for *Nortextil,* a textile enterprise. (NOR)
692) Trade mark for *Armaver* plastic tubes. (SWI)
693) Emblem for Rush-Presbyterian-St. Luke's Medical Centre, alluding to donors. (USA)
694) Trade mark for *Erber's* camera shop. (USA)
695) Trade mark for American Films, Ltd. (USA)
696) Logotype for Drugstore Montreux SA. (SWI)
697) Logotype suggesting waves for Bayhead Yacht Corp. (USA)
698) Logotype for a fashion store in Zurich. (SWI)

686) Logotype für *Irihama*-Küstenrestaurants. (JPN)
687) Schutzmarke für die *Bredanardi*-Helikopter-Fabrik. (ITA)
688) Schutzmarke für *Delta,* eine pharmazeutische Firma. (GBR)
689) Logotype für *Asilin*-Kunststoffröhren. (SWI)
690) Emblem, das auf Wasser und Sonne basiert, für eine Sommerkunstschule der Universität von Minnesota. (USA)
691) Schutzmarke für *Nortextil,* ein Textilunternehmen. (NOR)
692) Schutzmarke für *Armaver*-Kunststoffröhren. (SWI)
693) Emblem, das sich auf Spender bezieht, für das Rush-Presbyterian-St. Luke's Medical Center. (USA)
694) Schutzmarke für *Erber's* Kamerageschäft. (USA)
695) Schutzmarke für American Films, Ltd. (USA)
696) Schriftzug für das Drugstore Montreux SA. (SWI)
697) Emblem mit Anspielung auf Wellen, für Bayhead Yacht Corporation. (USA)
698) Namenszug für das Modegeschäft *Grieder* in Zürich. (SWI)

686) Emblème des restaurants *Irihama* au bord de la mer. (JPN)
687) Marque de l'usine d'hélicoptères *Bredanardi.* (ITA)
688) Marque déposée de la société pharmaceutique *Delta.* (GER)
689) Marque des tuyaux plastiques brevetés *Asilin.* (SWI)
690) Emblème combinant l'eau et le soleil, pour les cours d'été de beaux-arts de l'Université du Minnesota. (USA)
691) Marque de l'entreprise textile *Nortextil.* (NOR)
692) Marque déposée pour les tuyaux plastiques *Armaver.* (SWI)
693) Emblème du Centre médical Rush-Presbyterian-St. Luke's, avec allusion aux donateurs. (USA)
694) Marque du magasin de photo-ciné *Erber's.* (USA)
695) Marque déposée pour American Films, Ltd. (USA)
696) Logotype pour le Drugstore Montreux S. A. (SWI)
697) Logotype pour la Bayhead Yacht Corp. (USA)
698) Logotype pour un magasin de modes zurichois. (SWI)

Trade Marks / Schutzmarken
Marques et emblèmes

686

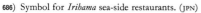

687

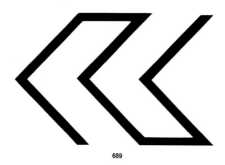

689

690

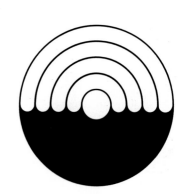

692

693

695

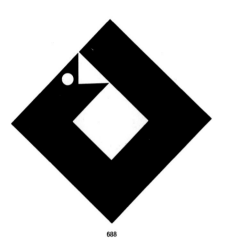

688

696

691

697

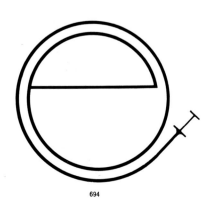

694

698

699

700

701

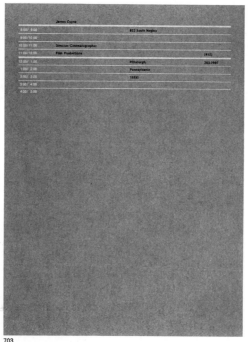

702

703

704

Artist / Künstler / Artiste:

699) 707) ALAN FLETCHER
700) MABEY TROUSDELL, INC.
701) TOM WOOD
702) NICOLE PRUDHOMME
703) J. MICHAEL ESSEX
704) JOHN NOWLAND
705) 706) TOM CARNASE / DONALD ADAMEC
708) WOODY PIRTLE
709) EDWARD HUGHES
710) DON ALMQUIST / DICK JONES
712) MERVYN KURLANSKY
713) OLA LAIHO

705

706

707

699) Stationery for a properties stylist. Yellow paper. (GBR)
700) Letterhead for WAPE Radio. Last figure in colour. (USA)
701) Letterhead for Marketplace Inc. Brown paper. (USA)
702) Stationery for *Lollipop* children's fashions. (FRA)
703) Letterhead for James Coyne, film productions. White and blue on brown. (USA)
704) Letterhead for Australian Meat and Food Industry Services Pty. Ltd. Black print. (AUL)
705) 706) Letterhead for the Art Directors Club, Inc. (USA)
707) Letterhead for The Riverside Group, a residential amenity society. Black on blue paper. (GBR)
708) Letterhead for Linda Pirtle. Black and red. (USA)
709) Letterhead for Evanston Hospital Challenge and Change fund raising campaign. Purple and yellow C. (USA)
710) Letterhead with Early American nautical motif in blue and olive for a seaside motor lodge. (USA)
711) Stationery range for Geersgross Advertising Ltd. (GBR)
712) Stationery for Tony Copeland, photographer. (GBR)
713) Letterhead for Adax Oy, an advertising agency. (FIN)

699) Briefpapier für einen Dekorateur. Gelbes Papier. (GBR)
700) Für einen Radiosender. Letzte Figur farbig. (USA)
701) Briefkopf für Marketplace Inc. Braunes Papier. (USA)
702) Briefpapier für *Lollipop*-Kindermode. (FRA)
703) Briefkopf für James Coyne, Filmproduktionen. Weiss und blau auf Braun. (USA)
704) Briefkopf für Australian Meat and Food Industry Services Pty. Ltd. Schwarz auf Weiss. (AUL)
705) 706) Briefkopf für den Art Directors Club, Inc. (USA)
707) Briefkopf für The Riverside Group, eine Organisation für bessere Wohnverhältnisse. Schwarz auf Blau. (USA)
708) Briefkopf für Linda Pirtle. Schwarz und rot. (USA)
709) Briefkopf für eine Spendenaktion des Evanston Hospital. C in Violett und Gelb. (USA)
710) Briefkopf mit frühamerikanischem nautischem Motiv in Blau und Olivgrün für ein Motel an der Küste. (USA)
711) Briefpapier für Geersgross Advertising Ltd. (GBR)
712) Briefkopf für den Photographen Tony Copeland. (GBR)
713) Briefkopf für Adax Oy, eine Werbeagentur. (FIN)

699) Papier à lettres pour un designer. Papier jaune. (GBR)
700) Pour un émetteur. Dernier personnage couleur. (USA)
701) En-tête pour Marketplace Inc. Papier brun. (USA)
702) Papier à lettres pour les modes d'enfants *Lollipop*. (FRA)
703) En-tête pour le producteur de cinéma James Coyne. Blanc et bleu sur brun. (USA)
704) En-tête pour l'Australian Meat and Food Industry Services Pty. Ltd. Impression noire. (AUL)
705) 706) En-tête de l'Art Directors Club, Inc. (USA)
707) En-tête pour le Riverside Group, une société de loisirs pour résidents du même quartier. (GBR)
708) En-tête pour Linda Pirtle. Noir et rouge. (USA)
709) En-tête pour une campagne de collecte en faveur de l'Evanston Hospital. C pourpre et jaune. (USA)
710) En-tête orné d'un ancien emblème nautique américain. Bleu, olive. Motel au bord de la mer. (USA)
711) Papier à lettres de la Geersgross Advertising Ltd. (GBR)
712) Papier à lettres du photographe Tony Copeland. (GBR)
713) En-tête de l'agence publicitaire Adax Oy. (FIN)

708

709

710

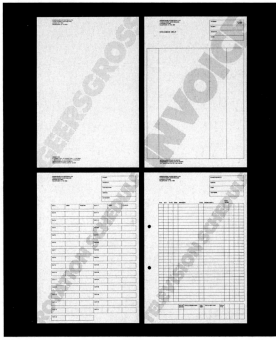

711

712

713

Art Director | Directeur artistique:

700) MABEY TROUSDELL, INC.
701) TOM WOOD
702) ANDRÉ CHANTE
703) J. MICHAEL ESSEX
704) JOHN NOWLAND
705) 706) DONALD ADAMEC
708) WOODY PIRTLE
709) EDWARD HUGHES
710) DICK JONES
712) MERVYN KURLANSKY
713) OLA LAIHO

Agency | Agentur | Agence – Studio:

699) 707) 712) PENTAGRAM DESIGN PARTNERSHIP
701) CREATIVE SERVICES, INC.
702) HOLLENSTEIN CRÉATION
703) CENTER FOR COMMUNICATION PLANNING
704) JOHN NOWLAND GRAPHIC DESIGN
705) 706) ADAMEC ASSOC.
708) THE RICHARDS GROUP
709) EDWARD HUGHES DESIGN
710) DORLAND & SWEENEY, INC.
713) G4 STUDIO

**Letterheads
Briefköpfe
En-têtes**

714) Container and folding boxes for cosmetic products made by Holiday Magic. (USA)
715) Display unit for six flavourings offered by Sunkist Growers, Inc. (USA)
716) Paper carrier bags for the *Sanyudo* confectionery store. (JPN)
717) Telescoping carton for *Frey,* confectioners in Basle. (SWI)
718) Box for a game made by Psychology Today Games. (USA)
719) Set-up box for food products of the Toga Folkart Company. (JPN)
720) Container for a beauty lotion by Dorothy Gray, Inc. (USA)

714) Töpfchen und Faltschachteln für kosmetische Produkte von Holiday Magic. (USA)
715) Ausstellungsständer für sechs verschiedene Gewürze von Sunkist Growers, Inc. (USA)
716) Tragsäcke aus Papier für das *Sanyudo*-Konfiseriegeschäft. (JPN)
717) Ausziehschachtel für die Konfiserie *Frey* in Basel. (SWI)
718) Schachtel für ein Spiel der Psychology Today Games. (USA)
719) Verpackung für Esswaren von Toga Folkart Company. (JPN)
720) Behälter für ein Schönheitswasser von Dorothy Gray, Inc. (USA)

Packaging / Packungen / Emballages

714

715

717

718

714) Conditionnement et boîtes pliantes pour des cosmétiques de Holiday Magic. (USA)
715) Présentoir pour six condiments offerts par Sunkist Growers, Inc. (USA)
716) Sacs en papier pour le magasin d'habillement *Sanyudo*. (JPN)
717) Carton-accordéon pour la confiserie *Frey* à Bâle. (SWI)
718) Boîte pour un jeu de Psychology Today Games. (USA)
719) Carton-présentoir pour des produits alimentaires de la Toga Folkart Company. (JPN)
720) Conditionnement pour une lotion de beauté de la Dorothy Gray, Inc. (USA)

716

720

719

Artist | Künstler | Artiste:

714) JULIE ANN ACH / LYNN SHOOK
715) JOHN ANSELMO
716) SHOZO KAKUTANI
717) PAUL STUBER
718) HOWARD SAUNDERS / TOM LEWIS
719) E. HASEGAWA / Y. SHIGEHARA / K. UMINO
720) EDWARD C. KOZLOWSKI

Art Director | Directeur artistique:

714) TOM ROBBINS
715) JOHN ANSELMO
716) SHOZO KAKUTANI
718) JOE Y. TAKAHASHI
719) EIICHI HASEGAWA
720) HERBERT R. NUBEL / EDWARD C. KOZLOWSKI

Agency | Agentur | Agence – Studio:

714) SOUTHERN CALIFORNIA CARTON
715) JOHN ANSELMO DESIGN ASSOC.
716) KAKUTANI DESIGN OFFICE
718) COMMUNICATIONS, RESEARCH, MACHINES, INC.
719) MADISON AD & CREATIVE AGENCY
720) EDWARD C. KOZLOWSKI DESIGN, INC.

721) Hanging dispensers for ISS mouth guards. (AUL)
722) Bottle styling for *Puschkin* vodka. (GER)
723) Bottle styling for a wine marketed by Alois Lageder, Bolzano. (ITA)
724) Bottle styling for a cordial made by Alphonse Orsat SA. (SWI)
725) Bottle styling for a wine marketed by Bourgeois Frères & Cie. (SWI)
726) Bottle styling for a rosé wine made by *Suntory*. (JPN)
727) Sample packs for *Astor* lipstick. (ITA)
728) Package for confectionery made by Yasima Climbing Railroad Co. (JPN)
729) Styling for half-litre and litre bottles of *hexy* fruit juices. (GER)

721) Dispenser-Packung zum Aufhängen für ISS-Tabletten gegen Mundgeruch. (AUL)
722) Flaschengestaltung für Wodka der Marke *Puschkin*. (GER)
723) Flaschengestaltung für einen Südtiroler Wein. (ITA)
724) Flaschengestaltung für einen Marc von Alphonse Orsat SA. (SWI)
725) Flaschengestaltung für einen Walliser Rotwein von Bourgeois Frères & Cie. (SWI)
726) Flaschengestaltung für einen Roséwein von *Suntory*. (JPN)
727) Musterpackungen für *Astor*-Lippenstift. (ITA)
728) Verpackung für Konfektwaren von Yasima Climbing Railroad Co. (JPN)
729) Gestaltung für Halbliter- und Literflaschen *hexy*-Fruchtsäfte. (GER)

721) Distributeurs muraux de tablettes ISS contre une mauvaise haleine. (AUL)
722) Etude de bouteille pour la vodka *Pouchkine*. (GER)
723) Etude de bouteille pour un vin commercialisé par Alois Lageder, à Bolzano. (ITA)
724) Etude de bouteille pour un cordial fabriqué par l'Alphonse Orsat SA. (SWI)
725) Etude de bouteille pour un vin commercialisé par Bourgeois Frères & Cie. (SWI)
726) Etude de bouteille pour un rosé *Suntory*. (JPN)
727) Echantillons de rouges à lèvres *Astor*. (ITA)
728) Boîte de confiserie pour la Yasima Climbing Railroad Co. (JPN)
729) Etude de bouteilles d'un litre et d'un demi-litre de jus de fruits *hexy*. (GER)

722

723

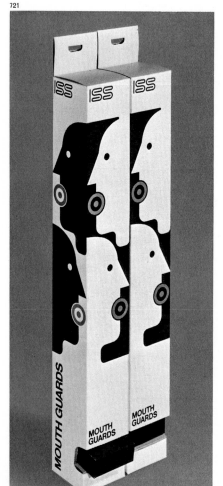

721

727

Artist | Künstler | Artiste:

721) EMERY, FOWLER-BROWN PTY. LTD.
722) WOLFGANG GESING
723) 725) EMANUEL BOSSHART
724) ERNEST WITZIG
726) SHIGESHI OMORI
727) DANTE VERNICE
728) SHOZO KAKUTANI
729) MANFRED DIETZE / WERNER WÜRDINGER

Art Director | Directeur artistique:

722) WOLFGANG GESING
723) PETER STRICKLER
724) 725) MICHEL LOGOZ
726) SHIGESHI OMORI
727) DANTE VERNICE
728) SHOZO KAKUTANI
729) WERNER WÜRDINGER

Agency | Agentur | Agence – Studio:

721) EMERY, FOWLER-BROWN PTY. LTD.
722) SPECIAL DESIGN
723)–725) ROTH & SAUTER S. A.
727) STUDIO VERNICE DESIGN & PACKAGING
728) KAKUTANI DESIGN OFFICE
729) WERBEAGENTUR GOTTSCHLING

Packaging
Packungen
Emballages

724

725

726

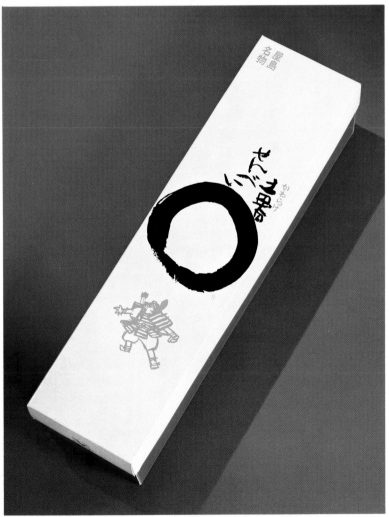

728

729

730) Folding carton for ISS ear muffs, which filter noise. (AUL)
731) Bottle design for a *Mennen* after-shave lotion. (USA)
732) Tube, container and cartons, showing the rainbow pattern that can be created in display rows, for *Juvena* cosmetic products. (SWI)
733) Specimens of packaging for *Berthier-Derol* pharmaceutical products. (FRA)
734) Range of tubes, containers and cartons for *didi* baby care products. (SWI)
735) Can design for *Merit* motor oil. (USA)
736) Range of containers and cartons for *Beauty Basics* made by Prue Acton Cosmetics. (AUL)

730

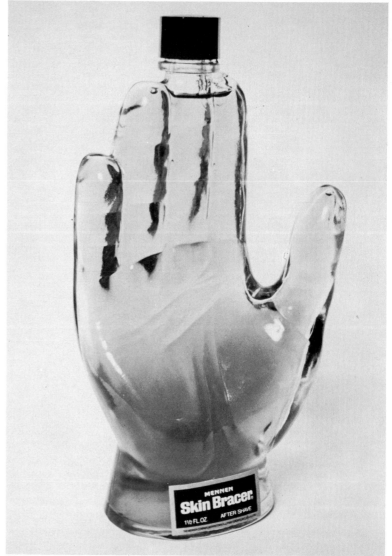

731

734

735

730) Folding carton for ISS ear muffs, which filter noise. (AUL)
731) Bottle design for a *Mennen* after-shave lotion. (USA)

730) Faltschachtel für ISS-Ohrenschoner, die den Lärm filtrieren. (AUL)
731) Flaschengestaltung für ein Rasierwasser von *Mennen*. (USA)
732) Tube, Behälter und Schachteln für kosmetische Produkte von *Juvena*. Durch Aneinanderreihen der Packungen kann ein Regenbogenmuster gebildet werden. (SWI)
733) Packungen für die pharmazeutischen Produkte von *Berthier-Derol*. (FRA)
734) Tuben, Behälter und Schachteln für *didi*-Produkte für die Säuglingspflege. (SWI)
735) Dosengestaltung für *Merit*-Motorenöl. (USA)
736) Behälter und Schachteln für *Beauty Basics* von Prue Acton Cosmetics. (AUL)

730) Carton pliant pour les protège-oreilles ISS filtrant le bruit extérieur. (AUL)
731) Etude de flacon pour une lotion après-rasage *Mennen*. (USA)
732) Tube, conditionnement et cartons montrant l'arc-en-ciel que constitue la gamme des cosmétiques *Juvena* mis côte à côte. (SWI)
733) Echantillons d'emballages pour les produits pharmaceutiques *Berthier-Derol*. (FRA)
734) Gamme de tubes, conditionnements et cartons pour les produits *didi* pour bébés. (SWI)
735) Etude de boîte pour l'huile à moteur *Merit*. (USA)
736) Gamme de conditionnements et cartons pour produits cosmétiques. (AUL)

Art Director | Directeur artistique:

733) CHRISTIAN SCHMUTZ
735) EUGENE J. GROSSMAN

Agency | Agentur | Agence – Studio:

730) EMERY, FOWLER-BROWN PTY. LTD.
731) CASE & MC GRATH, INC.
733) CREATION 3 S.A.
734) E. + U. HIESTAND
735) ANSPACH GROSSMAN PORTUGAL, INC.
736) NEISH, TUTT, GRUNWALD

Artist | Künstler | Artiste:

730) EMERY, FOWLER-
BROWN PTY. LTD.
731) HELMUT KRONE
732) RICHARD SIGG
733) CHRISTIAN SCHMUTZ /
LAURENT CEPPI
735) WILLI KUNZ
736) HEINZ GRUNWALD

732

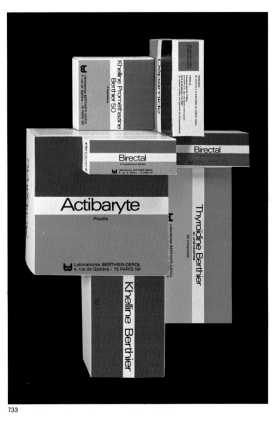

733

736

737) 738) Record cover and inside sleeve with lyrics (red and yellow cow on pale blue ground) for music by Ferguslie Park (Gerry Rafferty and Joe Egan). (GBR)
739) Cover for a record based on the original sound track of the film *Twister,* which deals with rodeos. Real jeans cloth with sewn-on pocket and loose yellow label. (USA)
740) Cover for a record album containing Gluck's opera *Orpheus and Eurydice.* Black, white, yellow, brown and red on blue. (SWI)
741) Full-colour record cover for a selection of songs by Kurt Weill for the operas and plays of Bert Brecht, including *Mac the Knife.* (USA)

737) 738) Schallplattenumschlag und Innenhülle mit Texten der Songs (rotgelbe Kuh auf hellblauem Grund) für Musik von Ferguslie Park (Gerry Rafferty und Joe Egan). (GBR)
739) Hülle für eine Schallplatte mit Originalmusik zum Film *Twister,* der von Rodeos handelt. Richtiger Jeans-Stoff mit aufgenähter Tasche und losem, gelbem Etikett. (USA)
740) Umschlag für ein *Ex-Libris*-Schallplattenalbum für Glucks Oper *Orfeo ed Euridice.* Schwarz, weiss, gelb, braun und rot auf Blau. (SWI)
741) Mehrfarbige Schallplattenhülle für eine Auswahl der Lieder von Kurt Weill für die Opern und Schauspiele von Bert Brecht, darunter *Mackie Messer.* (USA)

737) 738) Pochette de disque et chemise intérieure avec les paroles (vache rouge et jaune sur fond bleu pâle) de la musique de Ferguslie Park (Gerry Rafferty et Joe Egan). (GBR)
739) Pochette d'un disque utilisant la musique originale du film *Twister,* qui présente des rodéos. Vrai tissu de jeans avec poche cousue et étiquette jaune attachée. (USA)
740) Pochette d'un album de disques renfermant l'opéra de Gluck *Orphée et Eurydice.* Noir, blanc, jaune, brun, rouge sur bleu. (SWI)
741) Pochette polychrome pour un choix des chansons de Kurt Weill pour les opéras et les pièces de Bert Brecht, y compris *Mackie Messer.* (USA)

737

Artist | Künstler | Artiste:

737) 738) JOHN BYRNE
739) RON SULLIVAN
740) HANS USTER
741) DON IVAN PUNCHATZ / ACY R. LEHMAN /
GEORGE ESTES

Art Director | Directeur artistique:

737) 738) MICHAEL DOUD
739) STAN RICHARDS
740) OSWALD DUBACHER
741) ACY R. LEHMAN / GEORGE ESTES

Agency | Agentur | Agence – Studio:

739) THE RICHARDS GROUP

Publisher | Verleger | Editeur:

737) 738) A & M RECORDS LTD.
739) FORTUNE MUSIC CORPORATION
740) EX LIBRIS AG
741) RCA RECORDS

Record Covers
Schallplattenhüllen
Pochettes de disques

738

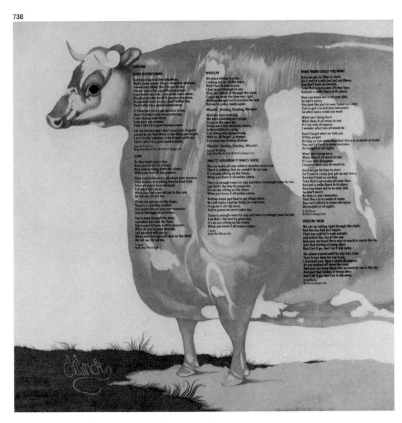

739

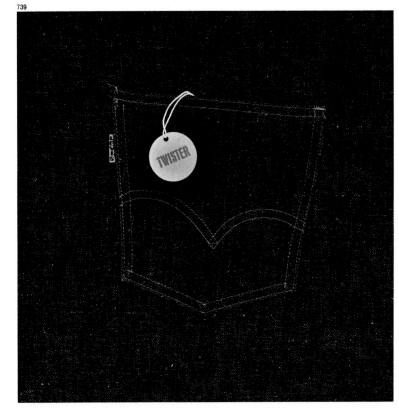

740

741

742

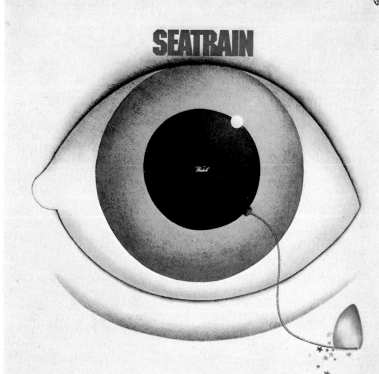

743

745

746

Artist | Künstler | Artiste:

742) FERDI AFFLERBACH
743) ETIENNE DELESSERT
744) ROGER HANE / ED LEE
745) CHARLES E. WHITE III / JOHN BERG
746) HENRIETTA CINDAK
747) J. MC MULLAN / J. BERG /
    R. MANTEL / H. MORISHIMA
748) R.A. PARKER / J. BERG /
    H. MORISHIMA / R. MANTEL

Art Director | Directeur artistique:

742) FERDI AFFLERBACH
743) ETIENNE DELESSERT
744)–748) JOHN BERG

Publisher | Verleger | Editeur:

742) HUG & CO.
743) WARNER BROS. RECORDS, INC.
744)–748) COLUMBIA RECORDS

742) Cover for a recording of the 1972 Carnival in Basle. Bright colours with real lace, steel wool and glass eyes. (SWI)
743) Record cover for music by a beat group. Pale turquoise iris, yellow flame. (USA)
744) Complete record cover (both sides) for songs by Billy Paul. Full colour. (USA)
745) Record cover for music by the Gentle Giant group. Chiefly grey-green and beige shades, carton die-cut in the form of a jar of preserves. (USA)
746) Record cover for a Prokofiev symphony. Black on silver. (USA)
747) Record cover for Beethoven's *Eroica* symphony conducted by Leonard Bernstein. (USA)
748) Record cover for suites from Stravinsky's *Firebird* and *Petrushka*. Bird in red, dancers in dullish colours. (USA)

I See The Light • War Of The Gods • The Whole Town's Talking • I Was Married • Thanks For Saving My Life • Peace Holy Peace

War Of The Gods

Billy Paul

744

747

748

Record Covers / Schallplattenhüllen / Pochettes de disques

742) Umschlag für eine Aufnahme der Basler Fastnacht 1972. Bunte Farben mit richtigen Spitzen, Stahlwolle und Glasaugen. (SWI)

743) Schallplattenhülle für Musik einer Beat-Gruppe. Iris in Helltürkis, gelbe Flamme. (USA)

744) Vollständige Schallplattenhülle (beide Seiten) für Lieder von Billy Paul. Farbig. (USA)

745) Schallplattenhülle für Musik der Gruppe Gentle Giant. Hauptsächlich graugrüne und beige Schattierungen. Hülle in der Form eines Einmachglases ausgestanzt. (USA)

746) Schallplattenumschlag für eine Symphonie von Prokofieff. Schwarz auf Silber. (USA)

747) Schallplattenhülle für Beethovens Sinfonie *Eroica,* von Leonard Bernstein dirigiert. (USA)

748) Schallplattenhülle für Suiten aus Strawinskys *Der Feuervogel* und *Petruschka.* Vogel in Rot, Tänzer in dumpfen Tönen. (USA)

742) Pochette d'un enregistrement du Carnaval de Bâle 1972. Couleurs vives; dentelle, laine d'acier et yeux de verre véritables. (SWI)

743) Pochette du disque d'un groupe beat. Iris turquoise pâle, flamme jaune. (USA)

744) Pochette polychrome complète (recto et verso) d'un disque de chansons de Billy Paul. (USA)

745) Pochette d'un disque du groupe Gentle Giant. Prédominance de tons vert-gris et beiges, carton découpé en forme de bocal de conserves. (USA)

746) Pochette de disque pour une symphonie de Prokofiev. Noir sur argent. (USA)

747) Pochette de disque pour l'*Eroica* de Beethoven, dirigée par Leonard Bernstein. (USA)

748) Pochette de disque pour des suites de *l'Oiseau de feu* et de *Pétrouchka,* de Stravinsky. Oiseau rouge, danseuses en tons mats. (USA)